The Aesthetic Pleasures of Girl Teen Film

The Aesthetic Pleasures of Girl Teen Film

Samantha Colling

BLOOMSBURY ACADEMIC
NEW YORK • LONDON • OXFORD • NEW DELHI • SYDNEY

BLOOMSBURY ACADEMIC
Bloomsbury Publishing Inc
1385 Broadway, New York, NY 10018, USA
50 Bedford Square, London, WC1B 3DP, UK

BLOOMSBURY, BLOOMSBURY ACADEMIC and the Diana logo
are trademarks of Bloomsbury Publishing Plc

First published in the United States 2017
Paperback edition first published 2019

© Samantha Colling, 2017

Cover design: Eleanor Rose
Cover image: Film Confessions Of A Teenage Drama Queen 2004 © George Kraychyk/
Walt Disney Pictures/REX/Shutterstock

All rights reserved. No part of this publication may be reproduced or
transmitted in any form or by any means, electronic or mechanical,
including photocopying, recording, or any information storage or retrieval
system, without prior permission in writing from the publishers.

Bloomsbury Publishing Inc does not have any control over, or responsibility for,
any third-party websites referred to or in this book. All internet addresses given
in this book were correct at the time of going to press. The author and publisher
regret any inconvenience caused if addresses have changed or sites have
ceased to exist, but can accept no responsibility for any such changes.

A catalog record for this book is available from the Library of Congress.

ISBN: HB: 978-1-5013-1849-8
PB: 978-1-5013-4901-0
ePDF: 978-1-5013-1851-1
ePub: 978-1-5013-1850-4

Typeset by Deanta Global Publishing Services, Chennai, India

To find out more about our authors and books visit
www.bloomsbury.com and sign up for our newsletters.

Contents

Author's Note and Acknowledgements — vi

1 Introduction — 1
2 Cinderella's Pleasures: The Power and Pleasures of Costume — 23
3 Celebrity Glamour: Space, Place and Visibility — 47
4 Sporting Pleasures: The Body as Aesthetic Surface — 71
5 Musical Address: Expansion, Confinement and Kinaesthetic Contagion — 91
6 Music Video Aesthetics: The Affects of Spectacle — 113
7 Conclusions and Future Research — 131

Filmography — 143
Bibliography — 148
Index — 166

Author's Note and Acknowledgements

This book has come about, in part, as a response to my own pleasure in girl teen films. This pleasure has come with a confused sense that although these films are, for the most part, ideologically conservative, more often do not include characters with whom I consciously identify, nor involve events, scenarios or people with which I am especially fascinated, I still find them appealing. Teaching the film *Mean Girls* (Waters, 2004) – a quintessential millennial girl teen film – to A-level film studies students I found that neither I nor the students could satisfactorily explain what we enjoyed about the film. At the same time, with the same group, I was also teaching a unit on British Cinema, and the crime film *Bullet Boy* (Dibb, 2004). Set in East London, *Bullet Boy* is a moody and claustrophobic tragedy about a young man's entanglement in a culture of crime. The differences in the ways that students engaged with these films are indicative of broader critical approaches to film. They found it difficult to discuss or explain the comedy, bright and polished mise en scène or light-hearted tone of *Mean Girls*, where, in comparison, the simmering violence, aggression and bleached-out urban landscape of *Bullet Boy* was much easier to address. The students felt that in analysing *Bullet Boy* there was more to discuss, to explicate and to understand. *Mean Girls* seemed too 'obvious', but also difficult to explain in its very obviousness. The intentions of this book have developed in response to a desire to gain a practical hold of girl teen films, to be able to articulate joy or fun in the same ways that violence or aggression seems comprehensible. With these thoughts in mind this book does not describe why I, nor my students, like girl teen films but explores the pleasures that these films are designed to provoke. I would, therefore, like to thank the students whom I taught at that time as well as those now, who keep me thinking and questioning.

From Manchester School of Art, I would also like to thank Felicity Colman, Joan Ormrod, Emily Brick and Jim Aulich. From Bloomsbury, Katie Gallof and Susan Krogulski. For reading versions of this book and providing very helpful feedback, Rachel Moseley, Catherine Driscoll, Sarah Thomas and one anonymous reader. For friendship and support, Amber Roberts, Leanne Green,

Gary Bratchford, Mary Ikon, Laura Guy and Jenny and Mark Wilkinson. For teaching me things along the way, Jeff Fox, Adrian Baker, Iain Fox, Linda B and Keith Moulton. My family: Mum, Mark, Rosie, Lenny, Hobie, Geraldine, Andy, Dad, Michelle, Maud and Merry. And finally Leonie-Jade Leigh, without whom this book would have been completed a lot sooner.

1
Introduction

You know, I've never been to one of these things before. And when I think about how many people wanted this [removing tiara atop her head] and how many people cried over it and stuff ... I mean, I think everybody looks like royalty tonight. Look at Jessica Lopez. That dress is amazing. And Emma Gerber, I mean, that hairdo must have taken hours, and you look really pretty.

Cady, *Mean Girls* (Waters, 2004)

Adapted into fiction from the parental self-help guide, *Queen Bees and Wannabees: helping your daughter survive cliques, gossip, boyfriends, and other realities of adolescence* (Wiseman, 2002), *Mean Girls* follows Cady (Lindsay Lohan) who, after being home-schooled throughout her childhood, must navigate the social hierarchies of American high school. After manipulating her way to the top of the social ladder, becoming increasingly scheming and glamorous as she does so, Cady is eventually crowned as spring fling queen at the school dance. She has, however, lost all of her friends along the way and finds herself facing penance in the form of social ostracism as a 'Mathlete'. When she is crowned as spring fling queen, she stands centre stage in a tiara and her Mathlete uniform (Figure 1.1), personifying the balance of innocence and glamour that the film projects as appropriate for girls. Seeking redemption from her fellow high school students she recites the speech quoted at the beginning of this chapter. This moment of redemption, of taking it all back, feels hollow. All the fun and affective force of the film is in the scenes where Cady is being a mean girl, in the scenes where she struts, dances and makes a spectacle of herself. This final sentimental speech cannot undo the pleasures of the glamour that has come before it. This book explores what those pleasures are.

Teen film, and more especially Hollywood girl teen film, is generally critically dismissed as silly and trivial, the implication being that girl culture is silly and

Figure 1.1 *Mean Girls* (2004), Cady's redemption.

trivial, and in turn that girls are silly and trivial. Instead, this book takes the pleasures of these films seriously and explores how they are designed to create fun for girls.

Girl teen film

Teen films can be defined by their thematic focus: coming-of-age narratives, rites of passage and maturity as a narrative obstacle. The types of teen films that this book examines are mainstream, commercial films in which girls are the protagonists. Not all the films that I refer to are made in Hollywood, but they all follow the Hollywood paradigm. As I will detail throughout, they all present us with the same 'fun' version of girlhood, they are all essentially Cinderella stories, they repeat the same moments of fun over and over, and they are designed to create specific affective pleasures.

Within the tradition of film studies the aesthetic and affective pleasures of teen film have gone unexplored. Studies usually focus on what films mean, taking an approach which assumes that teen films play a pedagogic role in the lives of young people – believing that they are good or bad for them (Considine, 1985; Lewis, 1992; Shary, 2002, 2005). Where a less moral approach is taken, the intent is to define teen film through theme and narrative; again the focus remains on what teen films mean and their relation to ideas about adolescence, rather than the films' appeals (Doherty, 2002; Driscoll, 2011; Martin, 1989). In the film studies context, youth is often implicitly taken as male, but where teen films about girls are explored, methodologies usually ignore aesthetics and instead critique the films, finding them feminist or misogynist, empowering or not for the imagined teen girl audience (Hentges, 2006). Where aesthetics are examined, this tends to be in relation to independent or art-house teen films; the aesthetics of the mainstream are usually taken for granted (Kearney, 2002). A notion of what is 'typical' and ostensibly unsuitable for aesthetic analysis goes unquestioned. I want to rectify this gap and explore the aesthetics of mainstream millennial girl teen film.

The millennial focus of this book is in part a response to literature that already exists on the subject of teen film. Film studies often fixes on teen films of the 1950s – the decade to which the teen film is often cited as being created; the 1980s – especially the John Hughes films of that period, and/or the plethora of teen films of the late 1990s that followed the financial success of *Clueless* (Heckerling, 1995): made for approximately $12 million, the film's domestic box-office gross was $56, 631, 572, (boxofficemojo.com) (See e.g. Doherty, 2002; Lee, 2010; Lewis, 1992; Kaveney, 2006; Shary, 2002, 2003, 2011). This book addresses the proliferation of girl teen films at the turn of the twenty-first century.

I focus specifically on girl teen films released between 2000 and 2010. It is well documented that, since the 1990s especially, girls are everywhere in the media (Aapola, Gonick and Harris, 2005; Driscoll, 2002; Gonick, 2006; Harris, 2004; Projansky, 2014; Tasker and Negra, 2007). The development of cable television and the growth of channels such as Disney and Nickelodeon in the 1990s produced multimedia girl celebrities (Projansky, 2014: 12–13); this girl thrived at the turn of the century and as part of the digital era. In combination, from the late 1990s onwards, a third wave of feminism that focused on youth – loud, young, sexy, feminine – has been packaged and sold in all facets of the media and commercial culture. At the turn of the twenty-first century, the ubiquity of girls in film and media was unparalleled.

The proliferation of girls in the media means that girls have become a topic for discussion in academia. What has emerged as girls studies over the last twenty years or so combines the traditions of feminist criticism and critical youth studies to explore the construction of girls' subjectivities in specific social, cultural and historical contexts and locations. Girls studies has articulated, in a number of ways, the contrary depictions of girlhood present in popular culture (Aapola, Gonick and Harris, 2005; Douglas, 1994; Harris, 2004; Nash, 2006;

Projansky, 2014; Renold and Ringrose, 2011). Representations coexist whereby girls are simultaneously exalted and abject. These representations express the ways that girls are often objects of curiosity, pleasure and anxiety in culture. The version of girlhood we see in millennial girl teen films is similarly constructed by contradictory qualities. Taking a new approach, this book examines how these contradictions are designed to feel good.

In her article 'Girl as Affect' (2011: 3) Monica Swindle asks, 'What is a girl?' Girl, she suggests, is a signifier but also a distinct affect in excess of the signifier (4). In its present Western, late capitalist, twenty-first-century incarnation, girl exists as a discernable affect. Rather than focus on what girl means, I seek to describe how girl feels. Or, more specifically, how the late capitalist commercial Hollywood version of girlhood feels. To answer the question very simply: girl feels fun. This book takes a film studies approach to detail how this fun is created and what it feels like.

Because I am dealing with an *idea* of what adolescence is – the Hollywood version of the teenager – it is not essential to demarcate strict temporal boundaries around who is in, or who watches, these films. Catherine Driscoll (2011b: 2) and Adrian Martin (1994: 66) suggest that the teen in teen film really refers to a mode of behaviour, which can be characterized as a contradiction between maturity and immaturity. Teen film works through contradictory qualities that define ideas of adolescence: immaturity and maturity, independence and belonging, innocence and knowingness, rebellion and conformity, expansion and confinement. The teen I refer to is a figure that embodies these contradictory qualities. The Hollywood version of adolescence is structured by interlinking antinomies that, in their relationship, create tensions, energies and frictions specific to the commercial idea of the teen. The teen figure holds two extremes in balance and at the hinge of their meeting becomes the idea of adolescence and embodies particular feelings specific to 'the teen'. The appeal of this embodiment of adolescence can be understood in Joseph Roach's (2007: 8) description of the balance between mutually exclusive extremes in the dance term contrapposto: 'a pose in which the performer turns in different directions simultaneously at the knees, the hips, the shoulders, and the head, making an interesting line of the body'. The fusion and friction of opposites create intensity: their combination is what makes them interesting. Applied conceptually, contrapposto explains the residual energies created by the combination of and resistance between contradictions. The antiphonal friction held in the idea and embodiment of adolescence is what makes the teen a powerful and intriguing figure, generating

Introduction

feelings of promise, potential, expectation and possibility. These feelings central to understanding the pleasures of teen film.

Driscoll (2011b: 112) and Martin (1994: 68) describe teen film as fashioned by the notion of liminality. The characters of teen film, they suggest, are recognizable in Victor Turner's description of the liminal position: 'Neither here nor there; they are betwixt and between … in the realm of pure possibility' (1967: 95, 96). Generically, teen films can be described by their focus on transformations, transitions, boundaries and crossing thresholds from childhood into adulthood. I propose, however, that, according to the Hollywood version of the teen, these spaces and times in between are more static than the term liminality suggests. Teen films often create characters and situations that feel like the shift and transition of liminality but fix the teen figure to prescribed sets of contradictory qualities. Therefore, rather than being in the 'realm of pure possibility', the Hollywood teen figure is defined by specified, regulated and uniform combinations of contradictory qualities. Where boys must learn to balance their hedonistic desires and sense of responsibility, girls are required to create the 'appropriate' combination of innocence and experience: not between, but both. When Cady stands centre stage at the end of *Mean Girls* to make her speech of redemption, that wraps the narrative of the film up into a neat bow, the character regulates her extrovert impulses and sexuality. She manages to project the 'appropriate' balance of innocence and experience to be deemed worthy of forgiveness.

In this book the girl that I refer to is the Hollywood version of girlhood, a fictional figure foremost structured by the contradictory qualities of innocence and experience, expansion and confinement. Girl teen film is a label that consciously identifies the genealogy and embedded relationship with the broader category of teen film and also provides the distinction that recognizes the girl-centred narratives that these films provide. The girl teen film descriptor is an awkward turn of phrase, but it emphasizes the Hollywood notion of girlhood that these films create. The label does not imply that the appeal of these films is only to girls or indeed to people aged thirteen to nineteen but stresses that the films are structured by notions of girlhood. The girlhood that I refer to here is a concept. Girl teen films give us images and ideas of girls; they create a version of girlhood, rather than represent actual female desires, memories or fantasies. Instead, they aim to create affective experiences that feel as though they express desires, memories or fantasies that girls supposedly share in common.

Millennial girl teen films exist in a number of modes that can be understood based on how the subject of female adolescence is treated on screen. In the

.tives are tragic and handled earnestly, for example: *A Walk* ... *k*man, 2002) or *Twilight* (Hardwicke, 2008). In comparison ...ms deal with female adolescence in an overtly political or ...m, for example: *Thirteen* (Hardwicke, 2003) or *Water Lilies* ...). This book focuses specifically on girl teen films in the fun mode. In ... un mode films are structured around visibility and performance (dancing, singing and sport) and girlhood is handled comedically, with a lighter touch. Films such as *Mean Girls* are connected by an emphasis on pleasure and fun and are structured around requisite moments of visibility that make the girl figure the centre of attention. These moments of visibility are presented as key forms of fun for the girl figure.

In girl teen films in the fun mode, 'fun' has a distinct character. The kinds of fun that the girl figure is shown to enjoy lead up to or are fundamentally moments of visibility: the makeover and catwalk, girls' sports, musical or dance performances. It is in these moments that girl teen films are designed to generate their greatest affective force. These moments of 'fun' are often rites of passage: the girl figure's ability to present herself (her body) successfully marks her out as having achieved appropriate levels of maturity. Essentially whether these moments reflect a narrative rite of passage or not, it is here that the girl figure is shown having fun and it is these moments that are designed to be the most affectively loaded. We can observe how these moments are specifically prescribed as 'girl fun' as opposed to 'boy fun' if we compare the boy teen film *Superbad* (Mottola, 2009) with the girl teen film *Sleepover* (Nussbaum, 2004). *Superbad* follows three male friends over the course of twenty-four hours. Moving between high school, house parties and the boys' attempts to buy alcohol, the film charts their misguided quest to have sex with girls for the first time before the two key characters are separated to attend university. *Sleepover* follows four female friends who celebrate their graduation from junior high with a sleepover party, before one of them moves away. Over the course of the night the friends compete against another group of girls in a scavenger hunt, for which they must be the first to complete a number of set tasks. As a sex comedy *Superbad* has a UK 15 certificate, compared to *Sleepover*'s PG rating. Appropriate to its certificate and assumed tween-teen target audience, *Sleepover*'s romance is presented without any reference to sex or sexuality. In relation to both films what is set forth as fun, therefore, is restricted based on the ages of the characters and the age of the audiences as defined by certification. Nonetheless, the very similar plot devices and narrative time frames make these films' comparison illustrative of what is deemed fitting as boy fun in juxtaposition to girl fun. Where boy fun centres around rites of passage that are age restricted by law, explicitly aggressive or fundamentally based around male bonding, girl fun (even where it includes female bonding) pivots around visibility. Even in girl teen films that reach a higher certification and include sexual references, girl fun still includes the same moments of visibility. Like *Superbad*, *Easy A* (Gluck, 2010), for example, is a UK certificate 15 and includes a number of sexual references, but Olive's (Emma Stone) fun revolves around a catwalk moment, a musical number and kissing a boy. There are no girl teen film equivalents to *Superbad* because, regardless of character age or certification, what is created as appropriate as 'girl fun' (and 'boy fun') is restricted.

As a sex comedy *Superbad*'s humour revolves around a number of embarrassing and humiliating scenarios, but the film does show the boys having fun. 'Boy fun' involves: drinking at a bar, shooting a gun, being praised for bringing alcohol to a party, getting drunk, having sex, orchestrating a scene that shows one of the boys getting arrested and therefore giving him notoriety, and setting a police car on fire. In *Sleepover* the main character Julie (Alexa Vega) describes the events as 'my Cinderella night'. 'Girl fun' is: painting toenails, putting make-up on, dancing in wigs, a makeover, putting clothes on mannequins at the mall, skateboarding (and consequently being noticed by a boy), strutting into a school dance, dancing with each other and with boys and kissing a boy.

Millennial girl teen films in the fun mode have a lineage that connects them to the 'clean teen' (Doherty, 2002: 145–86) films of the 1950s and 1960s, epitomized by the *Gidget* franchise (1959–85) and the AIP beach party series (1963–6). Driscoll (2011a: 14–25) illustrates that many of the traits found in the clean teen films are foreshadowed in earlier cinema, including films starring Lillian Gish and the early Andy Hardy films (ca. 1938–46). Clean teen films focus on white, affluent, middle-class teens. These are well behaved, comic but predictable and trustworthy characters. The films include elements of romantic comedy, humour is based around mild innuendo and slapstick, and the premise and characters are carefree. Clean teen films are branded as escapist, conventional and conformist. They reflect a light-hearted version of youth in comparison with those films that depict 'youth as problem' (Driscoll, 2011b: 29–38). Similarly millennial girl teen films in the fun mode maintain a white, middle-class perspective and the same carefree version of youth.

In millennial girl teen films fun is presented using double coding techniques. The late 1980s saw an increasing development of self-consciousness in teen films in general. The 1988 girl teen film *Heathers* (Lehmann) parodies the earnest treatment of adolescence found in the John Hughes films released earlier in the decade, films such as *The Breakfast Club* (1985), *Pretty in Pink* (1986) and *Some Kind of Wonderful* (1987). *Heathers* pokes fun at the sentimental attitude of the earlier films, to create an ironic take on depictions of American high school culture. The film follows Veronica Sawyer (Winona Ryder) as she attempts to end the tyranny of the 'Heathers' clique at Westburg High. After Veronica meets J. D. (Christian Slater) they 'accidentally' kill the top Heather and cover up the murder as a suicide. Veronica soon realizes that J. D. is a psychopath when he arranges further 'suicides' at the school. With grotesque teen characters and adults alike, and music such as 'Teenage Suicide (don't do it)', the film marks a distinct shift in tone and reflects the increasing knowingness of girl teen films during this period.

Another recognizable point of genealogical development in girl teen film is *Clueless*. An adaptation of Jane Austen's *Emma* (1815), the film is overtly self-conscious and knowing. In its opening montage, for example, the film creates a pastiche of the affluent America often depicted in commercial teen culture: cutting between shots of shopping, lounging poolside and driving expensive cars. Towards the end of this opening montage Cher's (Alicia Silverstone) narration emphasizes the film's knowing attitude: 'So OK, you're probably going ... is this like an Oxema commercial or what?' The film then cuts to Cher in the 'present' and she continues: 'But actually I have a way normal life for a teenage girl.' Having pointed out the knowing hyperbole of the opening montage, the film makes fun with Cher's idea of a 'normal' life, cutting to her opulent bedroom and racks of designer clothing. *Clueless* is not a parody but a pastiche that double codes its use of teen culture conventions (as well as its Jane Austen origins). Double coding is a form of irony that works to revisit the 'already said' (Krutnik, 1998: 28). Umberto Eco (1992: 227) describes double coding in reference to a man declaring his love to a woman in an age of lost innocence:

> He cannot say to her, 'I love you madly,' because he knows that she knows (and she knows that he knows) that these words have already been written by Barbara Cartland. Still there is a solution. He can say, 'As Barbara Cartland would put it, I love you madly.' At this point, having avoided false innocence, having said clearly that it is no longer possible to speak innocently, he will nevertheless have said what he wanted to say to the woman. ... If the woman goes along with this, she will have received a declaration of love all the same.

For Eco double coding offers a means of enjoyment that is not escapist: literature that both disturbs and delights (Brooker, 1992: 229). In contemporary girl teen films, however, double coding techniques do not eschew 'escapist' pleasures. Pleasure is found in the hyper-imitation of girl teen film conventions, in combination with the films' original affective sentiments. This is pastiche in Richard Dyer's (2007) sense of the word: imitation that signals itself as imitation and in doing so makes this self-consciousness central to its affects and pleasures. In this context self-consciousness and affect, feeling and emotion are not mutually exclusive, as Dyer (ibid.: 180) describes: pastiche 'imitates formal means that are themselves ways of evoking, moulding and eliciting feeling, and thus in the process is able to mobilise feelings even while signalling that it is doing so'.

Pastiche is the aesthetic imitation of other art, not of life or reality (ibid.: 2). It is distinct from parody in that the latter makes fun *of* that which it imitates, where pastiche makes fun *with* its imitation. Pastiche, unlike parody, does not question the mode that is being mimicked (ibid.: 40). Pastiche makes a point of its being a copy but still uses the techniques of that which is being imitated. As a consequence it 'facilitates an experience of the imitated work' (ibid.: 100). *Clueless* makes fun with conventional depictions of American teen culture but retains the affective pleasures of presentations of youth and wealth all the same. Dyer explores pastiche, not as necessarily negative as Frederic Jameson (1985) describes it, as 'blank parody', but as an affective form that potentially articulates a 'sense of living permanently, ruefully but without distress, within the limits and potentialities of the cultural construction of thought and feeling' (Dyer, 2007: 180). Likewise, I suggest that pastiche and double coding techniques are necessarily neither innately positive nor innately negative; instead I explore double coding here as a means to facilitate pleasures that can either be taken up or be rejected. The audience can choose to go along with them or not.

As suggested earlier in this chapter, the surprise success of *Clueless* had a noticeable impact on the number of girl teen films produced in the late 1990s. The year 1999 saw the release of a number of films that followed the cheerfully affective attitude and double coding techniques used by the film. *She's All That* (Iscove), *Never Been Kissed* (Gosnell), *10 Things I Hate About You* (Junger) and *Drive Me Crazy* (Shultz) continued the trend, and in the same year *Drop Dead Gorgeous* (Jann) and *Jawbreaker* (Stein) took a slightly more acerbic tone and *Jawbreaker* can be seen as a direct descendent of *Heathers*. Girl teen films made between 2000 and 2010 have further conventionalized double coding and it is now an essential element of films in the fun mode.

Method and approach

Audiences, academics and producers predominantly consider girl teen films to be conformist, unoriginal, commodity entertainment. As a consequence, the comparatively scarce academic analysis that does exist tends to focus on the ideological implications of the films as industrial products – an approach that points away from their aesthetic dimensions. Bill Nichols (2000: 45) describes attitudes to art as symptomatic of the symbolic economy of culture: 'The more a thing is valued as art, the less it is acknowledged as a commodity; the more we value a film aesthetically, the less we want to treat it as an industrial product like any other.' The inverse of this argument is that the more explicitly commercial a film is, the less it is aesthetically valued, the less we want to treat it as an aesthetic product. We bind the object to its commodity status and forget that it is designed with aesthetic intent. We forget that producers know that the more appealing something is, the likelier it will be to make money. Pierre Bourdieu (2000 [1986]: 1) makes clear that aesthetic hierarchies are class based, that is, the socially recognized hierarchy of the arts corresponds to the social hierarchy of consumers: art and cultural consumption legitimate social differences. Aesthetic hierarchies are tied inseparably to pleasure hierarchies. The kinds of pleasure an object offers distinguish it as valuable (or not) and the kinds of pleasures a consumer enjoys distinguish him or her as superior (or not). These distinctions are class based, whereby the rejection of popular, 'vulgar', 'easy', 'trivial' and 'silly' pleasures and the affirmation of disinterested pleasures confirm the consumer's superiority (ibid.: 7, 35). A further hierarchical entanglement that ostensibly distinguishes one film from another, one consumer from another and one pleasure from another is the hierarchy of affects, feelings and emotions. Where the appreciation of 'pure' art supposedly calls for distance and consequently induces responses that are detached or dissonant, industrial products are often regarded as seductive, producing vulgar or trivial emotions that are sentimental or fun. Just as these hierarchies are class based, notions of gender also support them: the masculine mind appreciates pure art, while industrial products are enjoyed through feminine overinvestment.

The pleasure hierarchies table (Figure 1.2) provides a visual representation of the interconnected aesthetic, pleasure and emotion hierarchies that explain why feminine forms of popular culture, including girl teen films, are often disregarded in reference to their aesthetic dimensions.

This book starts at the point of a triple aesthetic exclusion (also see Galt, 2011: 37) based on the commercialism of Hollywood teen film, the supposed triviality of girl culture and the connection of fun to subordinate class tastes and feminine pleasures. This book aims to rectify the aesthetic neglect of girl teen films, examine the aesthetics of fun with as much subtlety, care and detail as one would any other formal strategy, and work outside of these hierarchies so as not to reproduce gender- and class-based value systems. I examine girl teen film from a perspective that does not justify the focus on pleasure by reclaiming specified pleasures as ideologically resistant, empowering or conversely oppressive. I suggest that ideologies do not explain how and why these films are enjoyed. I ask instead what girl teen films do that offers particular types of pleasurable experience?

In its cultural and academic manifestations, notions of millennial girlhood are considered to personify post-feminism and this concept is seen to describe ideas of millennial girlhood (Projansky, 2007; Tasker and Negra, 2005). The millennial girl's position as always in process (Driscoll, 2002), her simultaneous reliance on and disregard of feminist gains, her personification of the marked sexualization of culture, her constant body work, self-surveillance, transformation and her associations with consumer culture: all of these things tie her to definitions of post-feminism (Attwood, 2011; Gill, 2011; Harvey and Gill, 2011; McRobbie, 2004, 2009; Projansky, 2007; Radner, 2010; Tasker and Negra, 2007). Girls studies also explicitly connects post-feminism, and consequently girlhood, to neo-liberal ideals. As Rosalind Gill (2011: 147) proposes: 'The autonomous, calculating, self-regulating subject of neoliberalism bears a strong resemblance to the active, freely choosing, self-reinventing subject of postfeminism.' The increased use of double coding techniques in millennial girl teen film, outlined above, is a typical trait of post-feminist media in which irony works as a kind of 'get out

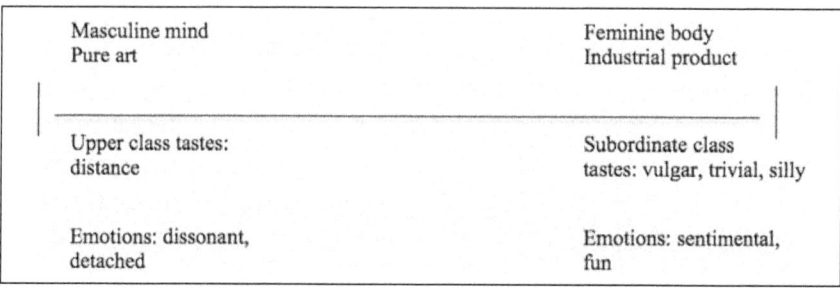

Figure 1.2 Pleasure hierarchies.

clause'. In post-feminist media any objection to exploitative or sexist imagery is pre-empted with irony (McRobbie, 2004: 159). Millennial girl teen films are typical post-feminist texts. Nonetheless, the post-feminist and neo-liberal values to which these films conform are not the reasons that pleasures are experienced. Instead, the ways in which the films are designed can explain how this post-feminist, neo-liberal version of girlhood becomes pleasurable. Approaching girl teen film from this angle, we can understand what (gendered) versions of fun these films create, what pleasures they offer and how the Hollywood version of girlhood is designed to feel good.

Laura Mulvey's (1986 [1975]) seminal essay 'Visual Pleasure and Narrative Cinema' brings pleasure to the fore to argue that the pleasures of mainstream Hollywood films reaffirm patriarchal ideologies already present in the spectator. Mulvey appropriates psychoanalytic theory as a political weapon to illustrate how 'the unconscious of patriarchal society has structured film form' (ibid.: 198). Her argument posits that the cinematic apparatus constructs woman as object of the male gaze and in doing so draws on and reinforces specific primal pleasures in looking. Voyeuristic pleasures in classical Hollywood cinema, Mulvey suggests, subject women to 'a controlling and curious gaze' (ibid.: 200). In this case scopophilic pleasures arise from sadistic impulses that use another person as sexual object. The second mode of looking – fetishistic – which, Mulvey argues, the cinema rearticulates, works to alleviate male fears of castration, to provide 'avenues of escape' from this anxiety (ibid.: 205).

Mulvey's application of psychoanalytic theory to film makes pleasure its focus, but this approach takes universal and monolithic structures of looking and pleasure and fits cinema to the theory. Mulvey's essay is representative of apparatus theory, an approach that performs from the outside in: starting with theory and fixing it to film. In this book I instead start with the films and through textual analysis explore the pleasures they aim to create.

Apparatus/classic film theory seeks to apply laws 'that help underpin all significatory work' (Metz, 1986: 247) and in doing so takes for granted the notion of finite pleasures that are structured by repressed and unconscious desires. Critiqued extensively in film and media studies (e.g. Evans and Gamman, 1995; Plantinga, 2009; Rushton, 2013; Shaviro, 1993; Stacey, 1994), such an approach does not account for the diversity of pleasures but seeks to explain psychological and ideological effects that pacify an unidentified audience. As Steven Shaviro (1993: 11) proposes, psychoanalytic and poststructuralist apparatus theory is founded on a basis of 'suspicion, disavowal and phobic rejection'. Metz and

Mulvey take an approach to cinema that sees it as a kind of ruse, a plot to trick us into believing in what we perceive. Both Metz and Mulvey object to the expert ability of Hollywood cinema to engage its audience, and in this context feeling becomes complicity with ideological and psychological structures. This book seeks to understand pleasure from a perspective that does not disregard, or is not nervous about engagement and emotion. I suggest that films create experiences that we do not have to *believe* but which, to be enjoyed, we do go along with. I want to understand why we might go along with the worlds of girl teen film.

A further, fundamental problem that apparatus theory sets up and that hinders explorations of pleasure and maintains aesthetic hierarchies is the logic of representation whereby film is positioned as only a reflection of pre-existing forces and structures of subjectivity. This approach, as Mulvey (2006: 145) describes it, finds 'the film behind the film'. As Richard Rushton (2013) suggests, the logic of representation relies on a distinction between reality and a film's representation of reality. Film is explained as a secondary mode, examined for what ideas or social issues are reflected by it (ibid.: 8). From this perspective films are not considered as important in themselves and as a result questions focus on what a film is evidence of, instead of what a film does. The consequences of solely exposing girl teen films with regard to their representations of girlhood in relation to real-world totalities, sees that pleasures and aesthetic experiences are guiltily reclaimed, rejected or ignored, and what the films *do* is overlooked. If girl teen film is only ever explored in respect of its relation to reality, if it is constantly exposed as ideologically conservative or secretly subversive, it will only ever be understood as a form that either reflects girlhood accurately or inaccurately, perpetuating the idea that accurate representations of girlhood are worth more. This approach maintains aesthetic and pleasure hierarchies: rearticulating the idea that some pleasures have more value than others. Pleasures that subvert mainstream ideologies that are 'behind' film are praised as valuable and those that conform to those same ideologies (patriarchal, capitalist, neo-liberal, post-feminist) are attacked. To counter these hierarchies I follow Rushton (ibid.: 10) and take an attitude towards films that sees them as part of reality, instead of (only) representations of it. From this perspective we can ask, not what is behind film, but what does film do? For Rushton (ibid.: 4), films 'do not re-present anything. Instead they create things; they create realities, they create possibilities, situations and events that have not had a previous existence'. Taking this attitude to wards film creates a position from which we can begin to ask what kinds of experiences, affects, feelings and pleasures do girl teen films make available. I also suggest that films can do more than one thing at once: they can represent and they can create. However, focusing on what girl teen films *create* gives us an opportunity to understand the types of pleasure they offer. The experiences and possibilities that films invite us to enjoy are gendered. The experiences offered by these films are limited and some experiences are only offered to some: restricted by race, class, gender and physical (dis)ability. This book is not in opposition to traditional film theory but explores similar questions from a different perspective. Shaviro (1993: 33) suggests that we cannot reduce the agitation of the senses and fascinations experienced by the cinema viewer to 'lack, disavowal, and ideological or Imaginary misrecognition'. We have to take the body and the senses into account.

The research is in dialogue with recent film phenomenology and affect theory (Barker, 2009; Brinkema, 2014; Bukatman, 2003; Plantinga, 2009; Shaviro, 1993, 2010; Sobchack, 2004) in that it is concerned with the materiality of the film experience, the role of the senses and precognitive sensation. Throughout the book I take the position that films create affective and embodied experiences. As Dee Reynolds (2012: 124) describes, affect is embodied in that 'it refers to that point at which the body is activated, "excited", in the process of responding'. Cinematic affect theory and film phenomenology foreground the senses and consequently the body: the ways in which film is perceived and the ways in which it transmits affects between film body and lived body (Barker, 2009; Sobchack, 2004). Where film phenomenology often focuses on how the film and viewer act together, this book concentrates on how films are designed to appeal affectively and physically. With the aim of maintaining a practical focus, rather than a philosophical one, I place attention on the aesthetics of girl teen film. I concentrate on what the films' aesthetics can tell us about the kinds of pleasure they aim to generate: not what the films *will* do but the kinds of experience on offer and what they invite us to feel. Following Carl Plantinga (2009: 11), I propose that by examining films' aesthetic features we can reasonably determine the intended affective response, without assuming that these intentions will be successful. Eugenie Brinkema (2014) points out that affect is often deployed in a singular, general way, taken as a synonym for force or violence. As a means to push at affect theory we should, she suggests, engage in close readings that explore affect as composed in specific cinematic texts. My approach here is to turn towards the details of affects.

A gap in film phenomenology and affect film theory is a neglect of the aesthetic dimensions of films that seem to be 'ordinary', mainstream and 'unremarkable'. Studies mainly (almost exclusively) focus on marginal art-house films or Hollywood genres that stress discomfort, and perceptual and physical disorientation. This neglect of the mainstream or 'unremarkable' maintains hierarchical notions of what is worthy of aesthetic and affective analysis. As a means to unsettle traditional aesthetic hierarchies and fill the gap, this book prioritizes 'fun' pleasures that are implicitly categorized as trivial and feminine, such as joy, delight, excitement and amusement. I do not intend to suggest that hidden depths or avant-garde aesthetics in these films have gone unnoticed. Instead I aim to move away from the assumption that feminine popular culture needs to be defended through ideological feminist critique or reclamation. I am interested in how the 'ordinary' use of film form and style in girl teen films produces affectively charged experiences and in turn how this creates restricted and gendered notions of fun.

Throughout this book I use Michel Chion's (1994) term 'audio-viewer' as a means to highlight and more accurately convey the kinds of sensorial experiences that girl teen films aim to achieve. Studies in cinema and sensation provide constructive frameworks from which to explore film in ways that equalize sensorial aspects of the film experience. Vivian Sobchack (2004: 65) stresses a cross-modal approach to cinematic experience, whereby the sensory exchange of perception means that seeing and hearing a film also entails feeling, touching, tasting and smelling. From this starting point, hearing and sound are brought to the fore to displace the hierarchical emphasis that film analysis often places on sight (Sobchack, 2012: 25). Consequently we can explore, for example, the ways in which music is designed in film to intensify our experience of visual textures, and visual textures can equally reinforce our experience of music. In this book I place particular emphasis on the relationship between music and image, and Chapters 5 and 6 detail the physical impact of this relationship. For this reason the term spectator seems inadequate to describe the people addressed by film.

Girl teen films embody feelings that lend affective force to specific, gendered ideas of fun. As well as staging representational ideas of fun (e.g. showing people laughing and smiling), these films create feelings around particular events that make them feel fun. Susanne Langer's (1953) framework for a philosophical study of art, *Feeling and Form*, offers a way of exploring the kinds of fun that girl teen films create. Langer seeks a means of examining the ways that abstract forms embody feeling. Forms are used, she suggests, 'to act as symbols, to become expressive of human feeling' (ibid.: 51). Despite being entirely abstract, structures of music, for example, can express vital experiences that verbal language is unsuited to convey: 'Feeling, life, motion and emotion constitute its import' (ibid.: 32). Art, Langer proposes, expresses not actual feeling (those of the artist for example) but ideas of feeling – expressions that are felt as a quality, rather than logically recognized as function (ibid.: 32), making cogent the verbally ineffable (ibid.: 39). In *Problems of Art* (1957: 25) Langer describes art as 'images of feeling, that formulate it for our cognition'. As Richard Dyer (2002: 21) explains, a problem with Langer's philosophy, is the presumption that feeling or emotion is universal – 'is not coded, is simply "human feeling"'. Dyer (ibid) suggests that emotion is coded to the same extent as the 'non-representational' signs that express them, in ways that explain 'how entertainment forms come to have the emotional signification they do', specific to the social, cultural and historical circumstances in which they are produced. I take the approach that films are sounds and images of feeling, affect and emotion, formulated for our experience. These embodiments of feeling are designed to generate specific pleasures and we can explore the films, embodiments of feeling as a means to identify what types of affect they aim to create. Combining these methodologies the study not only suggests how the films are designed to create affect but also details the specificity of those affects as a thorough account of the kinds of pleasure on offer.

Pleasure and aesthetics

This book uses pleasure as a means of exploring girl teen films. To this end it starts from the premise that pleasure is material and connected to the body. Pleasure as something biological, psychological, philosophical and experiential involves a substantial body of work, but it is also an idea that is taken for granted. Overviews of pleasure generally take a similar course to one another (see e.g.: Connor, 1992; Kerr, Kucklich and Brereton 2006; Maguire, 2011; Modleski, 2000; O'Connor and Klaus, 2000; Rutsky and Wyatt, 1990; Trilling, 1980). Though pleasure is approached from various perspectives and to different ends, studies commonly begin with reference to classical models whereby 'higher' forms of pleasure are linked to the mind and 'lower' forms to the body (in reference, e.g. to Plato, Aristotle and Descartes). Different types of pleasure are then referenced – again, often in allusion to the way that pleasure is evaluated dichotomously – some pleasures are considered to be seductive and others enlightening: in reference to beauty/sublime (Kant), pleasure/jouissance (Barthes, Lacan), false/real (Adorno). Studies of pleasure then usually move on to the idea of pleasure as rebellious or transgressive (Bakhtin, Barthes – depending on the author's position) with the aim of claiming one version or another as the 'other' of bourgeois ideology and pleasure (Rutsky and Wyatt, 1990: 15). Rather than repeat a similar synopsis and get caught among arguments that claim various versions of pleasure as the most valuable, I would like to put these arguments to one side, focus on pleasure as a physical experience and see how this enables us to rethink film pleasures. As Steven Connor (1992) makes clear, discussions of pleasure are caught in an infinite reproduction of either/or arguments. When evaluating art, pleasure is a problem because of the notion of value: 'Pleasure and value endlessly produce and reproduce each other' (ibid.: 219). Separating different forms of pleasure is the most common way pleasure is distinguished from value: 'Pleasure can only be valuable, or lead to value as a result of being concentrated, purified, sublimated or otherwise transformed from itself' (ibid.: 205). Approaches to pleasure most often try to attribute a level of seriousness to the concept, distance the author from lower pleasures, justify the study of it or even the existence of pleasure itself. The attitude taken here aims to avoid these problems of pleasure.

To circumvent the key problem of pleasure and value – constantly connected and coordinated in interlocking spirals of reproduction – the notion of value needs to be clarified. The idea that some pleasures have more merit than others (a position that can be traced from Plato, through Descartes, Spinoza and Kant: 'pure' pleasures take the subject beyond the limits of all possible experience and knowledge) is rejected. The relationship between pleasure and value is understood here in terms of capital. Pleasure can add exchange value to films. Pleasure is valuable as a commodity – we invest our time and attention in entertainment as a means of experiencing pleasure. In turn we are also paid in pleasure – looking and listening is labour, the audience are given a wage of pleasure in return for their attention (Beller, 2006a,b). I do not intend to justify or condemn pleasure but accept it – this is not a philosophy of pleasure but a practical way of thinking about it as a means of exploring film and understanding the pleasures films offer.

Further to avoiding the problems of pleasure, pleasure is taken to be autotelic, related only to itself and not to something else that it expresses. Plato's hedonic value scale, for example, sees 'impure' pleasures as part of a unidirectional process – pleasure only exists here in reference to pain, it always involves filling a lack (Erginel, 2011). In connection, Catherine Malabou (2009: 42) explains how Freud's pleasure principle can be regarded as 'a tendency towards death. To avoid unpleasure amounts to seeking the quietest state, the lowest degree of energy, the deepest rest.' The pleasure principle inextricably links pleasure to unpleasure. Similarly in psychoanalysis pleasure is connected to sadism and masochism, pleasure is 'lived as unpleasure' (Malabou, 2009: 41). I do not wish to deny that pleasure can be derived from pain or suggest that all pleasure can only be understood as connected to positive affect, feeling or emotion. However, in a way that is appropriate to the fun mode of girl teen film and as something that is missing in current literature, it is positive pleasures that I would like to focus on here. The central concern is pleasure as just itself, pleasure for pleasure's sake, rather than as pointing to something else. To this end the pleasures I explore in this book are defined as positive affects, feelings and emotions: pleasures to which we generally have positive attitudes. I want to stress that I am not suggesting that these pleasures are positive in the sense that they necessarily have a favourable impact on the world and nor do I propose that they have a negative consequence (though they could do either). By positive I mean that they are corroborative: that they aim to feel good and they potentially do feel good.

Pleasurable sensations are one aspect of how we experience popular culture (and the world) but positive pleasures are relatively underexplored. Sara Ahmed (2010: 13) suggests that feminist cultural studies often takes 'bad feeling' as its starting point. In *The Promise of Happiness* Ahmed (2010: 14) starts with 'good feeling', though she does not assume that a distinction between good and bad feeling will hold. Similarly, it is with the ways that films aim to generate good feeling that this book begins. Having a better understanding of the kinds of pleasure that girl teen films invite their audiences to enjoy can give us greater insight into the Hollywood version of girlhood, the types of fun offered and, fundamentally, *some* possible explanations for why we might choose to go along with these pleasures.

To pursue this approach it is necessary to distinguish between affects, feelings and emotions. Affect is produced through encounters – it does not reside in the subject or object (Ahmed, 2010: 14, 21–2; Massumi, 1987: xvi; Shouse, 2005; Skeggs, 2010: 40). It is pre-personal (Massumi, 1987: xvi), 'a non-conscious experience of intensity' (Shouse, 2005) – an autonomic experiential state of the body. Feelings are personal and self-referential (Massumi, 2002: 13) – 'sensation that has been checked against previous experiences and labelled' (Shouse, 2005). Emotion is social – the display of labelled feeling. However, the above descriptions could be misleading in that they suggest a knowable, linear process in the relationship between affect, feeling and emotion. Instead of conceiving these elements as distinct realms, Ahmed (2004: 6) describes the interconnection of bodily sensation, emotion and thought as 'a form of company'. In *The Promise of*

Happiness (2010: 44) Ahmed describes this form of company in the relationship between subjects and objects as 'impressions': 'Happiness is precarious and even perverted because it does not reside within objects or subjects (as a form of positive residence) but is a matter of how things make an impression.' In the context of this book pleasure is the intended physical consequence of positive, feel good, impressions and affects. It is not one type of feeling, affect or emotion; it can be experienced in many forms – joy, satisfaction, arousal and excitement, for example – the connection between them being that these pleasures feel good and are inextricable from the body.

Pleasure, Ahmed (2010: 231–2) suggests, is a sensation caused by objects, but it is also how we turn towards certain things. Sensation, she proposes, involves evaluation: 'To be affected by something is to evaluate that thing. Evaluations are expressed in how bodies turn toward things' (2010: 23). Films do not just cause pleasurable affects, feelings and emotions in some kind of hermetically sealed experience – pleasures cause evaluations and anticipations. Here, we can describe these evaluations and anticipations as 'fun': fun is the evaluation of pleasure, where pleasure moves into an idea, fun is the understanding that to get pleasure from something makes something good. In turn fun is performative: finding fun in certain places generates those places as fun (see Ahmed, 2010: 6). This approach also helps us to understand how particular objects of fun (e.g. girl teen films) continue to circulate socially: 'Certain objects are attributed as the cause of happiness, which means they already circulate as social goods before we "happen" upon them, which is why we might happen upon them in the first place' (Ahmed, 2010: 28). Fun is socially and culturally determined and made normative, specific to particular historical moments.

Rather than take pleasure as an axiom, or get lost in arguing against varied notions of pleasure, my focus here is on aesthetic pleasures. Historically, pleasure has been linked to the body and this connection has often been employed as a means of creating hierarchies of pleasure, for example Aristotle's pleasures of the body were 'lower': those shared with animals (Katz, 2009). Pleasure is tacitly thought of as corporeal, generally associated with sensations and feelings. We can use aesthetics to take a body-centred approach to pleasure and film. If aesthetics is originally 'anything that has to do with perception by the senses' (Regan, 1992: 5), then aesthetic pleasures are those that connect with the body. For the purposes of exploring pleasure in a practical way and avoiding hierarchical value systems, I am following Jill Bennet (2012) and focusing here on practical aesthetics. I therefore take aesthetics to be communication through the senses: a way of engaging with the relationship between culture, perception and sensation. Girl teen films, of course, include pleasures connected to narrative or cognitive engagement. One obvious potential pleasure of girl teen films, for example, is their use of language and word play that engages with (or creates) contemporaneous adolescent vernacular, for example, see '40 *Mean Girls* Quotes That Make Everyday Life Worth Living' (Lang, 2013). Nonetheless focusing on aesthetic pleasures creates an opportunity to consider how girl teen films work on the body, or more precisely how they aim to work on the body of the audio-viewer. Aesthetic pleasures are not ideological traps that make their audience impotent and pliable and nor are they a counterfeit of 'real' pleasures (Adorno and Horkheimer, 1997 [1944]). Empirical studies have shown time and again that popular culture does not have the 'brainwashing' capacities that studies following the Frankfurt school take as read. Neither is my aim to argue that the pleasures of girl teen films can be found in the 'cracks' of the texts – in the non-conformist moments that are read against the grain of ideological imperatives. The pleasures of girl teen films are one aesthetically designed, affectively charged encounter among a myriad of others in an age where style is a part of everyday life (Postrel, 2003: xiv; Thrift, 2008: 13). My interest is in understanding these encounters.

Chapters

This book investigates the pleasurable surfaces of girl teen film. Examining those moments that Hollywood constitutes as 'girl fun', I explore how surfaces generate pleasure. These surfaces lend affective force to particular ideas of fun – specific moments of visibility that continuously reoccur in girl teen films – by embodying pleasurable feelings and appealing to tactile and kinaesthetic pleasures. Each chapter gives attention to particular surfaces and to these specific moments of fun and, in doing so, references two or more films in detail, selected from the comprehensive filmography, as illustrative of the techniques discussed. As a film that influenced the research (see foreword), *Mean Girls* is used as a key case study throughout.

Chapter 2, 'Cinderella's Pleasures', frames the book and situates the fun mode of girl teen film in its fairy-tale context. The chapter begins by examining the legacy of Cinderella as a fairy tale that places particular emphasis on pleasure. It also introduces the notion that, like fairy tale, girl teen films encourage an enchanted mode of engagement and explores how the aesthetic pleasures of

Cinderella play out affectively in a twenty-first-century context, where coming of age is achieved through glamour. Here I argue that the nature of Cinderella's pleasures – those that the character enjoys and those that aim to appeal to audiences – are indicative of the types of pleasure regarded as appropriate for girls. Nonetheless, rather than focus on what Cinderella 'means', the chapter explores how she is designed to feel good. From this position costume is considered as an element of 'magic' conjured by the commercial sphere, and using *A Cinderella Story* (Rosman, 2004) and *The House Bunny* (Wolf, 2008) as key examples, the chapter explores the tactile and kinaesthetic pleasures that Cinderella's costumes invite us to enjoy.

'Celebrity Glamour' takes its cue from the Cinderella legacy laid out in the previous chapter and the argument that Cinderella stories have increasingly replaced fantasies of romance with visibility and fame as the central reward. The chapter begins by outlining the ways in which celebrity is classified as a 'normal' desire in the twenty-first century and how visibility is understood as the key means to power for girls. It then creates a framework that delineates the types of celebrity played out. The chapter argues that the glamour that surrounds celebrity makes visibility physically pleasurable. As a means to demonstrate this, it defines celebrity glamour and using a number of case studies including *Easy A* and *Confessions of a Teenage Drama Queen* (Sugarman, 2004) examines the surfaces that make visibility pleasurable in these films. These include glamorous spaces and places, and the material construction of visibility.

Chapter 4, 'Sporting Pleasures', highlights the pleasures offered by the active body, typically analysed for what it represents, the body on screen is explored here as itself an aesthetic surface. Sports performances in girl teen film provide the Cinderella character-icon with another moment of visibility and recognition and here it is the body itself that singles her out as special. I examine how these moments are often at odds with the physical inhibitions girls are usually conditioned and restrained by, creating feelings of expansion and freedom. The chapter explores the plurality of kinaesthetic pleasures that girl teen films draw on: pleasures that will be examined in more detail in Chapters 5 and 6. Using the case studies of *Blue Crush* (Stockwell, 2002), *Stick It* (Bendinger, 2006) and *Bring It On* franchise (2000–9), this chapter examines the kinds of kinaesthetic pleasure encouraged by sequences that create: the ideal, perfectly composed sporting body and the effortful body in training. Finally it considers the spatial compositions of collectivity evident in the films' sporting moments and the potential pleasures of girls moving together in synchrony.

Following on from the previous chapter, 'Musical Address' explores the body and its capacities and pleasures in relation to music and dance. The chapter begins by exploring the conventional organizations of music and dance in girl teen musicals, dance films and musical moments. Beyond structural conventions, the spectacles of performance in these films share in common an intended affective impact that draws on the embodied pleasures of music and dance, and on the spaces of possibility created by musical address. The chapter outlines the way that the pleasures of the musical have been identified as utopian and builds on this formulation of pleasure, to understand its physical dimensions. Comparing the original (Waters, 1988) and remake (Shankman, 2007) versions of the girl teen musical *Hairspray*, I establish the sanitized aesthetic mode of millennial teen musicals: films that consequently offer experiences that are less based on affective transgressions and instead founded on aseptic fun. The chapter then weaves an analysis of the conventional remake of *Hairspray*, alongside a musical moment in *Mean Girls* (Waters, 2004) to illustrate the experiences of expansion and confinement that these films offer and the kinaesthetic pleasures they encourage.

Chapter 6 draws together all the moments discussed so far, to examine the ways that 'Music Video Aesthetics' make a spectacle of specific, gendered ideas of fun. This chapter explores the ways that girl teen films are part of an intimate public of girlhood (Berlant, 2008) that aims to feel as though it expresses what is supposedly common among girls. Music video aesthetics lend affective force to those events, scenarios and ideas of fun that are part of this intimate public. The chapter introduces the notion of intermedia aesthetics and uses it to explain how music video sequences in girl teen films create spectacle through a convergence of music and image. It identifies different modes of spectacle and compares the 'post-continuity' (Shaviro, 2010) stylistics employed in action cinema and boy teen film to those in girl teen film, where music video aesthetics render the feelings of music and dance. Beginning with a case study of *Make It Happen* (Grant, 2008), the chapter explores how music video aesthetics present the ideal dancing body to create a type of kinaesthetic contagion that feels like dance. A girl teen film moment from the romantic comedy *13 Going on 30* then offers an illustrative comparison to *Make It Happen*, in which music video aesthetics make a spectacle of 'everyday' practices of femininity.

2

Cinderella's Pleasures: The Power and Pleasures of Costume

Introduction

The first known literary version of Cinderella, 'Yeh-hsien', comes from ninth-century China. Sociohistorical permutations of the tale abound but its essential structure has become a gendered script used and reused most especially in products aimed at girls. Girl teen films in the fun mode are essentially Cinderella stories: they follow a rags-to-riches trajectory in which a degraded heroine, who suffers at the hands of other women, manages to climb the social ladder through grace and good looks. In popular culture Cinderella is a character-icon: although her stories are not all direct retellings of the Cinderella fairy tale, their heroines are a type. The Cinderella character-icon enjoys an iconic status, she signals narrative trajectory, plot features, character traits and a particular version of girlhood. Dependent on cannons of virtue and standards of beauty, the qualities and capabilities of the Cinderella character change according to the time and place of the story's telling. She quite neatly indicates the kinds of girls deemed entitled to happiness and pleasure in any given time and culture. Yeh-hsien, for example, was valued for her pottery skills and intelligence. In twenty-first-century girl teen films the Cinderella character-icon is valued for her ability to sing, dance and wear clothes well. She is white, able bodied and slim, and she embodies middle-class propriety and heterosexist assumptions.

The versions of Cinderella commonly taken to be the most influential are those of Charles Perrault (1697), The Grimm Brothers (1812) and Walt Disney (1950) (Haase, 2004a; Preston, 2004). Girl teen films however often use the Cinderella story in ways that are not necessarily straightforward: evoking the memory or idea of the tale, rather than any one version. Some films use the exoskeleton of Cinderella – the infallible structure – to produce versions of the tale that conform to its formal functions, while others adopt elements of

Figure 2.1 *A Cinderella Story* (2004), Cinderella's moment.

the story more loosely. History has variously revised Cinderella, articulating and creating diverging expectations of appropriate feminine behaviours, but the story's pleasures have remained consistent. Cinderella is a fairy tale about pleasure: although the tale involves fear and despair, the character's joy and the pleasures that she delights in are what is stressed. Cinderella must deal with the jealousy of other women and her mother's death but these elements work to make her particular pleasures all the more intense and triumphant. Analyses of Cinderella have stressed the despair wrought in the tale by sibling rivalries (Bettelheim, 1976), evil women (Warner, 1995) and incestuous fathers (Tatar, 1999), but the story also emphasizes pleasure. Fairy tales that include a female protagonist often focus on fear and rites of passage that involve risk and violence (e.g. 'Little Red Riding Hood'). Other stories highlight fears that are a part of coming of age, sex and marriage (e.g. 'Bluebeard'), or girls embracing the animalistic elements in their nature (e.g. 'Donkeyskin'). The legacies of these fairy tales are evident in horror films (Short, 2006) such as *Carrie* (De Palma, 1976; Peirce, 2013) *Black Swan* (Aronofsky, 2010) and *Ginger Snaps* (Fawcett, 2000). In common with the Cinderella fairy tale, girl teen films in the fun mode emphasize coming of age through glamour. Where 'Little Red Riding Hood', 'Bluebeard' and 'Donkeyskin' foreground fright, anxiety and unease, Cinderella highlights joy, delight and triumph. This chapter explores what makes Cinderella so successful – told, re-told, appropriated and manipulated for more than 1,200 years? What can we learn from millennial girl teen film that explains the aesthetic appeals of Cinderella? And in turn, how do these pleasures play out in girl teen films? Cinderella's pleasures do not somehow recuperate or cancel out the conservative ideologies of the 'Disney-fied' version of the character but they do explain her success.

Generic compatibility and the pleasures of enchantment

Fairy tale is a pliable genre. Its lack of history or geography – 'Once upon a time. … In a land far away' – without a fixed author or text, makes it infinitely adaptable. The genre is nonetheless repetitive, episodic and formulaic: its narrative certainty and familiarity also make it durable. Fairy tale is both flexible and robust (Benson, 2003; Propp, 2000 [1928]; Tiffin, 2009), it is a mouldable form that essentially stays the same. Fairy tale's flexibility leaves its stories open to exploitation and a number of the genre's durable elements are evident in girl teen films.

Like teen film, fairy tales work through the simultaneous contradictions that create ideas of adolescence: immaturity and maturity, independence and belonging, innocence and knowingness, expansion and confinement. Descriptions of fairy tale can very easily be applied to teen film: the protagonists are 'young and inexperienced and, at the opening of the tale, often in a position of apparent weakness' (Brewer, 2003: 5). Fairy tales chronicle the emergence of young people from dependence into maturity and as Neil Philip (2003: 41) describes: 'The characters, by means of a series of transformations, discover their true selves.'

Fairy tale and the girl teen films I examine here are also constructed using a similar modality. Like fairy tale, the worlds of girl teen film are uncomplicated. Their modality is relatively straightforward; there is a distinct delineation of good and bad, beautiful and ugly, right and wrong. Characters are easily identifiable as Prince Charming, Wicked Stepsister or Cinderella equivalents with little psychological depth. Like fairy tales girl teen films stay at the surface but these are complex, intricate and pleasurable surfaces that require a particular mode of engagement to be enjoyed. The fairy-tale setting is particular in its relationship to 'reality'. The producer/consumer contract requires consumer complicity with a world that is deliberately constructed as 'nonreality'. Fairy tales are set in 'a fictional world where preternatural events and supernatural invention are taken wholly for granted' (Tatar, 1987: 33). No attempt is made at a claim for truth, instead with the line 'Once upon a time', a world of wonder is evoked. Fairy-tale magic is delivered flatly, without explanation or internal logic. By employing a mode of delivery that is authoritative, its magic is implicit and unquestioned (Tiffin, 2009: 7, 18–19).

Girl teen films invoke the magical spirit of fairy tale by conjuring the enchanted tenor of 'happily ever after'. Supernatural magic can be a narrative device. In *16 Wishes* (DeLuise, 2010), for example, Abby's (Debby Ryan) fairy godmother gives her the opportunity to attain her desires through magical wishes and in *Freaky Friday* (Waters, 2003), Anna (Lindsay Lohan) makes a mystical body swap with her mother (Jamie Lee Curtis). However, in millennial girl teen films, magic is more often conjured by the commercial sphere. Instead of relying on the enchantment of the supernatural, the magic of girl teen films is found in the promise and glamour of the commercial realm. In this context glamour (explored in more detail in Chapter 3) refers to attractive surfaces: constructed appearances that help to create 'enchantment without supernaturalism' (Thrift, 2008: 9). The magic in these films is a kind of fairy-tale realism that evokes the pleasures of magic within a modern-day context.

Enchantment is the attitude that these films invite the audience to adopt. For girl teen films (and fairy tales) to successfully entertain, for audiences to enjoy the form's intended pleasures, the audio-viewer must be enchanted. By this I do not mean a mystification that dupes or pacifies (Adorno and Horkheimer, 1997; Barthes, 1993), but a suspension of disbelief and willingness to go along with the illusion: a cognitive and bodily attitude that is open to the kinds of pleasures that are conjured by the commercial realm. Girl teen films are set in a world where the glamour and promise of commercial magic are taken wholly for granted. Enchantment is a feeling that girl teen films aim to generate: released from the limitations of the 'everyday', enchantment creates a greater sense of possibility. Enchantment is not a passive state found in the audio-viewer and nor is it simply a style that girl teen films possess. It is a mode of engagement, which the films encourage, that goes along with the fantasy of the worlds created.

Girl teen films use cinematic markers of enchantment: film equivalents to 'Once Upon a Time' that act as invitations to enjoy another world that will end 'happily ever after'. However fairy-tale enchantment and the realm of magic cannot be delivered earnestly in the twenty-first-century context. Girl teen film's enchantment must be double coded: a technique that invites the audio-viewer to laugh at the excesses of enchantment while simultaneously preserving its affective charge.

Double coding the fairy tale

In girl teen films released between 2000 and 2010, Cinderella themes and fairy-tale enchantment can no longer be delivered with the flat authoritative tone where 'Once Upon a Time' begins a statement of events that the audience are simply expected to accept. The traditional fairy tale is boundless, though specific tellings are historically and socially restricted; the genre is constructed to invite the audience's unquestioning acceptance of the worlds conjured and events that often seem to have little logical cause and effect. Consequently a girl can hide from her incestuous father in the skin of a donkey ('Donkeyskin') or retrieve her grandmother whole and alive from the belly of a wolf ('Little Red Riding Hood'). In the fairy-tale context the flat delivery of the supernatural provokes no surprise. Girl teen films' fairy-tale realism is more generically restricted than traditional fairy tale. These films are bound by conventional Hollywood cause and effect and magic has to be explained. Double coding techniques are an essential part of girl teen film because where Eco's lover cannot say 'I love you', girl teen films cannot say 'happily ever after'. Double coding techniques work as a means to express those sentiments and affects drawn from Cinderella and the fairy-tale genre that can no longer be expressed earnestly.

Even direct versions of the Cinderella story created in the girl teen film mould rely on double coding mechanisms to encourage the audience to accept its enchantment. The opening of *A Cinderella Story*, for example, begins by double coding its fairy-tale status, the voice-over declares:

> 'Once upon a time in a far away kingdom lived a beautiful little girl and her widowed father. ... OK it wasn't that long ago and it wasn't really a far away kingdom, it was the San Fernando Valley and it only looked far away because you could barely see it through all the smog.'

Similarly this opening makes a visual and aural juxtaposition between the idea of the fairy-tale kingdom and the modern urban location of the film's setting: cutting from the opening shot of blue skies, mountainous landscape and the turreted castle of a fairy-tale kingdom to a long shot of the smog-filled San Fernando Valley. In conjunction, soft ascending orchestral strings are cut sharply with the sounds of traffic and aggressive beeping horns. This opening evokes the idea of the fairy tale, using the conventions of the fairy-tale genre, only to disregard the notion of referencing its enchantment in earnest. The film presents a 'put on' of Cinderella but in using fairy-tale conventions it facilitates an experience of the Cinderella fairy tale all the same. The opening of *A Cinderella Story* evokes the magic of the traditional fairy tale but frames it as a greater fiction than the narrative of the film: as the camera zooms out, away from the fairy-tale castle, we see that it is part of a snow-globe scene – another layer of fiction within the film's narrative. The discrepancy between the idea of the fairy-tale kingdom evoked and the San Fernando Valley, in which this Cinderella character lives, highlights the impossibility of asking a twenty-first-century audience to accept fairy-tale magic flatly. Fairy-tale enchantment has been conjured nevertheless. By using double coding mechanisms girl teen films refute their thematic and aesthetic connections to traditional fairy tale but still become Cinderella stories and despite double coding those elements that are drawn from the fairy tale, they still create the affects, feelings and emotions that are part of the Cinderella story.

Cinderella's legacy

All fairy tales are about transformation, as Marina Warner (1995: xv–xvi) proposes: 'Metamorphosis defines the fairy tale.' What is particular about Cinderella's transformation is the glamour that surrounds her and the social ascent that she makes in the passage from invisible maid to high-profile princess. In its traditional form Cinderella's transformation is expressed through the makeover that reveals the 'grace' and 'beauty' dormant in the character, waiting to be uncovered. In millennial girl teen films Cinderella can also experience a 'glitzy' makeover whereby the 'authentic' version of femininity that the Cinderella figure represents is momentarily concealed and corrupted by a makeover that is 'excessive'. This type of makeover is eventually ameliorated because the level of glitz is found to be unsustainable and corrupting. The films can also include a make-under whereby characters' excesses are toned down or stripped away to reveal the Cinderella character-icon underneath. In all its forms Cinderella's transformation personifies in the familiar and easily identifiable tropes of the makeover and reveals the idea of the adolescent girl as a figure in process.

In the twenty-first-century context Cinderella's transformation is brought about through self-governance and product consumption: crafted by the magic of the commercial sphere (rather than the power of maternal love, as was the case in earlier versions). Rosalind Gill (2007: 187) points out the escalating emphasis on physical improvement and the ceaseless pursuit of beauty in millennial media: 'Increasingly, femininity is presented as a bodily characteristic, requiring constant work – and, crucially, constant expenditure on beauty products.' Cinderella is the girl with the prettiest dress, most sparkling accessories, coiffed hair and streamlined figure. Her value is played out upon, around, and manifest in the body: what she wears, how she wears it and how she is presented.

Classed and raced ideas of femininity are attached to the makeover. Regulation of the girl body is based on mythic notions of aristocratic imperialism compared with the idea of the excessive Other (McRobbie, 2005; Palmer, 2004; Weber, 2009, 2011). As Brenda Weber (2011: 138) suggests, makeovers contain and contribute to a variety of discourses – imperialism, neo-liberalism, post-feminism – that articulate normative iterations of femininity. Cinderella maintains class-based ideas about taste and distinction that regulate bodies and behaviours. The right products will let Cinderella's value become physically apparent. Wearing the clothes correctly, she exhibits the 'right' corporeal dispositions. For the Cinderella character-icon in girl teen films the spectacle of the self is the only way to access power. Her only value is her body.

Traditionally, Cinderella's value shifts through transformation from maid to wife and her pleasures are tied to Prince Charming and heterosexual romance. Simone de Beauvoir (1953: 56) proposes that the Cinderella myth 'encourages the young girl to expect fortune and happiness from some Prince Charming rather than to attempt by herself their difficult and uncertain conquest'. Nonetheless, Prince Charming is increasingly less important (if he was ever really that important at all?) in the current neo-liberal, post-feminist context where consumer products, self-management/presentation and visibility are the primary focus. In the twenty-first-century setting, where notions of girlhood have stretched to include younger girls and young adults, Cinderella's transformation in girl teen films has become less about marriage. The visibility that her makeover offers has itself become the reward. In the neo-liberal context, transformation is sold as self-empowerment. Exploring the rhetoric of wedding media, for example, Alison Winch and Anna Webster (2012: 54) suggest that the bride is encouraged to invest in the correct brands as a means of producing the appropriate branded spectacle of the self. Transformation is brought about through self-management and product consumption and consequently 'the bride can shed her inadequate bodily chrysalis and emerge as the perfect bride' (ibid.: 54). Importantly they suggest that this transformation is not about becoming the perfect spectacle for the groom but about profiling one's successful self-management for the approval of other women. In her influential study of *Jackie* magazine, McRobbie (1991) identifies the codes of romance that act as key structures of teen girl magazines. In *Jackie*'s picture stories, she suggests, romance is made up of 'moments of bliss': 'the clinch', 'the proposal', 'the wedding day' (ibid.: 96). As Gill (2007: 185) suggests of millennial teen girl magazines, that version of femininity is rarely prevalent any longer, giving way to a focus on pop, fashion, beauty and celebrity. Similarly, girl teen films are now more heavily structured by moments of visibility, instead of moments of romance. Although The Kiss is still an important moment in millennial girl teen films, a great deal of its affective force has been placed elsewhere and it is often tagged on at the end, rather than given the weight it received in the past.

Although Cinderella is often conflated with the idea of romantic love, her quest – and the theme that holds girl teen films in the fun mode in common – is to be recognized as important. In girl teen films the male love interest is often an obligatory but superficially outlined character. This is best illustrated by a moment in *Mean Girls*: having successfully renewed her Cinderella status at the school dance, Cady stands talking to her friends. As her love interest Aaron (Jonathan Bennett) approaches, her friend announces: 'Man candy stage right.' As with many Cinderella stories, Prince Charming is an accessory or prop that exists only as a romantic figure, rather than as a fully formed character. In Disney's (Geronimi, Jackson and Luske, 1950) version of the tale, he is barely defined at all. He is the outline of a man, lacking any real definition. The Prince Charming role is left

Figure 2.2 *Cinderella* (1950), Prince Charming drawn in outline.

formless because it is not his quest, not his 'happily ever after', that we are interested in. He is, instead, just a bonus to the other pleasures that Cinderella achieves.

That Cinderella's transformation gives her visibility and recognition works in accord with neo-liberal discourse surrounding the 'successful girl' (Ringrose, 2007). Corresponding with neo-liberal invention, success in the guise of fame and fortune have replaced fantasies of romance in girl-centred texts (Hopkins, 2002). Performance is a recurrent trope of Cinderella. In Perrault's 1697 (2002: 38) version of the tale, her ability to dance validates her character: 'She [Cinderella] danced with such grace that everyone admired her even more.' However, more so than ever, performance is now a central component of girl teen films and Cinderella derivatives. This focus on performance is symbiotic with the increase of demotic celebrity (Turner, 2010) and the commercial, synergistic, influence of popular television programmes such as *American Idol* (Fox, 2002–16) and *The X Factor* (ITV, 2004–). Shows that compulsively frame contestants' participation through a rags-to-riches narrative. In girl teen films, celebrity has become the key reward and narratives build up to and centre on moments of triumphant recognition.

Pleasures

The pleasures that Cinderella invites us to enjoy in girl teen film are the embodiments of feeling of potential and excitement that she generates, the tactility of glamorous surfaces that surround her and kinaesthetic empathy with her physical happiness. Not everyone buys into or goes along with these Cinderella pleasures, but these are the pleasures she is designed to offer.

To understand Cinderella's pleasures we need to explore the kinds of embodiments of feeling that she creates. Foremost the Cinderella character embodies the antinomies of innocence and experience, and feelings of potential, movement and change are created through this combination of contradictory qualities. The Cinderella character-icon's transformation does not complete her, it intensifies her 'poignant antiphony' (Roach, 2007: 181): she is both maid and princess, innocent and knowing, set free and confined. Anne Higonnet (1998) explores the idea of childhood innocence as a Romantic invention, one that has recognizably perpetuated into the twenty-first century. The Romantic version of childhood attributes innocence to the child's mind which is understood as a 'blank slate', and to the child's body which is innocent of adult sexuality (ibid.: 8). Romantic representations of childhood diminish the child's corporeality (ibid.: 33), because experience or knowingness is placed on the full, sexed body (ibid.: 24). Innocence is especially attributed to and prized in girls, as Higonnet (ibid.: 27) describes of Romantic imagery: 'Boys apparently, quickly become men, while girls remain girls.' Women and the idea of femininity are often infantilized and contradictorily: 'It becomes plausible to flip the equation and consider infants to be like adult women' (ibid.: 194). The Cinderella character-icon embodies a balance of innocence and experience that defines the Hollywood notion of appropriate female adolescence. Because the wicked stepsister defines Cinderella's appropriate character by contrast, she has remained an essential part of these stories (I am not aware of any twenty-first-century girl teen film that does not include at least one wicked stepsister type). The wicked stepsister is fundamentally 'too experienced' – a state that she embodies as a physical and narrative contrast to Cinderella. The 'correct' balance of antinomies that Cinderella embodies gives the character-icon the tension required to make her potentially interesting: the combination of innocence and experience creates residual energies that feel like potential and promise.

Disney's *Cinderella* is a paradigmatic example of how Cinderella's pleasures are conjured. Despite being more than sixty years old, this version of the tale offers a reference point for the ways that Cinderella's legacy has weaved its way through time in cultural products aimed at girls and especially millennial girl teen film. The scene in which she arrives at the ball is characteristic of how Cinderella's aesthetic pleasures are created. Cinderella stands distantly in the centre of a long shot that emphasizes the spectacle of the palace's grand entrance. Sumptuous and variously textured materials make apparent the glamour of the space: wrought iron gates, red carpet and tall columns. A mid shot foregrounds the magic of Cinderella's dress as it glitters and sparkles. Her costume and accessories have transformed her into a graceful princess-type, giving material shape to the idea of the Cinderella character-icon. Her blonde hair is neatly styled and effortlessly controlled and her skin is white and pale – everything on Cinderella is light and dazzling, including her hair and skin. As she steps into the palace and moves towards the opulent staircase, she is flanked on both sides by a row of guards and a close-up shows that they are watching her admiringly; she has been made visible. The music plays out an ascending scale, rendering the rising excitement of the scene. Her physicality embodies innocence and experience in a balance that defines popular versions of girlhood: her body moves both hesitantly and gracefully, projecting a 'natural' elegance and simultaneous unsure and unaware physicality. Nonetheless, she enjoys a positive bodily attitude in her new costume: she projects unaffected effortlessness and joy in what she is wearing. Her costume and accessories also give her access to the ball and provide her with opportunity and possibility: the necessary tools to expand out into the world. This expansion is within strict confines however – not only in the narrative device that restricts her enchantment temporally (the spell ends at midnight) – but also in the limitations that her costume puts upon her: she is physically restricted and only suited to specific and defined roles in these clothes. The scene embodies the interplay of innocence and experience, expansion and confinement that both limits notions of girlhood and lends the Cinderella character-icon the frictions that create a sense of promise and possibility.

Like the moment that Cinderella arrives at the ball in Disney's version of the tale, girl teen films make a spectacle of abundant and tactile surfaces. Cinderella is surrounded by especially glamorous (commercial) magic. The abundant surfaces in girl teen films encourage a sensuous encounter with the array of textures on display. As a character-icon, Cinderella is found in her outline: in the dress, glass slipper, glossy hair and smooth skin. These elements are not just component parts, they are constitutional facets that create the character and generate her pleasures. Describing the power of the Cinderella type, Roach (2007: 182) suggests that part of her appeal is that she has two bodies (before and after) – 'one of common clay, the other of pure magic'. Technologies of glamour, like clothing, accessories and hair, are the pure magic that constructs Cinderella as an enculturated body. They are also the things in which we are invited to take tactile pleasure.

Alongside these technologies of glamour Cinderella's bodily attitude also invites us to enjoy kinaesthetic pleasures. Kinaesthetic empathy is an embodied experience of physical processes on display. Matthew Reason and Dee Reynolds (2012: 18) describe kinaesthesia as referring to 'sensations of movement and position … informed by senses such as vision and hearing as well as internal sensations of muscle tension and body position'. Empathy, they suggest, can mean 'projecting one's self into the object of contemplation' (ibid.: 19). At its most intense 'empathy involves embodied simulation and imagined substitution of one agent for another' (Reynolds, 2012). In its more diffuse sense kinaesthetic empathy is a mode of perception whereby another person or object's action is experienced in one's own body. I would like to take an approach to kinaesthetic empathy that focuses on how the audio-viewer is *invited* to respond to bodies on display rather than make claims to how they *will* respond. For example, through kinaesthetic empathy we are invited to enjoy Cinderella's pleasures in her costume in our own bodies; it is these pleasures to which I turn now.

The powers and pleasures of costume

The Cinderella character-icon's magical body is constructed by various technologies of glamour, but clothing is particularly powerful in its enchantment and provides a useful practical example of how to understand what girl teen film feels like. The pleasures of costume in film have often been explained in reference to notions of excess. Psychoanalytic approaches have deconstructed the high-heeled figure of the femme fatale, for example, as adorned fetish, whose clothing is over-invested with meaning to alleviate male fears of castration (Bruzzi, 1997; Doane, 1992). The pleasures of costume have also been found in spectacular interventions that work against the grain of the conventional narrative (Bruzzi, 1997; Gaines, 1990, 2000). The idea of clothing as spectacular has, further, connected with the notion of clothing as a force of agency. Developing Elizabeth Wilson's (1985) feminist re-appropriation of fashion as a site of opposition, film theorists have found fashion in film to offer a means of agency: a way to define the self rather than marketing another aspect of passive consumption (Berry, 2000; Bruzzi, 1997; Gilligan, 2011; Jeffers McDonald, 2010; Stacey, 1994). Employing Judith Butler's (1990, 1993) concept of identity as an embodied performative practice, film scholars have found in clothing an important vehicle for performing identity and a means of subversion to traditional gender roles. From this perspective, costume can highlight gender performance and in doing so question the idea of fixed feminine or masculine identities. These arguments suggest that when characters play with costume they can present fluid rather than homogenous accounts of gender (Dole, 2007; Ferris, 2008; Gilligan, 2011). In these interpretations pleasure exists in those elements of costume that work against the flow of conventional narrative or traditional notions of gender and identity. Instead, I am interested in the pleasures of costume from a tactile and kinaesthetic perspective.

In girl teen films Cinderella's transformations are not radical, they are a prerequisite of neo-liberal modernity. As Zygmunt Bauman (2005: 3) illustrates, life in a modern society always involves the expectation of identity reinvention. Bauman describes this condition as liquid life: people in modern societies exist with the presumption that they will constantly shed, strip and change – a ceaseless exploration for individuality and a neo-liberal requirement to present adaptability. As McRobbie (2004: 261) suggests in reference to Bauman, choice is a modality of constraint, and individuals are expected to manage to make the 'right' choices. Similarly, modulation describes a shift within parameters. Shaviro

(2010: 13–14) applies Deleuze's (1992) term 'modulation' as a means to explain how particular cultural texts articulate a 'control society', whereby flexibility is the only fixed requirement (Shaviro, 2010: 14). Unlike metamorphosis, which is expansive and open-ended, modulation is shift and change controlled within a fixed set of criteria. Where metamorphosis or transformation offers the idea of unrestricted alternatives and possibilities, modulation involves an underlying fixity, change that continually shifts but goes nowhere. Becoming in the Cinderella girl teen film context is not escape or resistance from identities that imprison. The transformations that girl teen films create seem more appropriately described as modulations: they 'imply that no matter what happens, it can always be contained in advance within a predetermined set of possibilities' (Shaviro, 2010: 13). Liquid life requires the constant struggle for individuality through consumption. Liquid life demands the ability to adapt and change and individuality is a set task answered by consumption but never concluded: 'a permanently impermanent self, completely incomplete, definitely indefinite – and authentically inauthentic' (Bauman, 2005: 33). The condition of liquid life and the modulations of girl teen film bring us to the aporia of individuality, where 'in a society of individuals everyone *must* be individual' (ibid.: 15, italics in original). The more we try to construct ourselves as individuals the more we are like everyone else. The modulations that girl teen films create still *feel* like change but these films maintain the feelings of potential and promise, contained within a predetermined set of possibilities.

One way that the feelings of potential and promise are created is through costume. In *Mean Girls* there is an attempt to create comedy through a pastiche of the catwalk moment (a trope in which the Cinderella character-icon reveals her transformation/modulation). At home and for the approval of Gretchen (Lacey Chabert) and Karen (Amanda Seyfried) – members of the clique known as 'The Plastics' – Cady descends the stairs in a new dress, as the camera tilts up her body. Cady's makeover is exaggerated in its inauthenticity: she is over-accessorized, with big hair and a dress of synthetic fabrics and colours. The use of stairs and the body tilt are key conventions of the catwalk moment, but they are both employed here with an underplayed tone that indicates this scene as a pastiche of girl teen film conventions rather than an earnest coming-of-age moment. Nonetheless, the pastiche falls short because of the aesthetic power of clothes. As director Mark Waters explains: 'We tried to have this ridiculous costume joke, but she ended up just looking kind of really good in this outfit' (2004, DVD). Despite the attempt to derive comedy from the moment, the tactile and kinaesthetic pleasures of clothing maintain the 'magical' charge that the scene attempts to undermine.

In narrative terms the power of clothes has a legacy from fairy tale to girl teen film. What remains in girl teen films is the idea that the right clothes, if worn properly, have the power to shatter class boundaries and allow characters to climb social ladders (Berry, 2000; Jeffers McDonald, 2010; Moseley, 2005b; Scott, 1996). In *Mean Girls*, for example, clothes give Cady the necessary armour to become 'Queen Bee'. Clothes also have the power to signify and express characters' emotional developments (Moseley, 2005a). As Rachel Moseley (ibid.: 112) makes clear, clothes in film can articulate the transition from immaturity to womanhood in ways that are addressed to a 'competent feminine gaze'. At the end of *Mean Girls*, Cady describes the narrative journey her character has taken: 'I'd gone from home-schooled jungle freak, to shiny plastic, to most hated person in the world, to actual human being.' This journey is also expressed through costume.

Cady's first costume (Figure 2.3) uses warm earth tones and durable materials like denim and corduroy. She keeps her hair tied back and wears little make-up. This costume highlights her 'natural' femininity and her liberal middle-class status and covers her body in a way that makes reference to her lack of awareness – her innocence – at the opening of the film. Further into the narrative (Figure 2.4) her clothing becomes bright and ostentatious. Synthetic materials and garish colours signify her transition from Cinderella figure to artificial mean girl. This type of costume accentuates Cady's body, and meanness, artificiality and knowingness (adult sexuality) are conflated. Finally, at the end of the film (Figure 2.5) Cady's costume finds an 'appropriate' balance and she returns to a more 'natural' appearance. At this end point her hair is down and her costume highlights the appropriate balance between innocence and experience.

Costume signifies but it can also have affective impact. Clothes can be magical, not only in what they represent but also in what they feel like. Clothes on screen can enchant by way of look and feel, through appeal to our visceral understandings of shape, form, texture and heft. In girl teen films the glamour of clothing – of particular types of dress – is showcased in ways that aim to appeal to tactile and kinaesthetic pleasures. In its materiality costume can encourage tactile empathy: the audio-viewer is invited to enjoy a sensory encounter with the textures and physicality on display. Eugenie Shinkle's (2013) analysis of fashion photography that focuses on biological registers of image

Figures 2.3, 2.4 and 2.5 *Mean Girls* (2004), Cady's costume progress.

perception, provides an approach that can help us understand the pleasures of costume in film. Images, Shinkle proposes, do signify but their communications are not limited to rationalization, they also involve feeling. The fashion image can encourage a visceral response: 'a "feeling" about the image that is bound up with interpretation, but which is not easily teased apart from it or expressed in language' (ibid.: 84–5). The feeling that Shinkle explores is connected to an empathetic response of unease to the uncomfortable body expressed in the collaborative fashion photography of Kristin McMenemy and Jurgen Teller (2005). For Shinkle the affective charge of an image is in its 'excess'. Teller's and McMenemy's images belie the ostensible superficiality of the fashioned body by running 'counter to fashion's alleged obsession with spectacle' (Shinkle, 2013: 84). For Shinkle the intensity of the images is in their lack of spectacle and disturbance of the order of traditional fashion photography: in place of beauty, sensuality and luxury, the images present clothing and the model body as unsightly, uncomfortable and unappealing (ibid.: 80). Shinkle suggests that spectacle is an attention to surface, a superficiality that rejects depth and affect. First, Shinkle's application of affect suggests that appeals to the senses are excessive as a matter of course. I would argue that affect, feeling and emotion can be thought of as elements of communication that are not necessarily always excessive. Those facets in film that aim to move us bodily are often described as excess, but from the perspective of aesthetic engagement they are central. From the point of view of pleasure, how the audio-viewer is invited to feel is not in excess of communication but the main point of it. Secondly, Shinkle's analysis implies that spectacle, by the nature of its superficiality, lacks affective charge. The spectacle of traditional fashion photography, however, is constructed with the aim of creating affects, feelings and emotions that are appealing, based on conventional beauty, sensuality and luxury. Affects that make us feel good are no more superficial than those that make us feel disturbed. It is only the hierarchy of emotions that means that little attention is given to positively appealing affects.

What Shinkle does provide is a means of exploring the ways that clothing is worn to invite the audio-viewer to enjoy specific pleasures. Shinkle's consideration of embodied empathy can be applied to costume in girl teen film: 'We don't simply read postures and gestures, we translate our external perspective on the body into our own personal body perspective, incorporating its attitudes in our own skin and bodies, muscles and viscera' (Shinkle, 2013: 81). In girl teen films costume can enchant. The ways that costume is presented encourages a positive bodily attitude towards the films: open to enjoy the magic of clothes, and go along with the fairy-tale idea that clothes can change lives. In *A Cinderella Story*, for example, Cinderella's costume is made into a spectacle that invites the audio-viewer to enjoy an embodied experience of the textures and physical processes on display.

Cinderella's costume: A Cinderella Story

A Cinderella Story makes explicit reference to the Cinderella lexicon: we are encouraged to understand the dress and how Sam (Hilary Duff) wears it, in its fairy-tale context, but it also *feels* like fairy tale. Not through supernatural magic but by material enchantment. The makeover and reveal in *A Cinderella Story* offer a key example of how costume can be constructed as richly enchanting. Though it is set in present-day Los Angeles the film is a relatively straightforward version of Cinderella that uses all of the familiar characters and scenarios from the fairy tale. Sam's transformative dress is a classic ball gown silhouette (Figure 2.1). A design that Turim (1984: 7) calls 'the sweetheart line', the look of which 'depended on bras that were molded to a point and often strapless, corsets or girdles, and crinolines, layered, ruffled slips made of stiffened organza and net that supported the bell-shaped skirts to their great width at the hemline'. In *A Cinderella Story* Sam's transformation/modulation is illustrated most powerfully in her dress and the 'princess', 'debutante', 'true-woman' and 'bride' (ibid.) are all signified by it. The gown's shape moulds her into the Cinderella character-icon: its outline – two heart shapes that meet synched in at the waist over the bell-shaped skirt – embody, create and overstate idealized notions of adolescent femininity. The dress holds in balance innocence and experience: at once exaggerating feminine curves *and* obscuring the female form among the lengths and layers of skirt.

The dress is presented to invite the audio-viewer to enjoy a sensory encounter with the Cinderella costume: pleasures that are made more evident by the way that the film displays other types of clothing. Sam's makeover is illustrated through montage. In a rush to find a costume for the school Halloween dance, the makeover sequence presents a series of possible costumes: a matador, witch, porky pig, 'hula girl', nun and knight in armour.

These costume changes police the borders of appropriate femininity to make clear which versions of femininity are acceptable and which are not (see Moseley, 2002: 47), and they create comparisons that highlight the glamour of the Cinderella dress, revealed at the dance that follows. The contrasting look and feel of the various costumes emphasizes the pleasures that the sweetheart line has to offer. The costumes in the makeover montage are presented within a cluttered and unspectacular straight-angle mid shot. For the most part the costumes are made up of heavy, thick, dark and cumbersome materials. The cut of the clothes is concealing, with straight bulky lines. The relationship between Sam's body and this clothing is presented uncomfortably: a feeling with which we are physically invited to share. She wears the costumes with hunched shoulders and a lack of grace that accentuates their awkward fit and feel. In contrast the 'hula girl' costume is constructed of light and revealing materials but it is nonetheless presented as inappropriate: Othered and overtly sexualized, this costume reveals flesh and skin in a way that embodies notions of excessive experience, unfitting for the traditional Cinderella character-icon.

In comparison the Cinderella dress is displayed with a low-angle shot that jibs up Sam's body as she stands at the top of a flight of stairs. The drape and sweep of the bell-shaped skirt is smooth. The textured layers create a billowing flow. The lace of the corset is delicate and intricate, and the beadwork catches the light, giving the dress its sparkle. The dress is glamorous in its varied and rich textures, inviting the audio-viewer to enjoy a pleasurable sensory encounter in its abundance and luxuriance. The shape and proportions of the dress exaggerate feminine form in a way that appears effortless. Similarly, the relationship between body and clothing is presented as effortless. Sam wears the costume with apparent ease (ignoring the reality of discomfort in this kind of costume) and we are invited to enjoy an empathetic response with her positive physicality: we can experience a version of her physical joy and effortless flow in the dress in our own bodies. Her postures and gestures are graceful and controlled but also hesitant. As a spotlight illuminates the dress, she holds onto her necklace nervously. Similar to the Disney Cinderella of the 1950s this is a traditional expression of how Cinderellas feel in their costume. The moment personifies the Cinderella character-icon's embodiment of innocence and experience, creating a feeling of possibility that is restricted by the Hollywood version of girlhood but potentially feels pleasurable anyway.

Double coded enchantment: The House Bunny

A Cinderella Story is a double coded pastiche, but the Cinderella costume is one element that is treated as sacrosanct and the film's presentation of the dress is done in earnest. *The House Bunny* is exemplary of how double coding mechanisms in millennial girl teen films manage and maintain fairy-tale affects in conjunction with comedy that seems to laugh at the fairy-tale conventions it utilizes. Where post-feminist irony makes it difficult to deal with fairy-tale sentiments in earnest, double coding allows those affects to remain. The first film from Adam Sandler's Happy Madison productions (other Happy Madison films include *Deuce Bigalow: Male Gigolo* [Mitchell, 1999] and *Little Nicky* [Brill, 2000]) to focus on a female protagonist, the film uses slapstick, sight gags and body humour as part of its comic pleasures. The opening sequence of the film provides a characteristic instance in which the Cinderella fairy tale is concurrently cited as a source of comic pleasure and affective sentiment.

As mentioned in the introduction to this chapter, fairy tales are full of despair and part of their wonder is to relieve that despair with magic and enchantment. Magic is made all the more enchanting through its comparison with desperation. *The House Bunny* begins with a scrapbook image: a dour colour scheme highlights the desperate position of the protagonist, Shelley (Anna Farris), left on the steps of an orphanage. The camera zooms in gently and soft dissolves are accompanied by light, lilting, sombre music to highlight the character's pitiful position. The use of verbal irony in this moment, however, sets up a discrepancy, as Shelley's voice-over explains: 'I guess somebody didn't want me. I hear they did want the basket back though.' The protagonist's voice-over is delivered in a tone that is excessively sincere and innocent. Disparity and exaggeration signal the film's double coded mode. Humour is derived from the incongruity between style and content – between despair and the flippant way with which it is handled, and the exaggeration of the Cinderella figure's innocence.

The music score alludes to fairy-tale magic with a repeated light-tinkling chime, reminiscent of Disney fairy-tale musical scores. The use of soft water colours and traditional children's illustration makes reference to the organic textures of the ostensibly authentic, traditional fairy tale. There is, however, a discrepancy between this use of mise en scène and sound, and a simultaneous playful evocation of the fairy-tale genre. Shelley's voice-over begins by using the traditional language of fairy tale, but she and the visuals become confused and the sequence self-consciously highlights fairy-tale conventions as conventions: 'Then one day something magical happened, just like out of a fairy tale. Remember the one where the wolf huffed and puffed and blew the piggy's house down and he was wearing a glass slipper I think and he had a pumpkin plus there was that other thing? Well the same thing happened to me, only vastly different.'

The confusion of Shelley's fairy-tale imagery – the wolf as 'prince' turns out to be Playboy magnate Hugh Hefner – highlights fairy-tale sentiments as laughable.

Finally Shelley explains, with a continued tone of sincerity and innocence that she transformed into a beautiful young woman and eventually found the family she had always wanted. Here is the central gag of the sequence as Shelley reveals: 'Now I live in the Playboy mansion and this is where I want to live, happily ever after.' As the Playboy mansion and Shelley's occupation are revealed, a cosy, homely image is juxtaposed with a zoom-out reveal of the mansion. The classical strings that have underscored the sequence mix into a highly energetic, samba beat. As Shelley delivers her 'happily ever after', the camera tilts up into a brilliant blue sky and beach balls fly through the air to reveal the opening film credits.

This intense use of colour contrasts significantly with the soft water colours of the earlier fairy-tale images. The use of colour in this final shot accentuates synthetic, artificial, digital qualities and emphasizes a smooth flatness: alluding to the disparity between the idea of the 'earthy' fairy tale – its 'authentic' magic – and the plastic pleasures of the Playboy mansion that are to follow.

The classical notion of the pure and virtuous Cinderella protagonist is set in contrast to the hedonism, narcissism and ostentation associated with the Playboy bunny and the crude cynicism of the Playboy brand. The structure of this sequence draws on typical post-feminist irony: withholding until the last moment *how* Shelley has found her happily ever after emphasizes the discontinuity in speaking of Playboy as a fairy-tale dream. Shelley is both exaggeratedly innocent and exaggeratedly experienced: presented as though her life from orphanage to Playboy mansion has left her as a 'blank slate' (she is an extreme version of the 'dumb blonde' stereotype) but simultaneously 'overly' experienced.

Despite its post-feminist irony, through the use of double coding techniques the sequence still draws on fairy-tale aesthetics and affects: the soft water colours, the texture and sound of the storybook pages as they turn, the fairy-tale castle, all conjure aesthetic enchantment and draw on feelings of wonder. The techniques of enchantment are still in play. Although Shelley's voice-over is excessively sincere, innocent and optimistic, she *does* express the humble integrity of a Cinderella heroine. In its final moments the sequence becomes euphoric: in less than 2 minutes Shelley's dreams *have* come true, she *has* 'transformed' and her humble character *is* triumphant. The sequence, for example, economically renders Shelley's transformation/modulation, taking place over the course of a single 10-second shot. The speed with which the makeover trope is employed here emphasizes the playful way that Cinderella is referenced, but an experience of the fairy tale is created all the same. Aesthetically the pan across Shelley's makeover creates enchantment conjured by the material realm: light and assorted colours, various textures (felt, card, photo paper, silk ribbon), the sparkle of her dress and tiara, and camera flashes call on aesthetics of glamour and visibility. Though the power of the makeover is downplayed through double coding, its pleasurable affects remain. Those Cinderella sentiments that would be risible if expressed in a tone of sincerity are successfully rendered nonetheless.

Double coded costume

The House Bunny includes various moments of modulation, beginning with Shelley's change from orphan into Playboy Bunny. Shelley is tricked into leaving the Playboy mansion by a jealous rival and finds herself as 'housemother' to a local university sorority. Her role is to remodel the Zeta girls so that they will attract boys, make the sorority popular and save their home from closure. Shelley increases the girls' exchange value by refashioning their bodies as the only commodity that is available to them. The kind of makeover that Shelley performs on the girls is 'glitzy'. Instead of revealing their 'authentic' femininity, as the makeover in *A Cinderella Story* presents itself to be, the glitzy makeover is diegetically constructed as excessive and shallow. Much is made of the Zeta's makeover, but they eventually reject the Playboy model look as too superficial and ameliorate their provocative costumes and tone down their new looks to a type of attractiveness that is less overtly sexual (see Jeffers McDonald, 2010: 96). In narrative terms amelioration of the glitzy makeover is essential to answering the anxieties raised by inauthentic versions of femininity (Marston, 2012). The girl that is made over finds that excessive femininity obscures her supposed authentic self. With this type of makeover the films take the opportunity to make the most of the sensory pleasures of consumption and the tactility of clothes but deny this overtly constructed and sexualized version of femininity. Regardless of the narrative endings the affective force of these films is given to moments of visibility. When the films try to retract the pleasures of the makeover and catwalk with sentimental speeches, they often feel hollow, unable to compete with the pleasurable affects of those earlier scenes.

In *The House Bunny*'s glitzy makeover there are no sweetheart lines: on the surface the transformation appears to be quite different to that of *A Cinderella Story*. Nonetheless the powers and pleasures of clothes work in the same way:

creating the same version of girlhood and offering the same affects. The key catwalk moment in *The House Bunny* is aggressively double coded: the Zeta girls reveal their new looks and in the reverse shot the approbation of male onlookers is expressed by their slack jaws and inability to walk. In the makeover montage, previous to the reveal, the idea of the traditional Cinderella transformation is continuously undermined. Giving the girls a make-up lesson, for example, Shelley announces: 'First we must highlight your eyes. The eyes are the nipples of the face.'

Despite this double coding the same Cinderella powers and pleasures of clothes are maintained. Clothes are everywhere and in the central makeover montage clothes of a variety of textures and colours surround the girls. Clothing hangs from racks and lines of shoes fill the screen. Encouraging an empathetic tactility in the audio-viewer, the girls constantly touch and feel the fabrics, literally rubbing them on their faces: the sequence engulfs them in textures and offers a similar feeling to the audience.

As the makeover moment moves towards its climax, the intensity of the sensory encounter with clothes escalates. The camera tracks through an array of colourful shirts into a swirl of vibrantly coloured skirts. Cutting to a high-angle shot, the girls throw silk scarves towards the camera. The shot becomes a swirl wipe that transitions into the reveal. This transition embodies the power of clothes with the aim of feeling like material magic. This is an intensely tactile sequence and the fervent flow of materials invite the audio-viewer to enjoy the pleasures of a tactile richness and the enchantment of the commercial sphere.

As in *A Cinderella Story* the relationship between body and clothing is presented as affirmative in *The House Bunny*'s catwalk moment. Clothes are worn confidently – this moment does not involve Cinderella's physical hesitance – the

Figure 2.6 *The House Bunny*'s catwalk moment (2008).

girls strut, and we are invited to enjoy kinaesthetic empathy with the pleasure the characters take in their clothing and their catwalk moment: feeling a sense of their confidence in our own bodies. In this glitzy makeover the emphasis is on highlighting the female form conspicuously: flesh and skin are the main textures on display and the power of clothes is to mould and highlight the body. However in the shot before the reveal, Shelley and the Zetas run around playfully. The aesthetic mode is gleeful and childish before shifting into the hyper-sexuality of the catwalk moment. In *The House Bunny* the narrative particularly emphasizes the sorority girls' innocence. Even the fact that one of the sorority members is pregnant is glossed over. Her large belly is continuously referenced for comic effect, but beyond the fact of having a big stomach any other details of pregnancy are left out of the film. After the character has the baby it is conspicuously absent. Nonetheless, as a means to maintain the expected dichotomy, costume highlights the girls' adult bodies as embodiments of experience. Despite the differences between the classical and glitzy modulations in *A Cinderella Story* and *The House Bunny*, the powers and pleasures of clothes remain consistent – still in touch with their Cinderella legacy.

Conclusion

Cinderella's enchantment invites us to go along with the powers and pleasures of the commercial realm: the idea and feeling that clothes, hair, skin and accessories can change lives.

The success of the Cinderella fairy tale can in part be attributed to the affective attitude of the story and character that stresses pleasure above fear. Cinderella's pleasures are founded on glamorous and tactile surfaces, of which costume presents an illustrative example. The approach I have taken here to costume can just as easily be applied to the other tactile surfaces that are part of the makeover and catwalk moments in girl teen film. Hair, for example, represents the containment and ordering of female sexuality, but our immediate reactions to it are also intensely visceral, bringing with it its own particular type of uncanny and glamorous pleasures. When Sam enters the school dance in *A Cinderella Story*, her blonde hair falls to her shoulders in ringlets. Along with her sweetheart line dress and the sparkle of the event that surrounds her, it offers another pleasurable surface that offers tactile and kinaesthetic pleasures and invites us to go along with the powers and pleasures of the commercial realm.

As I have suggested, we do not have to believe this enchantment, but we do have to temporarily collaborate with it.

Cinderella is defined by the glamorous materials that adorn her, but she is also made glamorous by the spectacles that surround her. Central to the pleasures of Cinderella is the experience of visibility: Cinderella's transformation/modulation gives her the opportunity to enjoy celebrity. Cinderellas enjoy the glamour of being looked at and admired. Perrault's (1697 [2002]: 37) description of Cinderella as she enters the ball sums up this key element of the tale's legacy: 'Suddenly everyone fell silent. No one was dancing, and the violins stopped playing, because everyone was so absorbed in contemplating the great beauty of the unknown lady who had just entered.' In current neo-liberal, post-feminist and networked societies, the promise of celebrity has intensified. Celebrity has become an increasingly fundamental trope and pleasure of girl teen films. In the following chapter I examine how celebrity is constructed in the worlds of girl teen films as a type of glamour that creates spectacles of the self and generates pleasurable affects.

3

Celebrity Glamour: Space, Place and Visibility

Introduction

In *The House Bunny* when the Zetas reveal their makeover, Natalie (Emma Stone) becomes aware of how many people are looking at her. She declares: 'So this is what it feels like not to be invisible.' In girl teen film (following its Cinderella legacy) visibility, manifest as popularity and celebrity, is where fun is found.

In narrative terms celebrity and the labour of popularity are often employed as a site of pleasure, tension and contest in these films. In the 1980s girl teen film *Heathers* (a film that can be seen as a forerunner to those of the 2000s) the protagonist Veronica Sawyer (Winona Ryder) makes the labour of local celebrity explicit. Of her friends she declares: 'Well it's just like they're people I work with, and our job is being popular and shit.' The narrative of *Heathers*, as is typical of girl teen films, contradictorily struggles with the hazards and pleasures of popularity. Although Veronica is disdainful of the ways in which she must maintain her image, she is also compelled by the powers of celebrity that come with being a 'Heather'. Similarly, in *Mean Girls*, Cady is equally enamoured and repelled by the idea of her own celebrity. Although she admits her dislike of the Plastics, she also recognizes the appeals of being one: 'Because being with the Plastics was like being famous ... people looked at you all the time and everybody just knew stuff about you.'

The notion of celebrity as desirable is not specific to girl teen films of the twenty-first century but its narrative and affective importance has intensified and its aesthetic pleasures are increasingly employed. The spectacularization of girlhood in millennial media culture – the constant looking, picking at, deconstruction and regulation of girls – takes place within celebrity culture (Projansky: 5). At the turn of the twenty-first century, discourses of girlhood and celebrity have grown simultaneously. Like the ever-present girl, celebrity is not new but exists now in an intensifying and pervasive form. In girl teen film this millennial version of celebrity is played out as pleasure. In the Hollywood

Figure 3.1 *Bratz*'s red carpet glamour (2007).

film industry stars have often been exploited as key to gaining audiences for teen film and girl teen films often include actors that function as stars outside of the diegesis. For example between 2000 and 2010 (though their stardom waned and changed mid-decade) Hilary Duff and Lindsay Lohan variously operated as economic entities that existed in ancillary markets and other parts of the cultural economy. Duff and Lohan served as signs across the media, making abstract images, ideas and ideals appear tangible and lending their specific brands of girlhood to various products. Celebrity is a part of culture that thrives on affect: crafted out of passionate aesthetic signifiers, celebrity works to ignite and regulate desire (Redmond, 2015: 1). Rather than focus on the star as sign across the media and its economic function, I want to understand how celebrity is conjured within the worlds of these films. Through techniques of visibility and the generation of glamorous spaces and places, girl teen films create experiences that feel like glamour and make visibility pleasurable. This chapter explores how and what celebrity glamour is designed to feel like.

The powers of visibility

In girl teen film (as in our culture at large) visibility, and the intensified visibility of celebrity, as a 'normal' desire is an axiom. As Jo Littler (2003: 13) proposes, the desire for fame is constructed in popular media texts as desirable and 'ordinary': 'The idea that "to be ordinary" in our culture will probably entail "wanting to be a celebrity" … gets reproduced and naturalised.' In its twenty-first-century manifestation, public visibility has taken a 'demotic turn' (Turner, 2010) whereby being in view works as a central point of identity validation. The idea of visibility as glamorous, of being looked at as appealing, is nothing new but in the network of hyper-mediated spectacles of the twenty-first century, visibility is more available and more intensely endorsed (Couldry and McCarthy, 2004; Marshall, 2010). The spectacle of personas that defines celebrity has grown to become a norm – visibility and the mediated presentation of the self is part of the 'everyday'. It makes sense then that these films create experiences that draw on and develop the powers and pleasures of visibility, not just as a narrative means to successful romance but as a reward in and of itself.

Culturally, visibility and celebrity are constructed as a key means of substantiating social identity, and celebrity is presented as a significant means to acquiring symbolic capital, a way to 'really' exist, 'to mean something' as Littler (2003: 11) describes it. Being visible means being included, taken into account, talked about, looked at and considered. We grant celebrities time and cultural and social space. For those who can achieve it, visibility and celebrity can give access to powerful, social networks: what Holmes and Redmond (2006: 2) describe as the 'centre of meaning generation'. In girl teen films, where few other means of power are made apparent for girls, the spectacle of the self is *the* singular way of taking up time and space and accessing power.

Celebrity is identified in academia, like the girl figure herself, as a culture that neatly personifies post-feminist and neo-liberal discourse. Post-feminism and neoliberalism share de-classed and de-raced ideals of individualization. In the spectacle of contemporary celebrity the notion that freedom and choice gives everyone equal opportunity for success through self-management (Ringrose, 2007: 480) is markedly apparent. Discourses of bodywork, self-reinvention, adaptability and individual attainment that surround celebrity, express neo-liberal and post-feminist ideologies (Allen, 2011; Allen and Mendick, 2013; Attwood, 2011; Cronin, 2000; Gill, 2011; McRobbie, 2004, 2009; Projansky, 2014; Ringrose, 2007; Tasker and Negra, 2005). Girl teen films do not just express these ideologies: they create experiences of celebrity that aim to make the spectacle of the self feel fun. The girl figure's visibility is given affective force as well as narrative significance and through techniques of enchantment the audio-viewer is asked to go along with the idea that being looked at is important.

As we saw in the previous chapter, for the Cinderella character-icon, pleasure can be found in glamorous and tactile surfaces that adorn the body. Glamorous pleasures can also be created by celebrity aesthetics: by the way visibility is constructed on screen and on the kinds of spaces and places that surround the character. These celebrity aesthetics are a recognizable part of the Cinderella legacy – Cinderella is about being looked at after all – but here they take on a particularly millennial intensity in their use of spectacle and glamour. To understand the pleasures of celebrity aesthetics in these films, I will start by unpacking the form that celebrity takes.

The structures of celebrity in girl teen films

The experience of celebrity is played out in these films in recurring formats. How celebrity is constructed in girl teen films can be unpacked into three component parts: narrative events, modes and degrees of visibility. The first building block is celebrity *narrative events*: these are recurring narrative conventions through which visibility and celebrity are enacted. The most commonly recurring narrative events of visibility in girl teen films are: the catwalk, sports performance, and singing and/or dancing. In the catwalk, visibility is valued in and of itself – it is the task and the reward. The catwalk can take on different formats: the 'big reveal' that follows a character's makeover; the 'strut' that signifies an individual's or group's visibility and dominance of space; and the 'mediated catwalk', whereby characters are presented at red carpet events, garnering media attention. Tamar Jeffers McDonald (2010: 103–4) uses the term 'catwalk moment' to describe a facet within the big reveal – an instance of stasis that follows the makeover where the recipient pauses to show off her changes and receive admiration from onlookers. I am using the term a little differently as a moment understood by its design; the catwalk references the idea of motion and display that the fashion show origins of the word imply. It is not necessarily tied to the tropes that surround the makeover, it also happens at other moments. The second celebrity narrative event in girl teen films is the sports performance (analysed in detail in the following chapter). Visibility and celebrity is achieved here through hard work and made most intensely manifest in a final sports performance that displays characters' skills and bodies, to which their success is attributed. Finally singing and/or dance numbers represent another event that give the Cinderella character-icon their moment in the spotlight (the focus of Chapter 5). These numbers can take place as part of a school concert, a television show, nightclub performance, arena concert or as part of a competition or audition. In common with the sports performance, visibility is most often achieved through an industrious attitude that culminates in a final performance. In narrative terms the sports and dance contexts provide a framework for the coming-of-age narrative, whereby making 'mature' decisions gives the Cinderella character-icon her opportunity for celebrity and respect.

The second building block of celebrity in girl teen films is its *modes*: the type of celebrity enacted. The modes of celebrity performed in the narrative events outlined are identifiable using Rojek's (2001: 18–19) categories of celebrity: attributed – those that gain celebrity through exposure; achieved – those that gain celebrity through a 'talent'; ascribed – celebrity is assigned through ancestry and royal lineage.

The final component part of celebrity is the *degree of visibility*. Characters achieve visibility and fame in the diegesis of girl teen films to varying levels. Characters may enjoy localized visibility, concentrated in the public sphere of the school environment. Or they can experience levels of media exposure, from minor celebrity to international stardom. All girl teen films include one or more of these narrative events, one or more modes of celebrity and at least one point on the spectrum of degrees of visibility. At first glance it appears that modes and degrees of celebrity would correspond quite naturally and categorically with the narrative events in which celebrity and visibility are enacted. For example we might assume that a catwalk moment will most likely include attributed and local celebrity. However, single girl teen films can include more than one type of celebrity, enacted through a variety of narrative events, incorporating differing degrees of exposure variously. As the celebrity structures diagram (Figure 3.2) illustrates, the component parts of visibility and celebrity in the films overlap and play out in various formations. All girl teen films work at the meeting point at the centre of the Venn diagram because they are always about visibility.

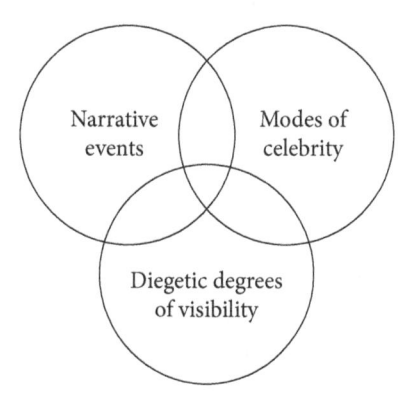

Figure 3.2 Structures of celebrity.

We can use the structures of celebrity Venn diagram to think about how celebrity is constructed in these films. In *Mean Girls*, when Cady as narrator declares that being a Plastic was like being famous, quoted above, she struts down the school corridor alongside the other girls as their peers watch them. This celebrity narrative event is a catwalk moment that represents the attributed celebrity and local visibility that Cady has achieved. These arrangements are generic: the same structures of celebrity play out over and over again in various combinations. Regardless of celebrity mode or degree, however, these films create the same experiences of celebrity based on the pleasures of glamour. I want to unpick how glamour makes visibility feel fun in girl teen film.

Celebrity and glamour

Celebrity is an abstract notion. The personas celebrities present feel material but can never be fully grasped. The concept of celebrity is both obvious and elusive. As Roach (2007: 48) illustrates, celebrity is a 'mediatized conception of a person ... not reducible to any one of the many icons that publicize it, but rather disseminated pervasively as a ghostly semblance, specific yet intangible, seen by not two people in exactly the same way, yet intelligible to nearly everyone'.

Celebrities generate an illusion of presence: they appear both available and unbiddable at once. They encourage intimacy – what Roach (2007) and Nigel Thrift (2008) call public intimacy – whereby the object displays particular qualities, which can be comprehended but at the same time suggests hidden depths beyond what we can see. Celebrities are singular and typical, ordinary and extraordinary, nowhere and everywhere. As Roach (2007: 22) explains it: 'The most charismatic celebrities are the ones we can only imagine, even if we see them naked everywhere.' It is in the combination of the abstract and the material – the possibility that fantasies and ideas can be housed in the material body – that the glamour of celebrity is conjured.

Appropriate in this context where we are exploring enchantment and the magic conjured by the commercial realm, the original eighteenth-century meaning of the word glamour was something like sorcery or magic (Dyhouse, 2011). It is a slippery term, the meanings of which have shifted and changed, though the connotations of charm, artifice and allure still remain. In the twentieth century its strongest associations were with the classical Hollywood cinema of the 1930s to 1950s, connected with luxury, excess, power and sexuality. These connections have continued into the twenty-first century but the word is not fixed, it can also have tacky, campy or seedy connotations, associated, for example, with soft-core pornography. Essentially though glamour is always about fantasy, desire and pleasure. Alongside the girl and celebrity, glamour has intensified and become a pervasive element of millennial culture. As Carol Dyhouse (2013: 155) makes clear, glamour is nothing new but with increasing affluence it has seemingly been democratized and become more available in the West. Where, she suggests, glamour was once offered as an imaginary escape from the banal routines of the everyday, modern imagery constructs reality itself as glamorous and the pursuit of glamour as an everyday imperative.

Glamour has the potential to turn people and objects into events, but it does not consist of a list of markers, nor exist as an object, but as sensation: glamour is perceived rather than possessed (Postrel, 2013: 12; Roach, 2007: 91; Thrift, 2008: 14). It is fleeting and transient, a moment rather than an entire narrative. It can tap into pre-existing desires, obscure the mundane and give us an experience of imagined ideals. In girl teen films, for example, celebrity glamour draws on and creates the longing to be admired. The films then momentarily answer that desire with an experience of admiration. Glamour feels like possibility because it furnishes us with enough to project our desires and fantasies into it but not so much to disillusion. It appears as though it were tangible, but it can never be fully grasped and consequently its promise never dissipates. This intangibility is key to the glamour of celebrity. Shaviro (2010: 10) describes the stars as ideal commodities because 'they always offer us more than they deliver, enticing us with a "promise of happiness" that is never fulfilled, and therefore never exhausted or disappointed'.

In girl teen film celebrity glamour makes visibility affectively pleasurable. Glamour takes many forms and is different to different people, though some versions are more widespread and enduring than others (Postrel, 2013: 19). Though we cannot describe glamour through a list of material markers, we can pinpoint its characteristics. The characteristics of celebrity glamour have been explored variously in academia, but like celebrity itself it can be difficult to fully grasp the components that make up its features. In the characteristics of celebrity glamour table (Figure 3.3) I identify the essential traits that define celebrity glamour. These are: public intimacy: the illusion of availability and proximity (Currid-Halkett and Scott, 2013; Dyer, 1979; Holmes and Redmond, 2006; Marshall, 1997; Roach, 2007; Rojek, 2001; Stacey, 1994; Thrift, 2008); the appearance of effortlessness (Dyer, 1979; Postrel, 2013; Roach, 2007; Thrift,

54 · The Aesthetic Pleasures of Girl Teen Film

1. Characteristics	2. How	3. Pleasures
Public intimacy: the illusion of availability and proximity	Creates platforms and opportunities for visibility: e.g. a podium, an audience, media attention, but also restricts access. Glamour creates a sense of mystery that illuminates as it conceals, highlights as well as veils	Feelings of promise
The appearance of effortlessness	A veneer of unselfconsciousness, effort is concealed, organised to disappear, traces of work are disguised	Ease, experience of moving through the world unrestricted
Practical inutility	Textural variety, luxury, and impracticality create a sense of opulence, use is to generate glamour only	Abundance, tactility
The embodiment of contradictory qualities	For example innocence and experience, expansion and confinement	Energies, feelings of potential and promise

Figure 3.3 Characteristics of celebrity glamour.

2008); practical inutility (Marshall, 1997; Roach, 2007; Veblen, 1925); and the embodiment of contradictory qualities (Dyer, 1979; Holmes and Redmond, 2006; Marshall, 1997; Roach, 2007; Thrift, 2008). The characteristics are achieved using particular techniques that I summarize in the 'How' column of the table, and these techniques aim to create specific pleasures that are named in the third and final column.

The end credits of *Bratz: the movie* (McNamara, 2007) (Figure 3.1) provide an ideal illustration of how the celebrity glamour table can be used to explore how celebrity is constructed as glamorous in girl teen film. *Bratz: the movie* is a live-action film based on MGA 'fashion dolls' that the company describes 'are all about rockin' the hottest fashion trendz with their friends and some serious attitude. With tons of confidence and style to match, the Bratz® make heads turn wherever they go!' (MGA). The film follows the 'Bratz' as they start high school, through to their graduation. As their final narrative reward they are invited to perform on the red carpet of a movie premiere. This glamorous backdrop is a mediatized event surrounded by press and camera crews. The space makes visibility possible: the Bratz are on stage, lit up, in a roped-off area. Creating a sense of public intimacy they are there to be seen but at a distance, available but remote, the girls positioning within the space creates feelings of promise. The stage also embodies contradictory qualities, creating unresolved intensities: the space makes the Bratz the focal point of the scene but conversely they are also confined, physically and metaphorically roped into a specific kind of space and performance. This combination of contradictory qualities creates the pleasurable feelings of potential and promise. The design of the space also embodies the characteristics of practical inutility and the appearance of effortlessness. As a night-time event the Bratz's performance space stands out in the darkness as a spectacle of the night-time economy. The red carpet, dry ice, circular stage, velvet curtains, decks and clusters of people create textural variety. In combination the array of light sources – footlights, fairy, neon, spotlights and flash bulbs – shimmer upon a water fountain to create effervescent shadows across the scene. The play of light and shadow is central to creating a sense of excitement and mystery, hiding imperfections and generating feelings of abundance and tactility. The space is also unproductive, or more accurately, it is a space that only produces glamour and its only utility is visibility. The scene is also effortless: the space appears, we do not witness its construction or workings. Cables, scaffold and power sources are kept from view. The Bratz also fit into the space effortlessly: the satin and diamante on their costumes and accessories match the glittering backdrop, and like the space itself, the girls just appear and perform without expressions of force or effort. This final scene in the film makes no real contribution to the narrative, but it aims to leave the audience with an experience of glamour.

Taking this systematic approach to how celebrity glamour is created in girl teen films allows us to be specific about how and what types of pleasure are made available. I want to pull apart what we take for granted as obviously glamorous to understand how it works. Celebrity is constructed in girl teen films in a number of ways but the use of space and place is especially important in terms of understanding how glamorous pleasures are created around the visibility of the Cinderella character-icon. In conjunction, visibility is itself designed cinematically in ways that draw on specific glamorous pleasures. In this next part of the chapter I will take the systematic approach outlined above as a means to articulate how and what types of pleasure the glamour of space, place and visibility in girl teen films offer.

Glamorous spaces and places

Place is exciting because it is a site of pleasure and possibility. Historically, girls were often confined to bedroom culture (McRobbie, 1991), but in millennial popular culture they have entered the public sphere. Nonetheless, in girl teen films girls are still restricted to institutional, domestic and commercial spaces and places. As Mitchell and Reutschler (2016: 9) make clear, place is a stage and practice of power. In girl teen films place is a stage for visibility.

Space and place can produce glamour. Exploring the geography of celebrity Currid-Halkett and Scott (2013: 2) propose that 'the stars themselves are often quite ephemeral but the system of stardom is maintained through the continual social reproduction of cultural and symbolic capital and the physical settings, or scenes, in which the system takes shape'. In girl teen films, space and place can surround the Cinderella character-icon with celebrity glamour.

Space and place are simple *and* complicated concepts, with multiple meanings and implications. For our purposes here a working definition of these terms will help us to understand how space and place are designed to invite us to enjoy the pleasures of glamour. Place is understood as a fixed location. A form of space with definite coordinates, created through acts of naming (Cresswell, 2004: 7). Space, as Tim Cresswell (2004: 8) suggests, is a more abstract concept: space is unfixed, mobile and fluid.

The features of glamorous spaces

The 'backdrops' to stardom, what Sean Redmond (2015: 5) calls 'enchanted environments', include: mediatized award ceremonies, parties, charity events, high-end fashion shops or exotic holidays. These star 'scenes' are the spaces of celebrity. Space is not a defined locality but 'a framing device in the creation of cultural imaginaries' (Kitchin and Hubbard, 2010: 2). The spaces of girl teen film that are designed as glamorous are not specific locations but are dressed to create glamour. Like the 'transformations' that these films offer, the spaces dressed as glamorous are contained within a predetermined set of possibilities. The typologies of glamorous celebrity space in girl teen films are specific: the dance (prom, homecoming, etc.), the red carpet, music concert, nightclub, manor house and mediated event. These glamorous spaces are designed to create visibility. Like the eighteenth-century pleasure gardens, glamorous spaces are constructed to offer a variety of spectacles, the most important one being the crowd itself (Conlin, 2013). Nightclubs for example are designed to create a 'synoptic frenzy' (Rigakos, 2008) in which the space (and nightclub culture itself) is designed to make its patrons objects of aesthetic consumption; those looking are also looked at, in a cycle of observation. In girl teen films glamorous spaces are all similarly designed to generate optimal visibility but here the Cinderella character-icon is the main spectacle, the most watched. The films surround the

Cinderella character-icon in spaces that maintain her visibility as the central pleasure and emphasize the girl figure's visibility as her main value. Drawing on the key characteristics of glamour, these spaces feel pleasurable.

Whether constructed around the idea of a high degree of stardom or surrounding local celebrity at a high school event, the celebrity glamour of space in girl teen films is designed around the same characteristics. Texturally loaded spaces position the Cinderella character-icon at the centre of a spectacle that is glamorously tactile. The spaces are loaded with all kinds of materials that range from glitzy textures that play with light, integrated surfaces of information technology, including LED screens, to the ornate and plush surfaces that surround princess characters.

The prom, for which *Starstruck* (Grossman, 2010) provides a typical example among many (Figure 3.4), is loaded with glitzy materials that play with light. These materials create mysterious glamour, not just by their association with precious metals and stones but also by permeating the scene with a distorting array of colour, light and shadow. The glitter and sparkle of the prom not only illuminates the scene, it also aims to create the appropriate sense of mystique that glamour requires, simultaneously highlighting and enshrouding the space. This colourful veil creates feelings of promise: illuminating just enough, without revealing too much. The play of light and dark also conceals effort, and the 'ordinary' that exists behind the veneer. The glamorous spaces of girl teen

Figure 3.4 *Starstruck* (2010), the prom.

film often work to utilize the semi-darkness of spaces that make up the night-time economy. As Conlin (2013: 8) describes, the play of light and shadow in eighteenth-century pleasure gardens was dangerous but exciting, covering 'a manifold of sins, it also revealed a "fairy-land"'. By highlighting some aspects and obscuring others the play of light distorts the scene, adding to feelings of promise and effortlessness.

The ornate, royal spaces in *The Princess Diaries* (Marshall, 2001) are pleasurable because of the glamour of complex materials such as marble or lapis lazuli that are layered and dense with history. This type of glamour embodies the notion of ascribed celebrity. Glamour, in this context, is built over time, over generations and through ancestry. The sense of history embodied in the materials that surround her lend the princess character a type of glamour that feels denser and more tangible though it relies on the very same characteristics that make up the glitzier version found in the prom. In *The Princess Diaries*, Mia (Anne Hathaway) is made over from awkward teenager to 'graceful princess' when she discovers that she is the heir to a small European country. In her final big reveal she stands at the centre of a grand ballroom. The space is texturally loaded with fixtures that bare the glamorous weight of practical inutility. The sumptuous materials of Mia's costume allow her to fit into the space effortlessly: as she moves into the space a smooth tracking shot follows her, emphasizing the appearance of ease and creating an experience of moving through the world unrestricted. Of course Mia is restricted by her role as princess, by the dress that she wears, and the type of femininity that she is constructed by, nonetheless glamour makes the moment feel effortless.

Whether glitzy or ornate, glamorous spaces hold the same characteristics and often include specific features. In glamorous spaces staged staircases are a prominent feature. Staircases have a Hollywood history, in particular associated with 'the specularization of the woman', where 'she is displayed as spectacle for the male gaze' (Doane, 1987: 136). Stairs act as a staging space and a visual trope that is particularly aligned with the makeover as a setting for displaying the transformation (Jeffers McDonald, 2010: 98). Jeffers McDonald (ibid.: 99) suggests that stairs are 'emblematic of *motion*, as a liminal place symbolising progress from one place or state to another and, therefore symbolising change' (Italics in original). The staircase offers characters the opportunity to make a glamorous entrance as though, Jeffers McDonald (ibid.) proposes, descending from heaven (also see Stacey [1994: 98] on the glamorous associations and materiality of the Hollywood staircase). It is not only through association that the staircase can make space and characters glamorous. Staged staircases are excessive, unproductive spaces personifying the practical inutility of glamour. The glamorous staircases of girl teen film are used in the spirit of the flamboyant, 1950s, staged staircases of Morris Lapidus. Influenced by the pleasure garden at Coney Island, Lapidus' designs were gaudy and glitzy ('Morris Lapidus,' 2013). One design at the Fontainbleu Hotel, Miami, described as 'a staircase to nowhere' (ibid.), led to a cloakroom from which guests could emerge to parade for the people in the hotel lobby below. Similarly in girl teen films, glamorous staircases are lavish and superfluous: designed for visibility and pomp rather than practicality. Acting as another facet of modulation, they create feelings of change and motion but effectively go nowhere. When Daphne (Amanda Bynes) becomes a 'lady' in *What a Girl Wants* (see Figures 3.6 and 3.7), for example, her visibility is affectively achieved when she stands at the top of ornate staircases.

Stages similarly play a prominent part in the construction of glamorous spaces, and like staged staircases, create a platform for the Cinderella character-icon. In both versions of *Freaky Friday* (Nelson, 1979; M. Waters, 2003), mother and daughter undergo a body swap and each must perform as the other. In the original, trapped in the body of her daughter, Mrs Andrews (Barbara Harris) must perform a variety of tasks that she is ill equipped for, including playing hockey and executing a water skiing routine. In the remake these sporting activities are replaced with the daughter Anna's (Lindsay Lohan) role in a rock band. The original denouement that takes place at a water park is replaced with a music competition and Anna's/her mother's (Jamie Lee Cutis) moment on stage. The visibility of the stage and the scenario of the music competition lends the scene its comic tension: with everyone watching Anna's mother (in her daughter's body) finds it difficult to perform. Nonetheless, the stage also contributes to the glamorous pleasures that the film offers. Performing here meets a desire for admiration and the stage presents us with a synthetic space that highlights the pleasures of performance and adulation but keeps its difficulties and stresses in shadow. The glamour of the concert space relies on a busy lighting design. Lighting literally provides a source of visibility and it also (again like the pleasure garden) supplies 'light entertainment' (Conlin, 2013: 8). The concert in *Freaky Friday* (2003) is illuminated using spotlights, follow spots, coloured gels and gobos (an outline projection of shapes). Lighting animates the space, creates shimmering and layered surfaces and imbues it with phosphorescent textures, all of which contributes to a texturally varied, abundant space that aims to create pleasurably tactile impressions. Stages also personify the illusion of proximity that is central to celebrity glamour, creating intense visibility but restricting access, and utilizing the feelings of promise that this generates.

Finally, mediation is also a tool that creates glamorous spaces. Many of the glamorous spaces in girl teen film articulate the basic media notion that 'mediated reality is somehow "higher" or more significant than nonmediated reality' (Couldry, 2004: 61). The diegetically mediated spaces in these films utilize the energy of greater visibility: more eyes and excessive focus on the Cinderella character-icon at the centre of a 'synoptic frenzy'. Mediated spaces often draw on the pleasures of effortlessness: as 'the media' scramble, push and shove, shout and yell, the Cinderella character-icon stands or walks through them relatively gracefully, and seemingly unhindered by comparison.

When Lizzie McGuire (Hilary Duff) has her moment on the red carpet outside the Colosseum in Rome, in *The Lizzie McGuire Movie* (Fall, 2003), this mediated space makes her visibility central, surrounded on all sides by the media and screaming fans. This is also a texturally loaded space: flash bulbs add to the play of light and shadow across the scene, it incorporates the glitz of products of conspicuous consumption such as limousines, in combination with the dense layers and rich residue of the Colosseum. This Cinderella moment uses techniques to create a glamorous space but it also draws on the glamour of the specific, exotic *place* of Rome.

The features of glamorous places

Celebrity has a distinct geography that plays out in urban places (Currid-Halkett and Scott, 2013: 5). The glamour in girl teen film is markedly located as metropolitan and the city itself is an object of glamour (though as I will discuss urban glamour is often brought into the suburbs). In girl teen film the typologies of glamorous places are specific cities, for example: New York, Los Angeles or London. Urban locations are set in contrast to suburban or mid-west America. The glamour of the city is made stark by its comparison to the rural mid-west or residential suburbs. Even where places are not specifically named in the films, 'the city' is set up as a fixed place, glamorous by its comparison to 'small-town' America. It is no wonder therefore that so many girl teen film protagonists leave small-town America to find success and visibility in major urban locations (see e.g. *Centre Stage* [Hytner, 2000], *Centre stage: Turn it up* [Jacobson, 2008], *Fame* [Tanchareon, 2009], *Josie and the Pussycats*, *The Lizzie McGuire Movie*, *Make It Happen* [Grant, 2008], *Save the Last Dance* [Carter, 2001], *Starstruck*). 'The City' is not just a backdrop but acts as a framework for organizing and generating glamour. As Postrel (2013: 152) suggests, seen or imagined from afar, the city shimmers. Like the play of light that makes up many glamorous spaces, the city skyline (especially at night) offers a place of promise: made translucent by the flash of lights that highlight its attractive elements and obscure 'everyday' reality. Cities like New York as they are imagined, on-screen and off, are the geographical embodiment of mystery and possibility. The city is not only mysterious at a distance; it is too big to be fully known even by its inhabitants (Postrel, 2013: 153). Because it is unknowable, the glamorous city offers feelings of promise: it gives enough to create an impression but is obscure enough not to disillusion.

The city skyline plays a prominent role in girl teen films. In *Confessions of a Teenage Drama Queen* (Sugarman, 2004: hereafter *Confessions*) Lola (Lindsay Lohan) moves from Manhattan, New York, to the suburbs of New Jersey. At the opening of the film the connection between New York and glamour is made explicitly. Grand helicopter shots sweep across the New York landscape in contrast to static, and boxed in shots that introduce residential suburbia. The city itself is a character in this film. New York is central to narrative development and defines Lola's attitude and actions. This New York character is a glamorous version that focuses on the city as the epicentre of entertainment, synthetic experiences, spectacle and promises of excitement. The film double codes this glamorous version of New York. At the opening of the film, following a typical helicopter view of the city, the camera moves in to present what we initially perceive as a 'real' place. Hyper-stylized and, ultimately we realize, a two-dimensional pop-up of the city, Lola's imagined version of New York is a cardboard model. Like the snow-globe scene in *A Cinderella Story*, *Confessions'* opening evokes the glamour of New York but frames it as a greater fiction than the narrative of the film. The differences between the 'real' New York in the film's narrative and Lola's pop-up version allow the glamour of the filmic New York to seem 'real' in comparison. The film highlights the artifice of Lola's New York, stressing its illusion, without destroying the city's glamour.

Consequently the New York skyline can be used to bring glamour into the suburbs. In the film's suburban high school production of *Pygmalion*, the New York skyline provides a glamorous screen backdrop. At the after show party, held in a suburban home, Lola dances with a celebrity and, delighted at being the centre of attention, her voice-over declares, 'When you're happy the whole world's New York.' The party cross dissolves into an imagined space framed by the city skyline and glamour is brought into the 'ordinary' space of the suburban home, surrounding Lola with the shimmer and promise of the urban landscape.

Confessions brings the affective pleasures of urban glamour into the domestic and institutional spaces and places of the suburbs. Consequently the conventional domestic spaces and places of girlhood can feel like the promise and potential of glamour. The film creates pleasures that feel like promise and change, contained within a predetermined set of possibilities. The glamour of space and place offers another form of modulation. Both create feelings of excitement, possibility and potential, but they essentially restrict the girl figure to spectacles of the self and the domesticity of the suburbs.

The pleasures of visibility in the catwalk

Visibility and its surfaces are fundamental to the creation of celebrity. Quoting Walter Bagehot, Roach (2007: 77) illustrates the glamour that was essential to the relationship between the 'mass of English people' and their rulers of the seventeenth century that is still a crucial element of conjuring celebrity in the twenty-first:

> They [the 'mass'] defer to what we may call the *theatrical show* of society. A certain state passes before them; a certain pomp of great men; a certain spectacle of beautiful women; a wonderful scene of wealth and enjoyment is displayed. … Courts and aristocracies have the great quality which rules the multitude, though philosophers can see nothing in it – visibility. (Italics in original)

Bagehot's description is still entirely accurate in summing up the key elements of glamorous visibility. It is a 'show', a performance that only exists as an event; it must be experienced to be at all. It is fleeting, a surface that cannot be probed too deeply, and it often consists of the female body.

In narrative terms the visibility that the catwalk moment creates is both task and reward in and of itself. In the catwalk, girls achieve visibility by means congruent with notions of 'feminine', attributed celebrity, where fame is valued in and of itself – ostensibly void of hard work and talent (Allen and Mendick, 2013: 1; Holmes and Negra, 2011: 2). In aesthetic terms visibility creates pleasure. In the catwalk, in its various versions, the practical techniques of visibility are commonly made up of three basic components of editing, cinematography and performance that cultivate glamour: slow motion, the body tilt and the effortless look back. These techniques make visibility a tactile and glamorous surface. In Hollywood cinema, slow motion is used in a variety of contexts with the intention of generating a range of effects. It is a gesture of display (Gunning, 1996: 77) that draws attention to the surface. The technique emphasizes the act of presentation itself. Slow motion can express dream or fantasy-like qualities, surreal states or highlight impressive bodily feats. The technique does not imply looking as a matter of course but it does often (and increasingly) provide emphasis and the opportunity to dwell on the moment. David Bordwell and Kristin Thompson (2004: 235) describe 'the slow motion scene of violence' as 'a cliché of modern cinema', with particular reference to the ways it is used to emphasize bodily power in action sequences. Similarly, slow motion in girl teen film is used to interrogate the moment of spectacle – the difference is that this is a spectacle of glamour that surrounds the feminine body. Another cliché of Hollywood cinema then is the slow-motion scene of visibility. The slow-motion scene of visibility is used across Hollywood cinema. Its features have been employed innumerable times across every genre. In this context slow motion implies a lingering look. Not necessarily because it is part of a classical point-of-view sequence (though it can be) but because slow motion gives its object time, it takes in intricacies and dwells on detail. In the context of the catwalk slow motion creates fluid movement and in doing so generates glamour and the feel of ease, of moving through the world unhindered. It also adds to this feel of glamour through its practical inutility. Slow motion takes up time. It goes beyond the necessary in terms of classical continuity and is a means of expression that exceeds what is essential. Slow motion is an excessive abstraction: it draws attention to the surface to 'prop up' the feeling of glamour being expressed.

The body tilt and the effortless look back are component parts of the slow-motion scene of visibility. In the body tilt, as the name suggests, the camera tilts or jibs smoothly up the body, sometimes (but not always) reproducing the point of view of onlookers. In combination with slow motion the body tilt works to intensify the feel of a lingering look. In girl teen films the body tilt may not be from any one characters' point of view but as a Hollywood cliché it maintains the signification and feel of looking nonetheless. When the point of view is made obvious, unlike the classical male approbation that is part of the traditional makeover reveal, it can be from either male or female character points of view. The attention to surface that the slow motion creates and the gaze of the body tilt work to add glamour to this type of visibility. Generating the illusion of availability central to celebrity, they linger upon the details of the characters' bodies, contributing to the idea of access that this interrogation of detail suggests. As technologies of display they draw attention to the surface and make a point of visibility. However the very notion of technologies of display, this scrutiny of the *surface*, suggests that there is something else, something more concrete that the onlooker cannot quite grasp. This idea that there is something more is a key element of celebrity, embodied by the techniques that construct it. The techniques of visibility create the impression of public intimacy and consequently invite us to enjoy the feelings of promise that come with it.

The performance of the effortless look back exaggerates a cool nonchalance that implies a casual indifference to being the focus of attention. Celebrity must appear effortless though, contrarily, we are all too aware of the labour it requires. In the classical Cinderella mode in girl teen film this effortlessness is coupled with innocence. The traditional Cinderella's effortlessness is rendered by her unaware, seemingly uncontrived, grace. In contrast, other versions of celebrity glamour combine effortlessness with a knowing awareness: a look infused with confident sexuality. Within the narrative this appearance of ease can be feigned. Films often contradict the effortless look back with earlier scenes of the intense labour of the makeover, or double coded moments where, for example, at the end of their 'runway' characters fall over. Nonetheless the effortless look back maintains the *appearance* of composure and indifference essential to the construction of celebrity glamour. Although, in narrative terms, we are aware of the effort that goes into the catwalk, it is a passing moment that offers an instance of glamour. The makeover is itself Romantic; it removes the mundane, tedious and potentially painful elements of beauty regimens but enhances the enjoyment of success by playing out the effort that produces the transformation. The catwalk, in contrast, is the moment of glamour, an instance that creates an experience of admiration, effortlessness, public intimacy, and sensations of promise and possibility.

So overused are the techniques of visibility in moments that seek to emphasize the glamour of being looked at that these tropes are parodied in *Not Another Teen Movie* (Gallen, 2001). Each time Amanda Becker (Lacey Chabert) enters a room the moment is constructed through slow motion, the camera tilts slowly up her body and she glances from side to side with overplayed nonchalance. To play up the excess of the moment she is surrounded by a halo of golden light. This parody alludes to the ways in which the slow-motion scene of visibility is used more especially in teen films of the 1980s and 1990s whereby the glamour of visibility highlights the male point of view in reference to his object of desire. In millennial girl teen films the techniques of visibility make being looked at pleasurable in and of itself.

Visibility in the 'big reveal': **Easy A** *and* **Mean Girls**

In girl teen films of the 2000s the glamour of visibility is itself constructed as *the* key pleasure. The catwalk in *Easy A* is a typical example of the slow-motion scene of visibility in girl teen films. After generating a rumour that she has lost her virginity, the film sees Olive (Emma Stone) cultivate her new reputation found in her 'slutty alter-ego' (Olive, *Easy A*). This is a reputation that makes her notoriously visible to the student population. The catwalk moment here is a 'big reveal' that follows Olive's self-modulation: a glitzy makeover she undertakes as a means to accentuating her supposed aggressive sexuality. The catwalk begins with a slow-motion long shot of Olive making her way through a densely populated area of school. The scene then cuts to a close-up of her bustier and performs a smooth body tilt up to her face. The camera lingers, taking in the details of Olive and her costume. Close-ups accentuate the sense of proximity here, contributing to the feeling of public intimacy that this moment embodies. Olive's visibility is both known and felt through the use of slow motion and the body tilt. These techniques draw attention to the surface and generate fluid, sensuous motion, making visibility seemingly effortless and tangible. This attention to surface also perfectly enacts the illusion of availability central to notions of glamorous visibility: the techniques encourage observation of detail but stay at the surface, they do not allow us to go any further. The moment invites scrutiny but not enough to break the illusion. In combination, Olive's sunglasses maintain a distance that is essential to feelings of public intimacy. Sunglasses are a classic signifier and embodiment of glamour (Postrel, 2013: 109–10). They implicitly enlarge the eyes while simultaneously creating mystery, they draw attention and concurrently conceal. Olive's look back is both confident and veiled, with an air of seeming indifference. Although she is aware of the reactions that her catwalk moment elicits from her fellow students, the look back maintains her requisite cool nonchalance. The scene that directly precedes this big reveal shows Olive frustrated and angry, rummaging through clothes and sewing bits and pieces together to make her new costume. Her makeover explicitly requires effortful construction. As an instance of glamour however the catwalk moment itself is successful in the *appearance* of effortlessness, necessary to generating glamorous visibility.

In *Easy A* exaggeration double codes the catwalk moment: playing up her role, Olive ostentatiously puckers her lips and kisses the air. At the end of the catwalk she greets a fellow student with 'Hey handsome', in sultry tones. She at once performs a surface knowingness and betrays her innocence through the exaggeration of that performance. The film makes clear its knowledge of the cliché of the slow-motion scene of visibility but the glamorous pleasures remain.

In *Mean Girls* the glamour of visibility is employed on a number of occasions, including Cady's catwalk moment with the Plastics. This is a makeover reveal to some extent but Cady's modulation is incremental rather than revealed in a single spectacle. This catwalk is also a 'strut' that works to embody the Plastics' attributed celebrity and dominance. In slow motion, the camera smoothly tracks across the four girls' feet as they walk down the school corridor towards the camera. The Plastics' theme, 'Pass That Dutch' (Elliott, 2003) accompanies the scene with a pulsating bass and syncopated hand clap that emphasizes the strut of the girls' walk and the moment's rising intensity. From a distance the camera track halts at Cady and then jibs up her body to her smiling face. Cut into the moment at this point is a volley of shots straight to the camera in which characters gossip about Cady and Regina (Amy McAdams) as figures of local attributed celebrity. The techniques used to create the slow-motion scene of visibility make the girls' presence feel like an event, alongside the explicit construction of the Plastics as school celebrities, played out in the accompanying straight to camera shots. Finally the scene cuts back to the catwalk moment and the slow motion resumes. Though students cross the corridor, obscuring full view of the Plastics, the girls dominate the space and their facial expressions exude the requisite confident, effortless nonchalance vital to celebrity (though in this case the look of indifference can also be attributed to character vacuity).

Still in long shot Cady looks across to witness Regina sharing an intimate gaze with Aaron (Cady's love interest). Cutting from a two-shot of Aaron and Regina, a mid-shot of Cady shifts back to twenty-four frames per second. When the slow motion stops, the glamour is gone and distracted Cady falls into a bin. The techniques of visibility contribute to the confident sexuality expressed but this confidence is double coded and undermined. Cady's assertive strut down the corridor is compromised by the ridiculousness of the cut-ins that describe her, followed by her own slapstick humiliation. Nonetheless as an instance, the glamorous pleasures of the moment remain.

The 'strut': St Trinians

St Trinians (Parker and Thompson, 2007) presents an unequivocal strut. The film is a reboot of the British franchise of films based on Ronald Searle's (ca. 1941) cartoons that depict the anarchic girls' boarding school. The *St Trinians* reboot provides a useful example because, being British, the film's mise en scène is conspicuously more grey and subdued in comparison to its Hollywood counterparts. However the film still employs the same techniques that make visibility a glamorous surface. The strut displays the St Trinians' girls as they walk through the glamorous place, Trafalgar square. The scene is not a big reveal: we have already seen the consequences of new girl Annabelle's (Talulah Riley) makeover, but like Cady's catwalk in *Mean Girls*, it consolidates Annabelle's inclusion in the school group. The girls dominate the space of the square unquestionably, not just by their numbers but also by their camaraderie, visibility and their effortless look back. The glamour of the *St Trinians* strut embodies feelings of unity: the girls strut in synchrony together, creating a sense of fellowship while simultaneously drawing attention to themselves individually. They stand out as special and fit into a group. The strut here taps into and creates a desire for the glamour of camaraderie and answers that desire with an instance of it. (This togetherness will be discussed in more detail in the following chapter).

This slow-motion scene of visibility is exemplary in the sense that the use of slow motion is entirely aesthetic. There is nothing new in shot that the audio-viewer needs time to appreciate or understand, nor is it shot from any one character's point of view. Slow motion is employed to make glamour only: it has no practical utility beyond generating the girls' visibility as an event. The girls perform the effortless look back – but not in reference to anyone in particular because there is no one else in the scene – but more generally to create the indifference required for glamorous appeal.

The 'mediated catwalk': What a Girl Wants

In the mediated catwalk, slow motion is replaced with the glimmer and sparkle of flash photography to generate spectacle around the Cinderella character-icon. The flicker and click of flash bulbs signifies mediation – visibility on a grand scale – and creates visibility as a physical, tangible event. Mary Celeste Kearney (2015) identifies the ubiquity of sparkle in millennial mainstream girl's culture. Vying with pink as the primary signifier of youthful femininity, sparkle, she suggests, demonstrates materially the increase in celebrity discourse and signifies late modern femininity associated with visibility, empowerment and independent wealth. Sparkle can also add affective force to moments of spectacle. Instead of the fluidity of slow motion and the body tilt, the flash bulb aesthetic is intended to create jerky rhythmic impact. Accompanied by the diegetic sounds of calls and shouts from photographers the technique creates a flurry of attention around the Cinderella character and invites the audio-viewer to enjoy a tempo shift – a fitful pulse that is both a visual and physical spectacle of glamour. The flash bulb technique, like the slow-motion scene of visibility, generates celebrity glamour by conjuring the illusion of availability and making visibility a visceral event. Again, the technique draws attention to the surface, generating a momentary overexposure that hints at accessibility. The technique also resembles the glamour of supernatural magic – the twinkle and glow of mystical enchantment. This is an overt example of the spells cast by the commercial (media) sphere. The glimmering punctuations of flash bulbs are a commercial rendition of the magic that accompanies Cinderella's transformation/modulation, where, as Warner (1995: 361) describes: 'Her perfections find themselves materialized in the immaterial dazzlement of light.' In girl teen films, the technique creates feelings of promise, highlights perfections and simultaneously obscures faults.

In *What a Girl Wants,* New Yorker Daphne goes in search of her long lost father and discovers that he is a British Lord. The film follows Daphne as she experiences her ascribed celebrity and becomes a 'Lady', including a number of coming-of-age catwalk moments that become progressively more 'graceful'.

First, Daphne mistakenly interrupts a fashion show and takes to the catwalk runway (Figure 3.5). She is not elaborately dressed or made up (aspects that would conventionally bring glamour to the moment) and the scene is performed for comic effect. The flash bulb technique nonetheless creates her visibility as glamorous and the punctuations of the camera flash make a visceral spectacle of the scene. Daphne's second catwalk moment (Figure 3.6) is both a 'big reveal' and mediated. Attending her first aristocratic function, Daphne has made herself over and attempts to impress her father. In this instance the flash bulb technique signifies her makeover as a success and renders her presence as an event.

In terms of its narrative, *What a Girl Wants* presents Daphne's visibility in the 'princess' role as restricting. She is physically and emotionally constrained: her previous freedom, associated with her Americanness, is restricted by an imagined British austerity that the film positions her against. In her final catwalk moment (Figure 3.7) Daphne has achieved the outline of the Cinderella character-icon. In the narrative this is set up as a hindrance to her individuality. However, as she descends the stairs at this final event, sound, performance, cinematography, mise en scène, accessories, clothes, hair and skin, all perform to generate the glamour of the moment. Orchestral strings work towards a

Celebrity Glamour: Space, Place and Visibility 69

Figures 3.5, 3.6 and 3.7 *What a Girl Wants* (2003), the glamour of flash photography.

crescendo as she descends the ornate, excessive and unproductive staircase. Her costume is a classic sweetheart line silhouette that incorporates the glamour and sparkle of rich silk textures and a bejewelled bodice. Her hair is elaborately but neatly styled: embodying effortless control. Flash bulbs punctuate, overexpose and distort the character's visibility, while she maintains the required effortless look back. Despite the narrative's emphasis on the restrictions of celebrity it is still constructed as an aesthetic pleasure.

Conclusion

Celebrity glamour is designed in the worlds of girl teen films using the particular techniques examined above to conjure the characteristics that make glamour: public intimacy, effortlessness, practical inutility and the embodiment of contradictory qualities. In these films glamour is used to create celebrity and visibility as a material and affective experience consisting of specific pleasures: feelings of potential and promise, of moving out into the world unrestricted, and of textural abundance. To enjoy these pleasures, celebrity glamour invites us to take up a mode of enchantment that goes along with the illusion of availability, or the appearance of effortlessness, for example, without questioning the 'magic' too deeply. In these films celebrity glamour fundamentally acts as another form of modulation. Its characteristics create feelings of potential and promise, movement and change, but it restricts the girl figure to specific (institutional, domestic or commercial) spaces and places with little room for actual manoeuvre, and perpetuates the notion that her visibility is her only recourse to power and pleasure by making visibility pleasurable and giving it affective weight.

In the next chapter I explore sports performances as another moment of visibility and flesh as another pleasurable surface.

4

Sporting Pleasures: The Body as Aesthetic Surface

Introduction

In the previous chapter I pointed out that the Cinderella character-icon's quest is to gain visibility and celebrity. Celebrity is constructed in these films as the key means to substantiate social identity, a way of acquiring symbolic capital, and fundamentally as *the* primary position for girls. Sports performances in girl teen films provide another framework from which Cinderella enjoys a moment of celebrity, visibility and recognition. In this moment the phenomenal body becomes a source of aesthetic pleasure. In the sports context it is the body itself that singles the Cinderella character-icon out as special. Typically ignored or analysed for what it represents, the body on screen is explored here as a surface.

At an aesthetic level the active girl body encourages particular pleasures grounded in physical work and physical perfection. In millennial girl teen films sports also provide a context in which girls are choreographed into synchronous formations, which offer up the pleasures of collectivity. This chapter examines the strategies employed to present the athletic girl body, with a particular focus on how the films render what it feels like to train, what it feels like to achieve moments of physical success and what it feels like to move together.

The girl body

The sporting contexts in girl teen films raise questions about the depictions and pleasures of the athletic girl body. Iris Marion Young (2005 [1980]) argues that girls' and women's experiences of their bodies in patriarchal societies is different to that of boys and men. Girls are conditioned to be physically inhibited, restricted and restrained. In her phenomenological examination of

Figure 4.1 *Ice Princess* (2005), the ideal body.

the basic modalities of feminine comportment, manner of moving and relation to space, Young (2005: 42) suggests that 'as lived bodies we [women] are not open and unambiguous transcendences that move out to master a world that belongs to us, a world constituted by our own intentions and projections'. She proposes that despite individual differences, geographical contexts, experiences, opportunities and possibilities, or anecdotal evidence of particular women that do not comply with normative modalities of bodily comportment, 'the situation of women within a given sociohistorical set of circumstances ... has a unity that can be described and made intelligible' (ibid.: 29). How we experience our bodies is influenced by enculturation. As Dee Reynolds (2012: 126) describes, 'Even if responses feel spontaneous or are automatic, they are to some degree learned.' Consequently girls' physicality is experienced in specific ways.

Girls, Young (2005: 43) suggests, are not given opportunities to use their full bodily capacities in the same ways that boys are. Girls are taught that they are fragile and as a consequence learn to hamper their movements. Due to objectification a girl cannot live herself as mere bodily object and so is distanced from her body – a body that exists dialectically as both subject and object (ibid.: 44). Rooted in their understanding of their body as a mere thing women experience their bodies as disconnected, as separate limbs and body parts that lack unity. Simultaneously experiencing herself as subject and object engenders hesitancy and repression of bodily energy. The feminine body is also constricted by imagined space in that the space available is usually bigger than the space the feminine body inhabits and women tend to make themselves smaller (ibid.: 40).

The feminine body is experienced as rooted and closed (ibid.: 41): rather than experiencing herself as a body that constitutes space, feminine existence positions itself *in* space (ibid.: 39). The phenomenal enculturation of girls does not encourage them to push out unrestrained into the world in the same way that boys are encouraged to do so. Girls in sport offer something different, pleasures connected to mastering the body, physical confidence, coherency and power. Athletic activities in girl teen films offer ways of experiencing the girl body in a new way.

Women's sporting bodies, in general, are represented in contradictory ways. Sports provide depictions of female bodies that are strong and confident. Ideologically, women doing sports on- and off-screen, is potentially empowering because, as Judith Butler (1998) describes, 'Women's sports ... call into question what we take for granted as idealized feminine morphologies.' Leslie Howe's (2003: 93) description of sports practice as an experience 'of reaching the self out beyond its apparent boundaries', sums up why sport is understood to counter the ways that girls' experiences of their own bodies is limited and hindered. The depictions of the female athletic body that women doing sports provide push at the boundaries of feminine gender ideals and contest gender norms.

Despite the empowering possibilities of female athleticism, the gendered body presented in the sports context also reinforces traditional gender boundaries. Particular athletic activities, Katharina Lindner (2011a: 322) illustrates, remain tied to traditional gender ideals. Activities that include physical contact and aggression such as rugby or boxing are commonly considered to be masculine or male appropriate, while non-contact activities that emphasize grace and form such as figure skating or synchronized swimming are customarily regarded as feminine or female appropriate (ibid.). The types of body form associated/ required for these types of sport further reaffirm gender boundaries: with masculine activities perpetuating an ideal that is muscular and strong, and feminine activities encouraging a tight and toned figure (ibid.). Media coverage and media representations of women in sport also compulsively re-frame the female athletic body by focusing on athletes' sex appeal (Carty, 2005) rather than their performance. Millennial girl teen films create similar confused and contradictory representations. Nonetheless the pleasures offered by depictions of sport in these films are connected to the active and athletic girl body. To unpack how the sports body works I need to define what I mean by sports and sports (in) film.

Defining sports and sports films

Lindner's (2011a) overview of female athleticism in film offers a useful framework from which a detailed examination of the aesthetic pleasures of women in sports films can be undertaken. Sports film is difficult to define because sport itself is a contested category. Lindner (2011a: 323) offers a broad definition of sport to include those that are competitive and non-competitive: 'spectator sports, and those pursued privately …, skateboarding and running, football and dance, mountain climbing and cycling, boxing and bowling, cheerleading and tennis'. In creating an inclusive definition of sport, Lindner integrates a wide range of athletic activities that are often left out of overviews of sports in film. Creating a broader definition of what we can consider as sport makes it easier to identify and connect the ways that the athletic body is displayed and the potential pleasures derived from athletic activity in film.

Sports performances take place in girl teen sports films and films that include sports segments. Girl teen sports films are distinct from those girl teen films that only include 'sporting moments'. As a sporting equivalent to the 'musical moment' (Conrich, 2000), sporting moments are passages of athletic presentation in films that are otherwise not sports films. *John Tucker Must Die* (Thomas, 2006) for example, includes sports performances that display characters' expertise in cheerleading. The characters' abilities to perform athletic tasks help to define them, but sports play no other part in the film.

In sports films, narratives centre around sporting events, athletes and the sporting experience (Kennedy and Hills, 2009: 34). The protagonist's quest for success is directly linked to sporting achievement and the final game or competition is the route to prosperity and character validation. The sports context in film in general, often provides a framework for coming-of-age narratives and, Garry Whannel (2008) suggests, a common narrative goal in sports film is the attainment of respect. The films are often less about sporting victory but about winning the recognition and admiration of others. In girl teen films, sports can provide the catalyst for showing character 'worth', determination, and fair play and sports conditions provide a narrative structure in which the transition from immaturity into maturity is easily played out: characters have to 'make the right decisions' to be successful. As I suggested earlier, sports also provide another framework that allows the Cinderella character-icon to become the centre of attention.

The sports film context and girls' sports

Girl teen sports films perpetuate gender, race and class stereotypes. They also emphasize heterosexual romance, often as a means to counter possible anxieties raised by the gender transgressions that female protagonists make by their involvement in athletic activity (Lindner, 2011a: 329). The Prince Charming figure in *Blue Crush*, for example, highlights the Cinderella character-icon's sex appeal. When Anne Marie (Kate Bosworth) is with her love interest, her physical softness is stressed, in contrast to the strength depicted in her sports performances. In the romantic moments of the film Bosworth is shot in ways that accentuate her curves, rather than the sharp lines of her body that we see in training sequences.

Because the types of girl teen film that I explore here are mainstream Hollywood productions, the majority of films marginalize characters that are not white, offering up white, middle-class notions of girlhood. Few teen films include black girls as the Cinderella character-icon and those that do are rarely mainstream productions in the fun mode. One example is the MTV dance film *How She Move* (Rashid, 2007). The film employs a number of girl teen film conventions and focuses on moments of visibility and performance. However, in common with boy teen films that follow black male characters, *How She Move* is best described in the romantic mode: focusing on tragedy and loss, rather than the 'fun' that organizes the films that I explore here. In the films examined in this book whiteness and middle-class femininity are conflated and stereotypically associated with athletic activities that emphasize 'frigid control *over* the body' (Lindner, 2011a: 335, italics in original): activities such as figure skating, gymnastics and drill. In contrast working-class femininity and (predominantly) female blackness are also conflated in these films and stereotypically defined by the myth of the 'natural' black body (Anderson, 1997; Lindner, 2011a; L. Young, 1996). In girl teen films, stereotypical associations of blackness with 'natural' rhythm and particular types of dance that emphasize an assertive or sensual body are reinforced. *Bring It On* (Reed, 2000), for example, makes an explicit association between black, working-class girls and dance ability. The film takes the point of view of a white, middle-class cheerleading team who steal moves from black, working-class competitors. The protagonists' white 'frigidity' is a narrative detail set in opposition to their black counterparts' 'natural' abilities. Competitive black and working-class characters are usually absent from films that involve sports or types of dance that prioritize a particular kind of body control that 'foregrounds the mind in the body-mind relationship' (Lindner, 2011a: 335): such as ballet, gymnastics or figure skating. Black and working-class female characters are presented to excel in athletic activities that emphasize rhythm and in the main this consists of street styles of dance and cheerleading. Even in films that do include street dance and cheerleading, black characters are usually secondary to the white Cinderella character-icon and narratives foreground a white, middle-class point of view. The only mainstream millennial Hollywood girl teen film in the mainstream mode that I am aware of that bucks this trend is *Bring It On: Fight to the Finish* (Woodruff, 2009), in which the main character's Cuban identity is central to the film.

In girl teen sports films and sporting moments, non-contact athletic activities predominate. Films include cheerleading, figure skating gymnastics and drill. Accordingly the body forms in these films are, predominantly, tight and toned, rather than muscular and strong, though as I will explore, there are films that complicate this. Sports that involve contact and aggression are also part of the girl teen film landscape. A relatively recent affiliation between soccer and female athleticism has played out in girl teen films in the 2000s, with an increased number of films involving girls' soccer. Soccer is a relatively aggressive activity and in Europe, in particular, is a male-dominated sport. However, in the 1990s the US women's national soccer team gained increased media coverage after winning the 1996 Olympic gold medal and in 1999 the Women's World Cup. The success of the team in the 1990s made women's soccer in the United States more visible. As midfielder Julie Foudy (Heywood and Dworkin, 2003: viii) suggests, the 'World Cup was about more than soccer': it created a cultural shift in the United States and increased the association between soccer and female athleticism. We also see lacrosse and field hockey in these films. In comparison with an athletic activity such as cheerleading, which is the most commonly exploited sport in girl teen film other than dance, field hockey and lacrosse are relatively aggressive sports. They are, all the same, considered as both female-appropriate and middle-/upper-class sports. Involving the use of sticks, both of these games require players to be able to use equipment as an extension of their limbs. In the female versions of hockey and lacrosse, the use of sticks detaches them from the force and domination associated with body contact sports. In women's lacrosse, for example, players are permitted to check opponents' sticks but unlike men's lacrosse cannot barge or shoulder other players.

This overview of sports in girl teen films creates a position from which we can explore the framing of the sports girl body as a pleasure. Sports sets up a platform for the presentation of the body in process: the body being trained, controlled and given the opportunity to reach out beyond its limits but also constrained within the boundaries of training regimes and sports regulations. Girls doing sports embody the contradictory qualities of expansion and confinement quite neatly: pushing out beyond their physical limits and contained within regulatory perimeters.

Drawing on their Cinderella legacy, girl teen sports films and sporting moments create two kinds of bodies, a type of before and after we would usually identify in the makeover and reveal. These are: the body in process, with which films aim to create the feelings of effort in training; and the body mastered, which is designed to create the feeling of effortless accomplishment – the magical body rendered as momentarily complete. The presentation techniques and pleasures of the body in process are distinct from those of the body mastered. Girl teen sports films vary in the degrees to which they engage with the 'muscle and sinew' of the body in process but they all aim to render both: what it feels like to train and what it feels like to achieve moments of physical success. The audio-viewer is encouraged to be kinaesthetically invested in the exertion, endurance and pain involved in the body's becoming and in the uplifting delight of the body momentarily perfected. In either case the body itself becomes a surface, designed to generate kinaesthetic pleasures and experiences of the girl body reaching out beyond its apparent boundaries.

Sporting pleasures and kinaesthetics

The sports performances in both sports films and sporting moments present the athletic body using shared presentational strategies. The focus of sports performances is on the spectacle of the moving human body – on physical energy, ability and exertion, rather than specific character motivation or inner thoughts (though these facets do of course play a role). Being so focused on the body and what the body can do, sports performances promote an embodied engagement with the body's potential for action. As a means of exploiting the possible pleasures of the spectacle of the moving body, sports performances encourage a range of kinaesthetic pleasures.

Reason and Reynolds (2010) conceptualize kinaesthetic responses in plural, rather than singular terms. Their categories of kinaesthetic pleasure are identified through ethnographic research with audiences of live dance. Through analysing the audiences' responses Reason and Reynolds articulate different types of kinaesthetic pleasures that explain the kinds of enjoyment that the audience members describe. The pleasures that they identify can be applied to the filmic context.

Reason and Reynolds (2010) break kinaesthetic empathy down into three core and connecting pleasures: sympathy, empathy and contagion. Importantly Reason and Reynolds (2010: 72) point out: 'Whether sympathetic, empathetic, or contagious, *the kinesthetic experience can be described as an affect*' (Italics in original), that is, potential pleasures are embodied, reactive responses. Girl teen sports films and sporting moments use set techniques that depict various sports as a means to invite these specific physical pleasures.

First, kinaesthetic *sympathy* involves the admiration of virtuosity. Spectators enjoy the spectacle of what bodies can do, with a particular emphasis on 'perfectly executed movements and sheer athleticism' (ibid.: 58), rather than on the work and effort behind it. This type of pleasure can be produced by what Susan Foster (1997) calls the ideal body. In training, the ideal body is what the dancer aims to achieve and for brief moments the dancer – or, I suggest, sports woman – may feel that they have done so through 'mastery of the body' or 'feeling at one with the body' (ibid.: 237). The ideal body is a 'perspective *on* the body as object' (Lindner, 2011b: 5), a body that is imagined as complete and perfected (Butler, 1998). For the Cinderella character-icon of girl teen film, this is the magical body: a surface that generates glamour as a spectacle of perfection.

In girl teen film an example of a moment that encourages kinaesthetic sympathy is the final performance in *Ice Princess* (Fywell, 2005). Having reached a regional final figure skating competition, the protagonist Casey (Michelle Trachtenberg) successfully executes her most accomplished manoeuvre (Figure 4.1). To render the spectacle of the move, Casey's body is composed using symmetrical lines and synchronous movements. A slow-motion long shot is accompanied by music that uses an ascending scale to heighten the moment of achievement. These techniques encourage the audio-viewer to appreciate the perfect composition of the body as it achieves the action. The following shot shows Casey's coach in close-up, her reaction shot expresses surprised delight, accompanied by the sounds of the cheering crowd that accentuate the triumph of the flawless landing.

The second mode of kinaesthetic pleasure that Reason and Reynolds (2010) provide is a more specific definition of kinaesthetic *empathy* than their initial broader category. Kinaesthetic empathy is identified with 'experiences of embodied and imaginative connection between the self and other' (ibid.: 71). Kinaesthetic empathy can take the form of inner mimicry, whereby the audio-viewer is able to do things in the imagination 'as if possessed with the skills, the strength, and the muscle knowledge' required (ibid.: 61). Despite remaining still and seated, the audio-viewer imagines that they are the performer or imagines themselves performing, creating a feeling that the experience of perception is 'taking place through the object or person perceived' (ibid.: 60). The audio-viewer of *Ice Princess*, for example, can appreciate Casey's performance and perhaps imagine themselves in her position and feel in their own body a version of what it would be like to have her capabilities.

Third, Reason and Reynolds describe kinaesthetic *contagion*. Contagion is a form of engagement in which the audio-viewer takes pleasure in an awareness of their closeness to the performer (ibid.: 66) whereby heartbeats and breathing move 'in synchrony with their perception of the movement' (ibid.: 71). This is an embodied response or anticipation that impacts upon the 'postural condition of the muscles without actual movement taking place' (ibid.: 66), a visceral awareness of 'effort, muscle and sinew' (ibid.: 73). Its intense focus on the ideal body means that the *Ice Princess* does not invite this type of pleasure. The camera remains distant from the body and even when Casey falls there is no real sense of gravity, or of the push and pull of her body.

The opening training sequence in *Blue Crush* presents an example of a sports performance that aims to encourage kinaesthetic contagion. This sports performance emphasizes what Foster (1997: 237) calls the perceived body: that which is tangible and understood from sensory information: visual, aural, haptic, olfactory, kinaesthetic. The perceived body 'implies a perspective *from* the body and an emphasis on its materiality as *perceived*' by the character that performs (Lindner, 2011b: 5, italics in original). In comparison to the ideal body presented in moments that encourage kinaesthetic sympathy, kinaesthetic contagion is a response to the perceived body in process. To render the body in process there is an emphasis on what it feels like to train. The *Blue Crush* sequence begins with a long shot of Anne Marie (Kate Bosworth) who is training for the Pipe Masters surfing competition. Despite the distance of the shot, Anne Marie's effortful corporeality is aurally stressed by her heavy breathing. The scene moves into a medium close-up and slow motion makes a spectacle of the effort depicted on her face. The following shot tracks in behind her as she performs pull-ups. The shot then moves in to a tighter close-up that draws attention to the movement of the muscles in her back and shoulders. The next shot is a high-angle close-up:

Anne Marie pulls herself up into shot, accentuating the labour of the action and bringing the audio-viewer into close contact with the character's powerful corporeality.

Sporting pleasures: The body becoming and flow in *Blue Crush*

The sports performances in *Blue Crush* exemplify depictions of both the perceived body in training and the ideal body in girl teen sports films and sporting moments. The film pivots around surf numbers and sequences of physical training that lead to a climactic competition. Anne Marie's quest is directly linked to this final surf performance, which will give her a financial reward, visibility, recognition and win her the respect of her family, friends and the local and global surfing communities. The sports context of this film provides a framework for a coming-of-age narrative. Anne Marie must 'make the right decisions': discard a distracting romance and overcome her fears of failure. The sports context sets the character a challenge in which, like the dual-focus narrative of the musical (Altman, 2002 [1987]), a successful performance on the waves will also equate with success in 'real' life.

Despite the increasing number of female participants in surfing and representations of the female surf body as ideally feminine, surfing is still considered to be a masculine/male-appropriate sport (Evers, 2009; Waitt, 2008). As Gordon Waitt (2008: 76) suggests of surfing culture: 'Unchallenged are the normative ideas of masculinity associated with gruelling physical training, vanquishing fears of death, and expressing a competitive, aggressive edge through an ongoing desire to surf larger, never-ridden waves.' This normative gendered framework is made explicit in *Blue Crush* through the tense relationship Anne Marie shares with the male surfers in her circle. Nonetheless, surfing does not involve the body contact aggression of other masculine sports such as rugby or boxing and the sport has a legacy in girl teen film, going back to the *Gidget* franchise.

Blue Crush's representations of class, race and gender are stereotypical. The film highlights heterosexual romance to counter Anne Marie's involvement in gruelling physical training and puts the white Cinderella character-icon at the centre of the narrative. As is commonplace in sports films, working-class Anne Marie's involvement in Hawaiian surf culture is authenticated through her relationships with non-white characters. The film also makes conventional appeals to the male gaze: an unnecessary shower scene represents a typical example (though considering the young female target audience, this raises questions about the looking relations in girl teen film). Nonetheless this is not the only way that the girl body is made a spectacle of in *Blue Crush*. The sports performances also offer kinaesthetic pleasures connected to the active and athletic body: the pleasures of the body as muscle and sinew – the feelings of training, stretching out and becoming powerful – and as perfect surface – feelings of achievement and flow.

Blue Crush: *The becoming body*

As the earlier description of *Blue Crush*'s first training sequence makes clear, Anne Marie is presented using her full bodily capacities. Her body is depicted, not as hampered or fragile but as powerful and strong. In a number of its training sequences leading up to the final competition and the 'glory' of the final wave, *Blue Crush* highlights the perceived body, emphasizing blood and sweat, muscle and sinew, possible dangers to the body and vocal signs of effort. The perceived body of the sporting girl is presented in accord with Purse's (2011: 76–93) description of the action heroine, who (unlike the 'action babe') exerts a physical presence 'rooted in real-world physics and physiology' (ibid.: 89). *Blue Crush* uses techniques that create an experience of what it feels like to train. These techniques encourage the audio-viewer to enjoy kinaesthetic contagion with the effort on display. Close-ups pick out indicators of labour and the mobile camera maintains intimate proximity to the physical action.

The film begins with a motif that runs intermittently throughout the film, showing Anne Marie's memory/nightmare in which she is injured. Despite the nightmarish mode of the sequence it maintains a focus on fleshy corporeality and the potential pain inflicted on the body by the ocean. Close-ups frame the effort extended as Anne Marie attempts to fight the ocean's currents. A punchy edit rhythm moves between various perspectives to highlight the chaos of being under the water and point-of-view shots emphasize the weight of the roiling waves above. As her head hits coral there is a loud 'whack' that stresses the force of the impact and blood seeps from the wound. The film aims to encourage an embodied mode of engagement in the audio-viewer, making appeals to kinaesthetic contagion and the flesh and blood of the body.

The first surf performance in the film is made up of two distinct sections. The first section creates an experience of the ideal body. As Anne Marie and her friends surf, the pop song 'Cruel Summer' (Blestenation [remix], 2002) is to the fore and dictates the rhythm of the edit. It is worth noting that at the beginning of this performance the camera does get in close to the action and makes a momentary spectacle of the muscularity of Anne Marie and her friends as they rise up, out of the water, looking for their first wave. These shots employ typical conventions of the male gaze, again raising questions around looking relations and the Queering of traditional feminine ideals. Nonetheless, the use of music video aesthetics in this sequence underplays the impact of the girls' physicality. This surf performance is expressive and explicitly choreographed and the music video aesthetics (explored in more detail in Chapter 6) distance the audio-viewer from the work of the sports body in this instance. Each separate surfing move is held together through the use of music rather than by the effort required, moment to moment, between paddling to riding a wave. In the second section of this surf number, in contrast, the upbeat pop track fades out and as Anne Marie enters more dangerous territory, the sounds of crashing waves become prominent. The camera moves in close as she paddles, emphasizing the movement of her back muscles.

The following shot is under water and the sounds of her paddling motion are pronounced. Long shots stress the enormity of the waves and the potential danger to the body and close-ups emphasize the harsh consistency of water, rather than its fluidity. Stressing the demand that the ocean puts on the surfing body presents an invitation to enjoy kinaesthetic contagion with Anne Marie,

Figure 4.2 *Blue Crush* (2002), muscle and sinew.

rather than simply admiring the character's ability to surf. The harsh environment and the spectacle of Anne Marie's labouring body encourage embodied pleasure in an experience of the materiality of the girl body as powerful, as well as the physical investment derived from the anticipation of her failure or success. When Anne Marie falls – the wipe out is a common trope of surf films – the camera moves with her under the water. Again the camera is mobile, moving and twisting with the body and the wave. Shots from Anne Marie's point of view are cut with close-ups of the effort on the character's face as she struggles under the weight of the wave.

We can usefully compare this representation of the perceived body and creation of the body in training, to those in the gymnastics film *Stick It* (Bendinger, 2006). The film follows Haley (Missy Peregrym) as she trains for a national gymnastics competition. Like *Blue Crush*, *Stick It*'s training sequences sometimes emphasize the perceived body: close-ups highlight facial and vocal grimaces of pain and effort, the body being pushed, pulled, falling, tensing and stretching.

Both films focus on the body's capacity for pain and the constant failure that makes up training as the body is pushed and pulled. Despite this focus on pain and failure, the emphasis on the perceived body encourages an embodied reaction in the audio-viewer that takes pleasure in the thrill of the girl body's potential becoming: the ways in which it stretches out and exerts force as it is made powerful (Manning, 2007). In this way, girl teen films sometimes create experiences of expansion and power not usually expressed through girls.

Blue Crush: *Flow and the mastered body*

More common to girl teen sports films and sporting moments are techniques that create the ideal body and fantasies of empowerment that emphasize seemingly effortless perfection, rather than gruelling visceral effort. Depictions of the sporting body in girl teen films more frequently aim to create the feelings that come with sporting success. This success can be described as unity (Howe, 2003) or flow (Jackson and Csikszentmihalyi, 1999): for brief moments the sports woman can experience the imaginary ideal of the athletic body as momentarily complete. Sequences that render sporting success aim to create the feeling of flow, whereby the mind and body seem to work together effortlessly. Movements are executed as faultless and the body appears as optimal, creating a feeling that something special has occurred (Jackson and Csikszentmihalyi, 1999: 5). Flow is rendered with an emphasis on the composition of perfect bodylines. The audio-

Figure 4.3 *Stick It* (2006), body in the making.

viewer is detached from the work of the body, which is framed at a distance. The camera is usually employed in grand sweeping crane shots or frontal framing. As Lindner (2011b: 15) points out, the ideal body is conjured as ephemeral and transient. Depictions are comparatively removed from the muscle and sinew presented in performances that emphasize the perceived body.

In *Blue Crush*, when Anne Marie meets her last wave in the final competition of the film, slow motion executes her efforts as fluid and weightless. The tactility of the water is presented as smooth and the soundtrack accentuates a consistent flow and light trickle, rather than the intense crashing waves of previous training sequences. Long shots show the body in perfect composition and close-ups inside the tube lack gravity or weight. There is a sense of effortless flow and the sea takes on an evanescent and ethereal quality.

Finally, as the wave breaks, Anne Marie gracefully glides through the surf and at the centre of a frontal frame punches the air in delight. Aiming to produce an experience of flow, this surf number invites us to admire the virtuosity of the perfectly executed movement that Anne Marie achieves and encourages kinaesthetic empathy with the feeling of perfect unity, of moving through the world without resistance.

In both its ideal and perceived creations, the body is a source of aesthetic pleasure. In her analysis of how the ideal and perceived body is framed in the dance film *Centre Stage*, Lindner (2011b) explores the gradual shifts in the film

Figure 4.4 *Blue Crush* (2002), effortless flow.

that increasingly frame the body as abstract and stylized. The dance numbers, she explains, eventually lack the subjective experience of the dancers, becoming increasingly utopian and impossible (ibid.: 11). As Lindner (Lindner, 2009) stresses, in reference to the boxing film *Girlfight* (Kusama, 2000): where films render the body as abstract, they remove the subjective experience that the perceived body provides. In doing so, she suggests, they undermine character agency and the empowering possibilities of the athletic female body. Framed as they are by fairy-tale realism, Hollywood girl teen films are always already stylized and abstract, utopian and impossible. Where sports numbers accentuate the perceived body, flesh and blood, muscle and sinew are just another surface manipulated as part of the films' enchantment. Sports films and sporting moments in girl teen films in the fun mode offer potentially empowering experiences of the girl body, but they are also restricted by the Cinderella version of girlhood that these films create. Just as Cinderella is made over through costume, her maid body of common clay sculpted, refined and dressed to become pure magic, the sports body of common clay is pounded, pushed and pulled to create the ideal body of pure magic, revealed in the final performance.

The final competition in *Stick It*, the National Gymnastics Championships, provides an interesting and unusual example. Haley's teammate Mina (Maddy Carley) performs a vault manoeuvre. The gymnastics number creates both the ideal *and* the perceived body. It begins with a smooth tracking shot as Mina runs towards the vault and then moves into an extreme-low-angle shot. The actress performing the role is also a gymnast, removing the necessity for a body double that would keep the camera at a distance. The crowd is completely silent and the only sound is the tread of Mina's footfalls, rendered with an eerie echo. The performance moves to twenty-four frames per second as Mina reaches the vault. She executes the move, which is shown twice at twenty-four frames from different angles and then finally in slow motion before she hits the mat for a faultless landing. The emphasis on the silence of the crowd and the use of slow motion classically builds anticipation. These techniques are used here to generate suspense but slow motion in this example also performs a number of roles. The fluidity of the slow-motion tracking shot adds to the ethereal feel of Mina's performance, creating a sense that this is a moment of flow. However it also, as Sobchack (2006: 340) describes slow motion, interrogates the 'movement of movement itself'. Slowing the movement down amplifies the feeling of flow but simultaneously makes visible the power of Mina's body: its weight, gravity and muscle control. In combination the extreme-low-angle shot is oddly abstract, but it accentuates the movement of her muscles as she pounds towards the vault. Techniques that render both the perceived and the ideal body are used here to encourage a variety of kinaesthetic pleasures: contagion with the power and muscle of Mina's movements, admiration of the perfect body composition that she achieves and empathy with both. The body is a pleasurable spectacle in both its perceived and ideal manifestations.

Moving together

I would like to consider a third and final way that sports films and sporting moments exploit the possibilities of kinaesthetic pleasure. Compositions of collective formations are recurrent in these sports performances: girls move together in unison, creating a visceral sense of togetherness unusual in twenty-first-century Hollywood versions of girlhood (and womanhood). Gymnastics is an individual sport, yet some of the sports routines in *Stick It* are choreographed to include collective performances in which gymnasts move in time together, or formations that create an allied unit. Training sequences for example reflect Haley's gradual integration into the gymnastics group and become increasingly collective.

The gymnasts are rivals but in the first competition in which they participate the performance is edited to create collective compositions: each gymnast is superimposed to frame layers of moving bodies. These *Stick It* routines are identifiably 'Berkeleyesque': abstract formations of 'indissoluble girl clusters' (Kracauer, 1995: 75) that create kaleidoscopic organizations of bodies and colour. Feminist critiques of the Berkley style have stressed the ways in which the spectacle reduces women to endlessly exchangeable, vacuous doubles: flattened into an indeterminate mass, the body becomes merely a decorative surface (Fisher, 2000; Herzog, 2010: 165). The *Stick It* routines can certainly be regarded in this way, nonetheless these numbers not *only* create kaleidoscopic organizations of bodies and colour, they also embody group unity. We are invited to engage with the physical performance as the Cinderella character-icon's moment, and encouraged to enjoy the spectacle of girls moving in synchrony.

In *Keeping Together In Time*, William McNeill (1995) explores the visceral fellow feeling generated by prolonged and rhythmic synchronous muscular movement found in dance or military drill. The connection created between people who move together in time, 'moving big muscles together and chanting, singing, or shouting rhythmically' (1995: 2), he calls muscular bonding. Muscular bonding, McNeill (ibid.: 6) explains, is something felt rather than talked about: 'Our words fumble when we seek to describe what it feels like to dance or march.' Despite the difficulty of explaining the pleasures of collective movement, McNeill suggests that 'boundary loss' offers a means of explanation (ibid.: 8–10). Boundary loss, he suggests, creates the feeling of becoming bigger, giving the individual the opportunity to stretch out beyond their isolated capacities. In combination it produces a feeling of being one with the group: a merger and heightening of fellow feeling. Muscular bonding creates community cohesion, arouses shared feelings and consolidates groups. McNeill describes this as kinaesthetic undergirding: 'Ideas and ideals are not enough. Feelings matter too, and feelings are inseparable from their gestural and muscular expression' (ibid.: 152). Sports in girl teen films provide a space to take advantage of the pleasures of muscular bonding through kinaesthetic empathy. Part of the pleasure of many sports are the possibilities of shared fun and the coordination of one's own movements with those of others. Muscular bonding is essential to the requirements of many sports: teams win or lose based on their ability to synchronize their bodily movements. Butler (1998) describes the coordination of bodies in sport thus: 'The bodies that begin the game are not the same bodies that end the game. As they are made, established, sculpted, contoured, in relation to one another, they are established in a space that is neither fully or exclusively individual or fully or exclusively collective.' Through kinaesthetic empathy we are invited to experience a sense of muscular bonding with girls who move together.

Hollywood genre films commonly struggle with experiences of female friendship. Because women are traditionally the objects of a sexualized gaze, intensity between women on screen carries a potential homoerotic charge (Boyle and Berridge, 2012; Stacey, 1988). Consequently, in narrative terms, female friendships are often shown as a stage in life, marginalized after marriage (Boyle and Berridge, 2012; Winch, 2012b). There are few stories about female friendship, Karen Boyle and Susan Berridge (2012: 3) suggest, told in Hollywood film that are not also centrally about heterosexuality. When films do engage with women's sociality, as many girl teen films do, relationships are often complicated by aggressive and scrutinizing interactions. In the neo-liberal, post-feminist context popular culture exploits the notion of the 'girlfriend' to celebrate 'women networking in the service of post-feminist lifestyle industries which sell the allure of girliness, particularly through the mechanics of the makeover', rather than as a means to frustrate patriarchal systems. In this context the 'girlfriend gaze' (Winch, 2012a) is analytical and policing. Girls' relationships in 'girlfriend' texts are marked by competition and antagonism (Boyle and Berridge: 2), love, envy and shame (Winch, 2012a: 80).

In contrast the collective sports performances in girl teen film offer an experience of muscular bonding among girls: moments of felt partnership, affiliation and alliance. The *Bring It On* franchise of films (Reed, 2000; Santostefano, 2004; Rash, 2006, 2007; Woodruff, 2009) is organized by a set formula in which rival cheerleading squads compete against each other. The films are structured around cheerleading numbers and training sequences that lead up to a final competition piece. The teams often include male participants but the female team members are the focus. The films all include verbal aggression and physical competition among its female characters, within and between teams. Nonetheless the nature of cheerleading means that a team can only win if their members harmonize their movements in synchrony with one another. All five *Bring It On* films emphasize the ideal body, lacking any sense of real effort. Even when the films make a point of bodily injury (including broken bones, bloody noses and vomiting) this is produced for comic effect rather than for a feel of the materiality of the body. Numbers are choreographed to encourage the admiration of virtuosity with a spectacle of perfectly rendered moves and shapes.

The films create kaleidoscopic organizations of multiple girl bodies or 'indissoluble girl clusters', but they also emphasize a potentially pleasurable unity within the teams. In the final performance of the first *Bring It On*, for example, the team enters the scene jumping and cheering together. They arrange themselves into symmetrical formations and following the rhythm of the music they clap, stamp, jump, chant and perform athletic tricks in unison with one another. Close-ups and mid shots pick out primary characters, reminding the audio-viewer that the performance is not only made up of 'faceless' girls. The film frames the girls as a tight unit – despite their narrative animosities, in competition they feel collective and through kinaesthetic empathy the audience can enjoy an experience of that physical solidarity. I do not wish to claim that the kinaesthetic pleasure of muscular bonding somehow cancels out the neo-liberal and post-feminist versions of female friendship found in the narrative. Rather, I simply want to understand the pleasures that exist at an aesthetic level.

Muscular bonding is key to girl teen films in general. The composition of collectivity is also found in sporting moments in films that are otherwise not sports films. In *Wild Child* (Moore, 2008) (a British film that employs the Hollywood paradigm, though its mise en scène is distinctly British), for example, sports provide a context in which girls are shown allied with one another through moments that embody muscular bonding. The film follows Poppy's (Emma Roberts) progress as she moves from America to be 'made-under' at a British boarding school. The film includes a number of Cinderella moments (a makeover reveal, a catwalk moment, a dance), the last of which is a sports performance at the film's resolution. In the final of a school lacrosse competition Poppy rallies her team together and in a bid to scare the opposition they perform a version of the 'haka'. Chanting, shouting rhythmically and moving together in time, creates the camaraderie of the team that Poppy has become a part of, and aesthetically this moment embodies fellow feeling and the boundary loss engendered by muscular bonding.

Pleasure in unity and moving together in time is evident not only in sports performances but in other key moments across girl teen films. When girls perform the strut it is often in groups. As I suggested in Chapter 3, performed together the strut is a physical embodiment of groups' attributed celebrity and power in the social hierarchy of the high school. The strut creates celebrity as it conjures glamour for those who perform it, but its pleasures are also connected to the unity generated by the girls' moving in time together. In *Wild Child* for example, Poppy and her friends perform the strut together. They have made themselves over, ready for a school dance. However their catwalk moment is performed for the camera only. This moment is not for the affirmation of other characters, instead it creates a sense of fellow feeling and the pleasures of muscular bonding.

Conclusion

At the end of *Mean Girls*, being run over by a bus chastens Queen Bee (meanest girl) Regina. Following her recovery she joins the school lacrosse team and Cady's voice-over tells us she, 'channels all her rage into sports'. The film makes fun of Regina's aggression, but it also uses the pleasures of sports to ensure the film's ending feels positive, and in the final montage of the film we see Regina's teammates cheering and jumping on top of her in celebration. In girl teen films, sports provide another kind of Cinderella moment that shifts emphasis onto the flesh of the girl body. Sports performances create experiences of the girl body in action and generate kinaesthetic pleasures attached to feelings of power, flow and fellow feeling.

Girl teen dance films and musicals encourage similar pleasures to those evident in sports films. Pleasures are drawn from the active girl body, its stretching out and taking up space, and its relationship with music. In the following chapter I draw out the potential for kinaesthetic pleasures and examine how conventional Hollywood film musical techniques work as a form of enchantment.

5

Musical Address: Expansion, Confinement and Kinaesthetic Contagion

Introduction

In the previous chapter I explored how the spectacle of the body in sports performances invites particular kinaesthetic pleasures. The musical numbers in girl teen films rely on similar pleasures that bring the body in action to the fore. Distinctive to the musical number, however, it is the body and its capacities in relation to music and dance that are central to these pleasures.

Surprisingly dance films make less of the possible pleasures of muscular bonding between girls than one would expect. Instead, in accord with the traditional musical genre, dance numbers are more commonly focused on the development of the heterosexual romance. Traditional forms of dance are about heterosexual courtship and this is expressed in these films regardless of the types of dance performed. The dance embodies the couple's compatibility – their back and forth creates their fit as a couple. Even in *Step Up 2: The streets* (Chu, 2008), where the success of the dance crew centres around their ability to synchronize their moves, the girls' relationships with one another are marginalized. The film does include one dance section that draws on the pleasures of girls' collectivity, but the real focus remains on the individual success of the Cinderella character-icon and the heterosexual couple.

In contrast, 'musical moments' (Conrich, 2000: 47) – passages of musical performance in films that are non-musicals – in girl teen films often make use of the pleasures of muscular bonding between women. In *Legally Blonde* (Lutz, 2001) for example, Elle (Reese Witherspoon) encounters a great deal of animosity from other women on her arrival to Harvard University. This tension is countered in the narrative by her friendly interactions with women at the local beauty parlour, and is embedded by a musical moment that choreographs the women moving in time together. Demonstrating how to lure male attention, Elle

Figure 5.1 *Hairspray*'s joyfully affective attitude (2007).

performs the 'bend and snap' and eventually the customers and workers of the beauty parlour join in, making a collective musical moment.

Musical numbers also aim to create other kinds of pleasures. The films that I explore in this chapter are girl teen films that are also musicals and dance films or they are films that include musical moments. The structural and stylistic techniques that are used to engage the audience of musicals and dance films I call 'musical address'. Musical address cues a world captivated by music and dance to create a familiar, in-between space – a no place, no time similar to the 'Once upon a time … In a land far away' of fairy tale – where the confines of expression and sensory experience are temporarily unbound. Musical address invites the audio-viewer to enjoy this sense of boundless freedom through an enchanted mode of engagement that is responsive to the pleasures of music and dance. In girl teen film, like sports performances, musical numbers feel like freedom and expansion, but the experiences that they create are also restricted by gender norms.

Beyond structural conventions, the spectacles of performance in these films share in common an intended affective impact that draws on the embodied pleasures of music and dance, and on the spaces of possibility created by musical address. The chapter outlines the way that the pleasures of the musical have been identified as utopian and builds on this formulation of pleasure, to understand its physical dimensions. Comparing the original (Waters, 1988) and remake (Shankman, 2007) versions of *Hairspray*, I establish the sanitized aesthetic mode of millennial girl teen musicals: films that consequently offer experiences that are less based on affective transgressions and instead founded on aseptic 'fun'. The chapter then weaves an analysis of the conventional remake of *Hairspray*, alongside a musical moment in *Mean Girls* to explain the component parts that make up musical address. Finally I explore the experiences of expansion and confinement that these films offer and the kinaesthetic pleasures they encourage.

Organizations of music and dance

Conventional musicals and dance films are defined by the ways that sound and the spectacle of performance are distinguishable from other uses of music and dance in film. These arrangements are conventional in the sense that they draw on techniques that are a familiar part of the classical Hollywood musical films of the 1940s and 1950s, films such as *Meet Me in St. Louis* (Minnelli, 1944) and *Easter Parade* (Walters, 1948). Millennial girl teen films employ a variety of scoring techniques: from creating original soundtracks (traditional musicals like *Hairspray* [2007]) to compilation scores that use pre-recorded popular music. Regardless of how the score is composed, these films employ the same techniques of musical address in their musical numbers. In accord with these classical Hollywood musicals, conventional girl teen musicals and dance films position singing and dancing as the primary focus. Musical narratives are constructed around choreographed 'numbers': sequences designed to showcase singing and/or dancing. The musicals and dance films I explore here include integrated numbers, whereby the performances of singing and dancing support or develop the narrative. The integration musical sits in contrast to stand-alone revues in which the numbers appear as essentially disconnected from the story. Revue musicals use the platform of the musical to showcase the talents of the performers in individual routines. In contrast girl teen musicals use music and dance as a means of expressing narrative and character. *Hairspray* (Shankman, 2007), for example, is an adaptation of the stage musical (2002) of the same name, itself a reworking of the original John Waters film. The film follows Tracy Turnblad (Nikki Blonsky) as she pursues fame on a local television dance show. The opening song 'Good Morning Baltimore' introduces Tracy as she sings about her dreams for future stardom. Her tone is optimistic and impassioned, characteristics that are central to the character and narrative that follows. In fully integrated musicals, musical numbers are fundamental to narrative progression and character motivation, as well as aesthetic mode and tone.

The level of integration between number and narrative in some girl teen dance films is minimal. Numbers are often situated in nightclubs or theatres in which characters watch the performance along with the audience, or performances are explained through rehearsal or competitive events. *Step Up 2: The Streets*, for example, represents a typical example of girl teen dance film that makes use of backstage musical techniques. Numbers are mostly explained as rehearsals, competition performances or flash mobs in which dancers prove their worth. Dance performances do not come from characters' needs to directly express their feelings and emotions (although they can also do this) as in conventional musicals. These numbers appear to function as disparate units of spectacle, rather than as sequences that drive the narrative forward. Narrative and the spectacle of music and dance, however, are not mutually exclusive. Narrative can develop *through* spectacle (Smith, 1998: 13). The numbers in *Step Up 2*, for example, establish the skill and 'authenticity' of the performer(s), set up antagonisms, accentuate characters' developing maturity and effect character relationships. In the millennial musicals and dance films analysed, emphasis is placed on the numbers as structural components that are part of a larger narrative whole, which can *also* be enjoyed as discrete units. Importantly, the performance numbers in girl teen film retain an affective attitude that is congruous with the films' emphasis on 'fun'.

Together with these conventional teen musicals and dance films, comic girl teen films have redrawn and revised performance numbers as part of their repeated moments of 'fun'. Musical moments are a constituent part of comedy

Figure 5.2 *Mean Girls*' musical moment (2004).

girl teen films, rather than of primary focus. *Mean Girls* offers a typical example of a musical moment. Integrated as part of a high school 'Winter Talent Show' this musical moment is a stand-alone performance sequence. The school's group of popular girls, the 'Plastics', perform a dance routine to 'Jingle Bell Rock' (Beal and Boothe, 1957). Initially they perform a 'raunch' routine to a pre-recorded version of the song but part way through their performance the CD player from which the diegetic music emits (visible at the front of the stage) is accidentally kicked out into the audience and, unsure of how to proceed the girls are frozen mid-performance. The protagonist, Cady, begins to sing in place of the pre-recorded track and the other Plastics follow her lead and continue the routine. In turn, members of the school auditorium audience sing and clap along with the performance and finally the tune is taken up on the school hall piano, and the number ends with the diegetic audience in full chorus.

Musical performance is not something new to teen films of the 2000s, clean teen films of the 195.0s and 1960s, for example, generally contained at least one musical number. During the 1980s musical numbers in teen film mostly became integrated and contextualized as part of scenarios that could 'explain' these performances using 'real'-world logic, films such as *Flashdance* (Lyne, 1983), *Footloose* (Ross, 1984), *Girls Just Want to Have Fun* (Metter, 1985) and *Hairspray* (1988). As outlined in the previous chapters, performance and visibility have become increasingly prominent in cultural products aimed at girls: in line with neo-liberal discourse, celebrity has replaced heterosexual romance as the key reward. The idea that singing and dancing are key forms of fun for teenagers and central to notions of self-worth is generated in various forms of popular culture aimed at an adolescent audience. In the reality television programme *My Super Sweet Sixteen* (MTV, 2005–), the 'Sweet 16' performs a routine for their party guests as a component of the 'perfect' birthday party. Singing and dancing have increasingly re-entered cultural products aimed at the teen market, and accordingly have become a core component of girl teen film's repertoire of elements.

The pleasures of the musical are explained in academic discourse as stemming from the genre's utopian foundations. Discussions of the Hollywood film musical have been heavily influenced by three key texts: Dyer's 'Entertainment and Utopia' (2002 [1977]), Feuer's *The Hollywood Musical* (1993 [1982]) and Altman's *The American Film Musical* (1989 [1987]), which have by and large set the parameters of discourse on the subject. Dyer's instrumental essay suggests that entertainment (for which he takes the musical as his example here) 'offers the image of "something better"' (ibid.: 20), something that our day-to-day lives do not provide – alternatives, hopes and wishes. Dyer (ibid.) proposes that what the musical presents in its non-representational signs (colour, texture, movement, rhythm, melody, camerawork) is what utopia would feel like. The non-representational signs of the film musical embody utopian feelings. These feelings are: energy, abundance, intensity, transparency and community (ibid.: 23). Feuer and Altman also reference the 'utopian sensibility' of the musical, directly and implicitly, as a means of explaining the pleasures of the genre. To illustrate the ways in which this idea of pleasure is used, the musical moment in *Mean Girls* can be analysed with regard to the numbers' utopian pleasures.

The musical moment in *Mean Girls* retains the division between narrative and number: the 'Winter Talent Show' provides a context within which the performance is integrated. In narrative terms the number is not essential to the film; although it does contribute to various plot details, the sequence is not strictly necessary. However, as director Mark Waters describes it in the DVD commentary of the film: 'You end up kind of really needing, like, a breath in the movie with some music. …' The musical moment offers a 'breath' of energy, of human activity in contrast to the series of conversations that make up the majority of the narrative.

The first half of the performance that the sequence begins with sets the number up as 'artificial' (Figure 5.2). The synthetic costumes and 'inauthentic' dance moves, in combination with the use of the CD player propped at the edge of the stage, all suggest a lack of 'liveness' and 'authenticity' customary to the musical. The second half, however, offers feelings of intensity and transparency. When Cady begins to sing, the number becomes 'spontaneous'. A quality on which Feuer (1993: 3–13) proposes, musical films place a premium as a means of bridging the gap between folk art and mass entertainment. The girls sing a capella and in accord their dance moves become coordinated with the melody of their own voices, rather than with the beat of the pre-recorded song. The look of non-choreography lends the moment feelings of sincerity and 'authenticity'. It is in this spontaneous turn that the moment generates a sense of togetherness – among the Plastics and particularly between them and the school auditorium audience. As the audience joins in and sings out together for the duration of the song, the sense of a spontaneously conjured community is created. This feeling of community is extended out to the audio-viewer. Feuer (1993: 31, 34) suggests that the cinema audience is encouraged to identify with the diegetic audience of musical numbers (as well as the performers) and consequently this mode of identification involves them in the number. The *Mean Girls* musical moment briefly offers the feeling of community as a solution to the fragmentation presented in the narrative, and as a presumed problem in the 'real'-world lives of the audience.

The utopian pleasures of the musical provide a useful foundation from which to consider the pleasures of musical numbers and moments in girl teen film. However, it is possible to develop this formulation of pleasure further by considering the aesthetic mode of contemporary musical numbers and their appeals to kinaesthetic pleasures.

Musical address and aesthetic modes

Girl teen films made in the 2000s have played with integration devices in various ways but what holds these millennial films and their musical moments together in common is their cheerfully affective attitude. A comparison between the original 1988 version of *Hairspray* (J. Waters) and its 2007 remake, offers an illustrative example. The original *Hairspray* does not contain diegetic singing but includes dance numbers that are incorporated as part of the 'Corny Collins Show'. Although the film uses elements of musical address, it is fundamentally different to its remake in 2007. *Hairspray* (1988) renders 'a life pervaded by music' (Dyer, 2002a: 179) in comparison to the traditional musical structure which sets up problems in the narrative and offers escape and solution in the numbers. *Hairspray* (1988) is a highly stylized film, but there is little difference between the spaces of the numbers and those of the rest of the film – all maintain a similar affective tone.

In comparison with the 2007 version, *Hairspray* (1988) is visually and affectively less 'polished'. John Waters' film draws on musical obscenity and the grotesque. Although the mise en scène of the 1988 film makes use of the vibrant colours of 1960s décor, this is an altogether tatty version. John Waters is a 'trash art' filmmaker who aggressively exploits 'bad taste' (Benson-Allott, 2009). His work reveals a fixation with vulgarity and the 'improper', and *Hairspray* (1988) reflects these preoccupations in its narrative and numbers. In Waters' film, for example, hair is 'ratted' up to extreme proportions and close-ups reveal the sweat and grease of teen hair and skin. In the original film Divine performs the role of Edna Turnblad as a 'grotesque' drag persona (Cunningham, 2003). The discrepancy between sex and gender ideals is constructed as a significant pleasure of the Queer performance. In the 2007 version, John Travolta plays the role made

Figure 5.3 *Hairspray* (1988), the Record Hop.

up as a woman. Travolta's masculine form is obscured underneath padding and prosthetics, obfuscating his real fleshiness beneath a cleaner synthetic version of the character. Travolta's performance maintains traditional gender boundaries, where Divine's drag makes fun of them. Both films draw attention to surfaces, as teen films generally do, but where the surface of the Waters' film is sticky and carnal the 2007 film feels like a smooth, simulated fabrication. I do not mean to suggest that all 1980s teen musicals are affectively transgressive, but the contrast between the two versions of *Hairspray* makes stark the sanitized aesthetic mode of contemporary girl teen musicals and musical moments.

The numbers in Waters' *Hairspray* use an aesthetic mode that affectively draws on musical obscenity and the grotesque. As Robin James (2013) proposes, *Hairspray* (1988) reflects that 'music was a gateway to racially transgressive corporeal practices and affective states'. The transgression of the original and the different aesthetic modes of the two versions of the film can be seen through comparison of equivalent scenes at the 'Record Hop'.

In the Record Hop number from 1988 the teens from the 'Corny Collins Show' dance the 'Madison Time' (Bryant, 1959) by jazz musician Ray Bryant; this is a song with specified dance steps. 'Madison Time' uses a jazz swing beat and the dance manifests the shape of the music. The dance is fundamentally constructed around 'buck' and 'wing' moves: these are black social dances that developed during the nineteenth century. Thomas DeFrantz (2004: 102) describes 'black popular music and movements' as

Figure 5.4 *Hairspray* (2007), the Record Hop.

unified in their approach through a shared percussive attack, allowance for individual expression within the group, repetition and intensification, strong reliance on breaks or abrupt ruptures of the underlying beat, and a highly complex rhythmic structure.

'Madison Time' relies on complex rhythms and a strong percussive beat, including repetition and intensification. In her movements Tracy (Ricki Lake) reveals her competence and comfort with the dance. Although the number is a line dance that the dancers perform in unison, it is Tracy's ability to respond with loose, improvised moves to the basic, regulated steps that gets her noticed. In response to the music, Tracy's body affectively transgresses racial, sexual and physical boundaries.

The Record Hop number in the 2007 film of *Hairspray* is recognizable as the same scene, but its aesthetic mode is distinctly different. The music, 'Ladies' Choice', uses elements that stem from black musical aesthetics, such as call and response, percussive attack and breaks in the underlying beat. However, sung by Link Larkin (Zac Effron) the song is an intensely upbeat 'Broadway number'. The dance that responds to the music here is a jazz routine in its contemporary sense: a controlled and commodified version of jazz dance. It does not involve the looser, spontaneous inventions associated with black social dances but the codified techniques, angular body lines and flamboyant technical virtuosity that DeFrantz (ibid.: 102) describes as prevalent on Broadway stages and Hollywood screens. These codified dance techniques that embody the brighter, upbeat music, lift the number away from affective states that are a possible consequence of musical and dance 'obscenity' and into sanitized 'fun'.

Dance films such as *Centre Stage: Turn It Up* or *Step Up 2: The Streets*, combine aesthetic modes of sanitized fun and music and dance obscenity. Structured around street dance and hip-hop routines these films exploit black aesthetics by focusing on the dynamics of breakdance choreography (rather than the political dimensions of hip-hop culture). In accord with musicals and musical moments dance films employ the techniques of musical address. However, these films' musical numbers are grounded in an aesthetic mode that emphasizes sexuality. In dance films, sexual identity and dance ability are conflated. The exploitation of hip-hop forms draws semiotically and aesthetically on racial stereotypes of the 'untamed, natural and raw sexuality' of black dance culture (Monteyne, 2013: 193). The aesthetic mode of the dance numbers in girl teen dance films bring in to play an aggressive sexuality that is not usually found in the conventional musical. The dance numbers in *Step Up 2* draw on the same music and dance obscenity that we see and hear in the original *Hairspray*. The dance provides a supra-diegetic space for the white Cinderella character-icon to create an aggressive sexuality. However, these classed, raced and gendered music and dance aesthetics are safely contained in the numbers. Beyond the music and dance, the films maintain the smooth polish and sterilization of contemporary musicals, despite their urban and working-class settings.

Contemporary girl teen musicals and musical moments share in common a core aesthetic mode that seeks to invite the audio-viewer to enjoy pleasures that are grounded in especially 'clean' and appealing affective states. In Waters' *Hairspray* (1988) the pleasures of the film are in part a residual component of the disgust that its aesthetic mode engenders as well as an affective response to music and dance obscenity. In comparison the 2007 version of the film appeals to pleasures connected to the openness, energy and happy promises that the enchantment of musical address offers.

Musical address and its kinaesthetic pleasures

Like Cinderella's modulations, her celebrity glamour and sporting successes, girl teen films' musical numbers often feel like promise, potential and expansion. Like the moments explored in the previous chapters these feelings meet with contradictory qualities and where the Cinderella character-icon expands out into the world through music and dance, she is also contained.

The techniques of musical address are particular to musicals, dance films and musical moments, and need to be outlined as a means to understand how musical pleasures work and the kinds of experiences they offer. Musical address is a form of enchantment cued by various techniques, including, and most obviously, a physical shift in character/actor mode of performance and expression: from walking and talking to singing and dancing. Raising a stage curtain, characters moving onto stage, or into a space as though it were a stage, can also create the necessary shift. Musical address will also make use of 'everyday' spaces and props in a way that they too become part of the enchantment: in *High School Musical* (Ortega, 2006), for example, the 'ordinary' school corridor becomes alive with music and dance, and basketballs become the source of the beat. The diegetic audience signifies how the audio-viewer should respond and how they should feel about the performance – showing their own delight and/or joining in with the number. Musical address also means that people's movements become coordinated or synchronous, with each other or with the music.

Another component of musical address is the use of 'audio' and 'video dissolve' techniques (Altman, 1989: 62–74) that help to smooth the transition from narrative to number. These techniques are used to allow characters to move almost imperceptibly from talking to singing, and walking to dancing. Tactics such as humming or rhythmical walking are employed to bridge the shift from narrative to musical performance. As a means of integration, film musicals also merge diegetic and non-diegetic music – mixing the two in ways that transform the image and sound hierarchy. This merger is what Altman (1989: 71) calls supra-diegetic music. *Hairspray* provides an illustrative example: when Tracy walks into auditions for the 'Corny Collins Show', Velma Von Tussle (Michelle Pfeiffer) leads the show dancers in rehearsal. Diegetic music plays underneath their footfalls. As Velma assesses the inadequacies of auditionees her vocals become increasingly rhythmic until she moves from conversation to singing, with a shift that lifts her voice in accompaniment to non-diegetic orchestration. In the supra-diegetic space of the musical the sound and image relationship is fundamentally changed. Music is to the fore and dictates the image. Altman (ibid.: 71) argues that supra-diegetic music transforms the 'real' world of film into an ideal world of pure music. The supra-diegetic space of the musical opens the diegetic world up, putting perceptual and expressive limitations aside for the duration of the number. The video dissolve, as Altman describes it, similarly enables the scene to bridge 'two separate places, times, or levels of reality' (ibid.: 74). This is an ideal space in which 'rhythm becomes contagious' (ibid.: 69). Musical contagion means that bystanders cannot help but tap their feet or sing along (1989: 68). Singing and dancing enchant the diegetic world with the possibilities and potential afforded by music and dance. The diegetic world responds to this enchantment by joining in, providing accompaniment or the necessary audience.

Girl teen musicals such as *Hairspray* also rely on 'musical logic' whereby space and time can be made to cohere through musical consistency rather than classical Hollywood continuity. Dyer (2002b [1976–77]: 51) describes the way that musical logic works: 'The action is telescoped to fit the song, the logic of the real world gives way to the logic of the song, of music.' Musical logic conveys the feeling that music takes over the world. In *Hairspray*'s (2007) 'Good Morning Baltimore' for example the disparate times and locations between Tracy missing her bus to school and riding atop a garbage truck are held together by an extended single note of the song. In combination the edit here is dictated by the beat of the music and the graphic match between shots emphasizes Tracy's continuous note. Although the cut elides significant movement in space and time, the transition between locations is held together through musical logic. Musical logic adds to the feelings of freedom and unrestrained expression offered by the supra-diegetic space of the musical. Musical logic further lifts the restraints of classical continuity – giving musical films and musical moments a greater sense of flexibility and movement.

Part of the pleasure of musicals is the ability of music and dance to shift the parameters and lend a sense of freedom to otherwise restrictive spaces. In line with Altman's (1989: 65) description of the supra-diegetic space as utopian, in the sense that the real and ideal are merged, Feuer (1993: 71) sees in the musical a resolution of dichotomies in the fusion of two value systems: the reality principle and the pleasure principle. Usually represented in the lead couple, rational, cognitive Puritanism stands in contrast to imagination, freedom, impulse and spontaneity. In musical film 'a world of music transforms a repressed world of silence' (Feuer: 72). The musical moment in *Mean Girls* for example, briefly, sees the world of the film taken over by music. When the diegetic audience is compelled to join in with the number, the 'repressed silence' – the tight restrictive hold of the hierarchical system of the school – is momentarily freed by the musical logic that overtakes the auditorium.

Girl teen musicals and dance films can also make use of a dual-focus narrative. A structure that is built around parallel characters of opposite sex and divergent values (Altman, 2002 [1987]: 42). *Another Cinderella Story* (Santostefano, 2008) represents a generic example whereby the contradictory values of the character stereotypes of 'jock' and 'geek' are resolved and merged through musical performance. Similarly the dance film *Save the Last Dance* (Carter, 2001) sees the duality of masculine/feminine, black/white, street/ballet resolved in the protagonist's final performance in which black aesthetics are appropriated and the two dance styles are merged. Through the creation of supra-diegetic spaces and the use of musical logic, difficulties, dichotomies and contradictions can be played out or overcome with seeming ease. It is in the numbers of these musicals and dance films that the characters find happiness (Dyer, 2012: 101). The narratives set up problems to which the numbers offer solutions, or at least respite (ibid.). For example, through the climactic number of *Hairspray*, 'You Can't Stop the Beat,' Tracy's mother Edna finds the confidence to perform that has so far eluded her. Her confident performance reflects that she is finally happy with herself. In the same number, the central and supporting couples confirm that they are in love, and the performance resolves national race segregation.

Millennial girl teen musicals also rely on pastiche to encourage an enchanted mode of engagement that goes along with the fantasy that musical address offers. To greater and lesser degrees, musicals and musical moments in girl teen films make use of double coding techniques. Double coding is not new to millennial teen musicals or musical moments. As Feuer (1993) has made clear the musical is a self-reflexive genre. Films like *A Star is Born* (Cukor, 1954), for example, (in particular the 'Someone at Last' number) use double coding techniques that pastiche musical convention while making use of the pleasures of these conventions all the same. What is unique to millennial girl teen films and their musical address is that double coding is fundamental. In contrast dance films are usually not double coded. The contexts in which performance takes place – rehearsals, nightclubs and competitions – require less of an affective gateway than that which is necessary in musicals and musical numbers. The settings are similar to those in sports films and provide a framework from which performance is more easily integrated and accepted.

Mean Girls uses double coding techniques throughout and its musical moment is no exception. As a pastiche the moment imitates the idea of musical film and in doing so makes this self-consciousness central to its humour. First, the scene parodies what Ariel Levy (2006: 21) refers to as a 'raunch aesthetic' and sets this up as at odds with the 'innocence' of the Christmas song to which the Plastics perform and the idea of the musical number as a sincere line to genuine emotion. 'Raunch', as Levy (ibid.: 5) describes it, is a 'cartoon-like version of female sexuality', an aggressive projection of 'kitschy, slutty stereotypes' (ibid.: 34) that has been particularly noticeable since the mid-to-late 1990s. The PVC costumes worn by the Plastics in combination with their self-choreographed 'raunch' dance moves, creates a discrepancy between the idea of musical numbers and this performance of one. Their costumes and dance moves, in the context of the school auditorium, parodies both 'raunch' culture and the idea of the sincere and 'wholesome' musical.

Mean Girls's musical moment also makes a pastiche of the supra-diegetic space of the musical, a space in which the 'real' and ideal are merged – where characters and onlookers are overcome by the spirit and intensity of music and dance. *Mean Girls* draws attention to, mocks and exaggerates the idea of musical contagion – the idea that the dream-like magic of music and dance infects the 'real' world of the film. Once the Plastics CD backing track has been kicked from the stage the performance is momentarily halted. When Cady begins to sing, the number becomes a spontaneous one and in doing so signals a further supra-diegetic shift. As Cady continues to sing, the other Plastics accompany her and, as if consumed by the power of music and dance, members of the school auditorium audience do so as well. Cutaways to the audience and their exaggerated facial expressions suggest they cannot help but join in with the number. This pastiche suggests that the use of musical techniques and sentiments is all done in jest: no longer really meant or accepted. The musical moment makes fun of the idea of the musical but still uses its techniques, and as such the moment facilitates the affects of musical address all the same.

Despite the cynical edge that *Mean Girls*' musical moment portrays and its light mockery of musical address, the scene still explicitly presents singing and dancing as fun in ways that are typical to girl teen film in narrative terms. Despite the momentary embarrassment caused by the CD player being kicked from the stage, the performance is successful in the sense that the diegetic audience responds enthusiastically with loud applause and cheers; the performance makes the Plastics centre of attention and provides Cady with a Cinderella moment that increases her position in the group and school hierarchy; it also provides a sense of togetherness that is lacking elsewhere in the narrative. Aesthetically the techniques of musical address also create fantasy spaces in which the world is momentarily experienced as unrestricting and expansive. Like sports performances that create flow, musical address creates a world in which girls can move through it without meeting resistance.

Kinaesthetic pleasures

We can extend Altman's (1989) concept of musical contagion discussed above, where rhythm becomes contagious and the musical world becomes infected by the possibilities offered by musical address, to include the audio-viewer. The techniques of musical address invite the audience outside of the diegesis to take up a specific physical watching position. The idea of generic expectation as a physical experience (Thomas, 2000: 9) works out not only across genres but also across individual film moments. Thomas (ibid.) proposes that our bodies attend to specific films in particular ways based on 'broad anticipation of the kinds of pleasure to be offered'. Some films and film moments invite our bodies to tense up, close-in and brace, while others invite a more relaxed or freer state. The techniques of musical address encourage a physical openness, attentiveness and sensitivity to the potential pleasures of music and dance.

This is a type of kinaesthetic contagion. In the previous chapter I explored kinaesthetic contagion as a visceral awareness of the effort, muscle and sinew of the sporting body. In this respect pleasure was connected to the feelings of physical power created by the effortful body of the sports performer. Reason and Reynolds (2010: 66–7) describe another type of kinaesthetic contagion, in their analysis of the pleasures of live dance performance, that provides a framework for understanding the pleasures of musical address. This second type of kinaesthetic contagion is a physically uplifting response to the general movement of the dance number. This category of kinaesthetic contagion can be connected to Barker's (2009: 74–5) notion of muscular empathy. Barker extends Linda Williams (1991) body genre categories to suggest that the audio-viewer's response is a type of embodied mimicry, not just of the characters but of the film itself. Williams' body genres catch the audio-viewer in mimicry of what they see characters perform on screen: pornography creates arousal; horror creates fear; melodrama creates tears. Barker broadens this idea to propose that audiences' responses can be triggered by the 'film's body'. In a similar vein Reynolds (2012) draws on Sobchack's (2004) work as a means to explore the affects of live dance and the audience's experience of the 'dance's body'. Reynolds (2012: 129) suggests that the movement of the dance as a whole can affect us. That we may internalize movement and sense its processes in our own bodies, not just the movement of one dancer or single component of the dance but the movement of the whole piece. This form of kinaesthetic contagion is a pleasure that musical numbers in girl teen films invite us to enjoy. The rhythm, energy and sense of freedom of the musical number does not only work on the diegetic audience. Musical address is designed to infect the audio-viewer, to invite a physical response to the uplifting aesthetic mode of the number as a whole.

Mean Girls's musical moment is neither particularly impressive in its use of dance, nor does it showcase singing talent that is exceptionally remarkable. Nonetheless, despite its pastiche of the musical, it provokes an uplifting, energized, physically free and relaxed mode of embodied engagement. The number cues a kinaesthetic contagion that responds to the general positive impulse of the number. When Cady, the Plastics and the audience sing, the expressive freedom and intrinsic pleasure of singing in general, lends the moment a quality of enchantment. As Dyer (2012: 3–4) explains, pleasure in other people's singing comes from one's own knowledge of what it is like to sing. Pleasure is inherent in singing, he suggests, because of what it physiologically involves: to sing requires relaxation of the vocal chords and muscles and so it implies a physically relaxed state. Moving together, the Plastics' dance also draws on feelings of muscular bonding that extend out into the diegetic audience: one member of the auditorium (a 'Plastic' mother) stands and mimics the girls' routine. Although this is clearly a comic parody of an over involved 'hip parent' (Wiseman, 2002: 51) it embodies the feelings of kinaesthetic contagion encouraged in the audio-viewer and a physical sense of togetherness and community.

Music is also a powerful element of kinaesthetic contagion. In bringing music to the fore musical address invites the audio-viewer to adopt specific physical and emotional modalities. In *Music in Everyday Life*, Tia DeNora (2000) provides a way of thinking about the affective dimensions of music that seems particularly relevant to the embodied shift that musical address invites. DeNora's (ibid.: 88–108) study examines the ways in which music is overtly employed as a means of state regularization in aerobics classes. In the context of aerobics, she explores the ways that specific musical materials work upon the body. The stylistic aspects of musical forms and genres, she demonstrates, have the potential to entrain the human body in slight, sometimes 'imperceptible micro-movements, such as how one holds one's eyebrows, cheekbones or shoulders, the tensions of one's muscles' (ibid.: 78). However, as DeNora (ibid.: 96) makes clear, music does not just act on the body – its effects cannot be strictly predetermined – it must be appropriated. That is to say, in the context of watching and listening to girl teen film the experience of the audio-viewer cannot be programmed. To have the impact the devices of musical address aim for, the audio-viewer must be appropriately engaged. What can be determined is that music does have affective and emotional possibilities.

As DeNora (ibid.: 106) examines, specific to the aerobics class, music helps to set up a series of shifts in embodied engagement for the participant, who (if the class is successful) is encouraged to move between states throughout the class, from: 'person-in-the-street, to aerobically enlisted and motivated'.

Music has the capability to create affective and emotional shifts. It can invite the body to take up specific modes of engagement. The musical address of girl teen film encourages a state that is 'musically enlisted'; a body that is on board to enjoy the positive possibilities of the musical number. The ways that music is employed in girl teen films suggests what pleasures the audio-viewer is invited to experience from it. As the body literally moves with the music in an aerobics class, the embodied engagement of its participants is more obviously recognizable. Nonetheless, as DeNora (ibid.: 107) points out, music has affective and emotional power over bodily states even while the listeners remain seated. Music can rouse the bodies it encounters because of the movement it implies (e.g. DeNora [ibid.: 107] suggests marching music may put listeners in mind of bodily states), but also because 'it is doing movement in a similar manner, because the materiality of how notes are attacked and released, sustained and projected partakes of similar physical movements and gestures'. The kind of movement music 'does' in girl teen film tends to encourage an open and positive embodied engagement.

The musical moment in *Mean Girls* for example invites a relaxed and uplifting physical mode of engagement. As a ubiquitous Christmas song 'Jingle Bell Rock' potentially provides the number with a comfortable familiarity, however previous awareness of the song is not an essential factor of its affective possibilities. The song uses a common 4/4 beat signature and the tempo remains at a consistent 140 beats per minute throughout, with a standard popular music structure: verse, chorus, bridge. These typical pop-song elements give the song and sequence an easy approachability. The body of the audio-viewer is easily oriented to feel the beat and rhythm of the number. The song is also in a major key and the guitar accents further add to its bright timbre. The use of female vocals (in both the recorded and 'live' versions) also contributes a light pitch. The song also uses a swung rhythm (rather than straight) – a 'looser' music formation that implies similarly swinging motion. This is not to suggest that we will literally sway in our seats as we watch and listen (although we could), but that the music and its movements encourage a relaxed, free and easy muscle tension.

The pleasurable simplicity of the number is furthermore evident when the backing track is cut and the characters are forced to sing a capella. The jaunty rhythm of the song is easily discernible in the vocal rendition – the regular beat is easily picked up – as expressed by the diegetic audience's accompaniment. This is a song that we are invited to clap or sing along with. Similarly when the auditorium piano is used to supplement the vocals it is done with ease. The accompanying piano adds to the feelings of spontaneity and a folksy 'authenticity' (Feuer, 1993: 3–13) that the opening of the number lacked, but it also adds further spring to the swing of the song – increasing the implied energy and momentum of the number.

Ultimately, the focus of musical numbers is on the spectacle of the human body and its relationship to music – on physical energy, ability and exertion, rather than specific character motivation or inner thoughts. Being so focused on the body and what the body can do with music, musical address promotes an embodied engagement with the pleasures of energy, tension and release, control, freedom and mobility connected to music and dance.

In musical numbers the body is generally constructed as ideal: seemingly complete and perfected in its organic capacity to create and respond to music. In accord with the ideal sports body the compositions of the body encourage an admiration of virtuosity but what is particular to the musical number in comparison to sports performances is the spectacle of what bodies can do with music. It is useful here to return to the sports film *Stick It* as the film offers a way to make the connections between sports performance and musical numbers explicit. *Stick It* includes both types of performance and although both rely on spectacles of the body in coordination, the film's musical number uses musical address techniques to place emphasis on the relationship between music and the body: music is fundamental to its pleasures.

Stick It's musical moment sees the protagonists of the film (a group of female gymnasts and two male friends) make a visit to a shopping mall. Unlike the *Mean Girls* musical moment (but common to girl teen film) the musical number in *Stick It* does not involve 'live' singing but makes use of pre-recorded, popular music to structure the scene. Musical address techniques integrate the number and the performance appears as though it is entirely 'spontaneous', it seems to emerge impulsively from the excitement of the characters. The shopping mall number is somewhat abstract: cut into brief dialogue the routine uses 'Berkelyesque' formations as a means of signifying 'fun'. Where in *Mean Girls* the pleasures of singing and dancing are connected quite clearly to being looked at and the positive responses of the diegetic audience, the performance of gymnastics/dance in *Stick It*'s mall number is used, in and for itself. That is to say, in combination with close-ups of smiling faces, giggles and high-fives, dance is used to connote fun. Where the *Mean Girls* sequence shows girls in control of a 'raunch aesthetic' the spectacle of bodies in the *Stick It* number, like those in *Hairspray* (2007), presents those bodies as moving out and taking up space through sheer exuberance.

In the musical numbers of girl teen films, girls can use their full bodily energies and capabilities. Through dance and music girls can make themselves bigger, extend their bodies outwards and take up space. Like the fantasies of empowerment and mastery of the body that we see in sports films, girls' bodies are presented in musical and dance numbers as agile, skilled and controlled. Music and dance create moments of expansion and power.

Musical address works as a prosthetic technology of the body. DeNora (2000: 103) describes how music functions as a prosthetic technology in 'everyday' life: as a material that extends what the body can do. In her ethnographic analysis DeNora explains that music can work upon the body, not just as a mere accompaniment but also as constitutive of agency. For example in aerobics classes, music can push the body beyond what it can usually do. Music is similarly used in working life: on the high seas for example the sea shanty was used for hauling sails or lifting anchor (ibid.: 104–5). In 'doing movement' (ibid.: 107), music encourages similar movement in the body. Through music, DeNora (ibid.) suggests, bodies are enabled and empowered. In the aerobics class we can see how music literally extends bodily capacities beyond the 'everyday': to create motivation, coordination, energy and endurance (ibid.: 102). Musical address similarly acts as a prosthetic in film, lifting the confines of expression and sensory experience, girls' bodies are constructed beyond the usual bounds, extending what the girl body can do and how it can be experienced. Cuing a world captivated by music and dance musical address enables young female characters to use their bodies' full capacities, to stretch out and beyond themselves.

Through music, singing and dancing, female characters can stretch out, fill space and occupy time. Dyer (2002: 2) proposes that 'the musical is unusual in assigning the experience of expansion to female characters.' He describes 'expansion' in *The Sound of Music* as 'the celebration of female energy and mastery of the world' (ibid.). In his study *In the Space of a Song* (Dyer, 2012) he explores the motif of expansion in the musical further. The feelings of expansion, he suggests, are blissful: 'to throw one's arms in the air, to rush out into the space around one' (ibid.: 113). The feelings of expansion are pleasurable, he proposes, but not innocent. Expansion is assumed to be an entitlement for some and not for others. Claiming space and time also involves 'the feeling forms of geographical expansion, of male going out into the world, of imperialism and ecological depredation' (ibid.: 101). Expansion is assumed as a white male privilege, rarely experienced by 'Others'. Singing and dancing in girl teen films offer a means of expansion, a way of inhabiting space and time, usually unavailable to girls.

The feeling forms of power in dance provide the female characters of girl teen film access to feelings of expansion, appearances of influence over space, and an ability to take control of the environment. Dance, Langer (1953: 187) proposes, 'is a play of Powers made visible'. Dance expresses ideas of specific emotion and initiates symbolic gestures, which articulate these ideas (ibid.: 186). The gestures of dance primarily, Langer (ibid.: 175–6) argues, express ideas of power: 'not actual, physically exerted power, but appearances of influence ... the subjective experience of volition and free agency'.

The fantasies of empowerment in the musical numbers of girl teen film do not just *show* bodies that are capable. Through kinaesthetic empathy the audio-viewer is invited to experience these feelings of dance – of power and expansion – in their own bodies; an experience not often expressed through girls. In these films' musical numbers girls' bodies are potentially experienced as unhesitant, in control and unified. Musical address emphasizes this unity: bodies on display appear organic, as one with, the music. As if spontaneously, bodies are able to respond to music in the supra-diegetic space of the number, capable of organic movement that unhesitatingly responds to the movement of the music. In this response, numbers show bodies that are in control, certain and cohesive. Showing bodies that respond as 'one with' the music, the numbers in girl teen films present girls' bodies, not as the disconnected and uncontrollable limbs that Young (2005) describes, but bodies that are capable of unified, organic movement.

In *Hairspray* (2007), when Tracy sings and dances she responds unhesitatingly to the music that surrounds her. She throws her body and voice out into the world to take up space and time. In *Step Up 2*, numbers are choreographed to be mimicked, as well as designed to display the protagonists' special abilities. For the audio-viewer music works on the body and in combination so do the dance moves. Routines are shot straight to camera and although the camera is mobile, there is an emphasis on showing the choreographed moves. The actors in the film are dancers foremost and consequently the camera can keep in close and let the performances unfold. These are ideal bodies and their abilities encourage kinaesthetic sympathy – admiration of the prowess demonstrated – but the skill of what the body can do with music also invites kinaesthetic empathy. The dance moves are shown in a way that the audio-viewer can experience the dance in their own body. The audio-viewer can feel in their own body, an experience of the power, capabilities and sense of expansion that the girls display.

Singing and dancing in girl teen films create the contradictory qualities of expansion and confinement. Expansion in girl teen films is physically freeing *and* claustrophobic. The musical numbers in girl teen films invite the kinaesthetic pleasures of physical expansion, unhindered movement and mastery of the body in space. The entitlement to space suggested by these pleasures however has its limits and girls' expansion is bound to commercial, domestic and institutional spaces.

In the mall sequence from *Stick It*, for example, musical address cues a number in which the young female characters expand out into the space of the mall. Using controlled and adept gymnastic manoeuvres the characters occupy space with a physical dominance that is unusual for girls. This sequence is clearly a fantasy of empowerment, a celebration of female energy and mastery of the body. Nonetheless these expressions of expansion and possibility are contained within parameters. Singing and dancing in these films feel like moving out into the world but they are confined to specific privatized public spaces (the mall, nightclub or beauty parlour), controlling institutional spaces (school or 'camp') or the domestic sphere (home). Unlike the expansion and celebration of female energy that can take place in traditional musicals (for example in the famous opening of *The Sound of Music* where Maria lifts her voice and throws out her arms to fill the hills with the sound of music), in girl teen films expansion is contained and numbers rarely leave domestic, institutional or consumer spaces. Even among those girl teen films that are conventional musicals, *Hairspray* (2007) is unusual in the ways that the protagonist is given freedom of movement and expansion into the public sphere. In girl teen dance films city streets are a generic backdrop and numbers often take place within an urban landscape. Narratives usually involve a containment of this public expansion however and girls (and boys for that matter) become institutionalized into dance schools or ballet companies.

Conclusion

Millennial girl teen films aim to create pleasurable affects based on a sterilized version of girlhood or a contained sense of sexuality. Obscenity of any kind is left implicit in forms of dance and music but the films' surfaces remain polished and sanitized. Musical address aims to create a form of enchantment that leaves the audience open to the kinaesthetic pleasures of expansion and power that the musical numbers encourage but the kinds of experiences that music and dance sequences offer are also fundamentally restrictive.

The mall moment in *Stick It* is a musical number but it is more accurately described as a music video sequence. Non-diegetic, pre-recorded music is brought to the fore and works in combination with the image to embody the energy and movement of dance. Appropriate to the spectacle of gymnastics/dance that the number is built around, the music implies regulated, deliberate and exact movements. Structured around a pop-rap, neo-electro cover, 'Nu Nu (yeah yeah)' by FannyPack (2005), as the girls flip through the air, their movements work in synchrony with each other and with the music. The song uses rap and syncopation which gives the number a sense of speed; half a beat behind the vocals the drum beat creates the feeling that it is trying to 'catch-up', lending the music a greater sense of momentum. This feeling of energy and pace is also expressed through the visuals, with constant movement that keeps up with the sound. This particular combination of music and image, the use of music video aesthetics, in girl teen films lends spectacle to prescribed moments and creates distinctive pleasures that I will explore in the following chapter.

6

Music Video Aesthetics: The Affects of Spectacle

Introduction

In the previous chapter I explored the ways that musical address offers a unique form of enchantment: unbound by the confines of expression and perception found in classical continuity, musical address draws on the affective, physical pleasures of music and dance. Music video aesthetics create another form of musical address through a shift in the sound – image relationship that similarly creates a 'supra-diegetic' space where the perceptual and expressive limitations of the classical Hollywood continuity system are put aside for the duration of the number. Music video sequences in film are associated with the direct address of spectacle and overt narration. Unlike the traditional score, composed after completion of the image track, this kind of sequence is identified with the use of pre-recorded, popular, self-contained songs. Teen film has developed with a distinct relationship to popular music and the music industry. The use of popular music in teen film is industrially recognized as both a selling point for movies themselves and a key to lucrative ancillary markets (For an analysis of the economic influence of popular music in teen film, see Caine, 2004; Dickinson, 2001; Doherty, 2002; Mundy, 1999, 2006). Music video aesthetics also encourage an intense form of kinaesthetic contagion that feels like music and dance. Rather than focus on the economic rationale behind the use of popular music and music video aesthetics in these films (of course, in this context aesthetic appeals have economic imperatives at their basis), this chapter explores the kinds of appeal this type of sequence aims for. The collaborative relationship between music and image in film is nothing new. The use of pre-recorded, popular music in films, however, is a relatively more recent practice that, since the 1970s, has become increasingly unexceptional (Inglis, 2003). The emergence of the pop promo in the 1960s and the form's stylistic influence on films like *A Hard*

Figure 6.1 *Make It Happen* (2008), Lauryn's first performance at 'Ruby's'.

Days Night (Lester, 1964) is also a fairly recent development in the relationship between sound and image that has become progressively common place, more especially following the launch of MTV in 1981. This chapter does not explore a history of music in film, or compare the use of pre-recorded popular songs to traditional scoring. There is extensive literature on music video, popular music in film and more specifically the relationship between music video and teen film (Dickinson, 2001; Henderson, 2006; Ross, 2011) but approaches focus on the pleasures of music video in relation to their ideological implications or seek to compare classical Hollywood scoring and the use of compilation scores in teen film. Consequently aesthetics and affect are left underexplored. I am interested in how this particular combination of music and image creates spectacle and the kinds of pleasures it aims to generate as a means to understand how girl teen films are designed to feel fun.

In *Bring It On: Fight to the Finish* the end credits role alongside a music video performed by Christina Milian, who plays the main character Lina, accompanied by her co-stars. This is a music video in form and structure: it is a staged performance that uses direct address, with Milian lip-synching straight to camera. The performers dance routines in front of studio sets that lack any sense of space or time but exist for the sheer spectacle of the performance. As with all music video the visuals are dictated by the music; music and dance are the driving principles rather than narrative or realism. Consequently the video, like the music itself, uses the repetition of short phrases and is edited to the beat of the music (for more on the characteristics of music video, see Railton and Watson, 2011; Williams, 2003). The purpose of this music video is to showcase the image and skills of Milian, and to further align her pop-star image with the film. The type of music video sequence I want to explore here are those moments that are not music videos in a formal sense but rather, they are moments that make use of music video aesthetics as a means to generate spectacle. In the romantic comedy/girl teen film *13 Going on 30* (Winick, 2004), for example, Jenna (Jennifer Garner) takes a shower, puts make-up on, looks through her wardrobe and walks down a corridor. Though this does not sound like the stuff of spectacle, music video aesthetics are used to present these 'everyday' activities in a mode that lends them excitement, creating intense experiences around a normative model of 'girl fun'. This chapter explores what music video aesthetics are, what they do and the kinds of pleasure they aim to create around gendered notions of fun.

Music video aesthetics

Music video aesthetics are one aspect of girl teen films that give moments of 'fun' greater affective force and explain these moments' physical appeals. Traditional Hollywood scoring fits image and music together in a way that aims to make the music 'unheard' (Gorbman, 1987). In music video sequences in film, music makes the image and the image makes the music: both media are reliant upon and transform each other. In this particular way of combining music and visuals, the differences between elements are not made visible but converge to create a general, coherent and intense impression. Music video stylistics are made by an intermedia process that creates this distinct relationship between music and visuals. Yvonne Spielmann (2001: 57) uses the term 'intermedia' to describe a convergence of separate art forms. She proposes that where multimedia forms cross borders and compare different media, each remains distinct. Intermedia, however, refers to an interaction and integration between different media, resulting in transformation: in their combination elements change to create a third aesthetic dimension that can be described as an intermedia aesthetic. Music video aesthetics create an audiovisual interaction in which music and image fuse and exchange. These sequences bring music to the fore to create an intense aural presence, but the music does not work alone to generate impact; it is the combination of image and music that produces an audiovisual spectacle. The intermedia fusion of music and image, where both seem to respond and correspond to each other, creates distinct moments of spectacle. In girl teen film spectacle surrounds the specific 'stuff' that makes up the intimate public of girlhood.

The intimate public of girlhood

As I have suggested throughout this book, the kinds of experiences that girl teen films offer are limited. That is not to say that the audio-viewer cannot enjoy experiences that I have not considered here, but those that we are invited to encounter are constrained by the Hollywood (Cinderella character-icon) version of girlhood. Girl teen films are Hollywood's version of girl culture, which starts from the premise that girls already have something in common. As Lauren Berlant (2008: viii) proposes, cultural products aimed at a particular minority work from a presumption that consumers of particular 'stuff' share qualities or experiences that are held in common. Girl teen films aim to feel as though they express what is common among girls, especially in the form of desires, fantasies and pleasures. Following Berlant (2008), we can describe these films as part of the intimate public of girlhood. As Berlant (ibid.: 5) describes: 'An intimate public operates when a market opens up to a bloc of consumers, claiming to circulate texts and things that express those people's particular core interests and desires'. The intimate public of girlhood aims to feel as though it expresses what is common among girls and in doing so it sustains the association of specific desires, fantasies, affects and pleasures with girlhood.

These films can feel like change, action, development, promise, potential, energy, possibility, choice, transformation, flexibility and freedom. What they create instead is a shift within parameters, a static movement. Berlant (ibid.: 13) describes the intimate public as a set of 'porous constraints', a term that brings us back to girl teen film's modulations. Berlant (ibid.: 3) suggests that the 'motivating engine' of scenes within a 'women's intimate public' is 'the desire to be somebody in a world where the default is being nobody'. The kinds of experiences that girl teen films create are about the spectacle of the self. Being somebody in these worlds always involves the girl body and its visibility at the centre. So far this book has examined how girl teen films create pleasurable experiences around the spectacle of the self through: the aesthetic appeals of consumer products that create the outline of the Cinderella character-icon; the celebrity glamour that surrounds her; the sports body as surface; and singing and dancing as forms of physical expansion and confinement. Music video aesthetics lend further affective impact to all of these things, giving them a heightened sense of significance.

Making and repeating fixed fantasies and pleasures as though they are common among girls, the intimate public of girlhood that these films are a part of gives force to a restricted version of girlhood. As Berlant (ibid.: 3, italics in original) describes 'the intimate public legitimates qualities, ways of being, and entire lives that have otherwise been deemed puny or discarded. It creates situations where these qualities can appear as luminous'.

The impact of music video aesthetics gives intensity to situations, trivialized by their connection to private, commercial or institutional realms, lending impact to these 'puny' and 'discarded' aspects of femininity. By contributing the physical impact of music and dance, music video aesthetics make actions and activities seem fun and more significant than they may otherwise appear. This brings us back to fairy-tale enchantment: both, fairy tales and girl teen films are simple in the sense that characters are clearly drawn and 'details, unless very important, are eliminated' (Bettelheim, 1976: 8). As Jessica Tiffin (2009: 14) points out, because fairy tale lacks embellishment, where details are given they gain a heightened symbolic force. The mirror, spinning wheel or slipper become meaningful, significant and compelling beyond their basic shapes. Tolkien (1966: 59) describes fairy tales in a way that is similar to Berlant's description of the intimate public: 'fairy stories', he suggests, 'deal largely ... with simple or fundamental things ... made luminous by their setting'. In girl teen films the simple or fundamental things that make up the normative Hollywood version of girlhood are made 'fun' and pleasurable through 'look and feel'. Music video aesthetics in girl teen film are, similarly, an ideal example of how the basic shapes that make up this intimate public of girlhood gain affective force. In these films a limited version of girlhood is designed to feel significant and through the magic conjured by the commercial realm, girl teen films create experiences from which girls can 'live small but feel large' (Berlant, 2008: 3).

Music video aesthetics aim to lend another level of intensity to the Hollywood version of 'girl fun'. They are used to make a spectacle of stereotypically gender-specific scenarios, moments and spaces. The spaces in which these spectacles take place are often sites of domesticity, regulation or consumption: the home, school, mall, nightclub or beauty parlour. As well as the catwalk, dancing and girls' sports, the things that they make a spectacle of are 'everyday' practices of femininity: shopping, trying on clothes or cleaning for example, creating spectacles of specific gendered ideas of fun.

Modes of spectacle

In film all spectacles are not the same but sequences that create spectacle are often considered to be more striking or intense – displays occupying distinct spaces that aim to directly arouse the audience (Buckland, 1998: 170; Gunning, 1990: 59). Within and between specific films and genres, spectacles come in different forms. Usually associated with action and blockbuster cinema, the 'impact spectacle' is an aggressive mode designed to encourage visceral reactions from its audience (Bordwell, 2006: 158; King, 2000: 95). To create spectacles that aim for impact, action and blockbuster films employ particular presentational strategies. These stylistic devices render specific moments as especially intense. For example, through the use of rapid editing and movement towards camera, explosions in action films build in intensity to create moments with increasing affective force (see King, 2000: 114). In girl teen films very similar presentational strategies are employed, but the things that these films make a spectacle of and the kinds of experiences that they create are restricted by traditional gender norms.

The presentational strategies that make impact spectacles can be described as 'post-continuity' techniques (Shaviro, 2010: 118–26). In *Post-Cinematic Affect* (2010) Shaviro introduces the concept of post-continuity to make explicit the connections between contemporary cinematic presentational strategies, affect and the body. Through reference to action and exploitation films Shaviro (2010: 118–26) suggests that cinema has now relegated continuity in favour of impact, with the aim of stimulating autonomic responses in the audio-viewer. Post-continuity techniques are used, he suggests, 'not towards the production of meanings (or ideologies), but directly towards a moment-by-moment manipulation of the spectator's affective state' (ibid.: 118). In the contemporary world, he suggests, the stylistics of image-based modes of presentation are used to engage full somatic participation (ibid.: 38). Action films, Shaviro proposes, aim to create the same visceral involvement as that of a computer game (ibid.: 104). Like computer games the stylistics of post-continuity are used to generate 'user excitement' (ibid.: 120).

The 'computer game' mode of post-continuity aesthetics is evident in the boy teen film, *Never Back Down* (Wadlow, 2008). In common with the girl teen films analysed here, *Never Back Down* is an exploitation film. Targeted at a male teenage audience, it was made with a relatively substandard budget and capitalizes on the increasing popularity of mixed martial arts in the twenty-first century. When Jake (Sean Faris) joins a new high school, he becomes involved in an underground fight club. The kinds of physical experiences that boy teen films offer and those moments that gain affective charge through the use of post-continuity stylistics are determined by gender norms. 'Boy fun' is created as different to 'girl fun'. Like all traditional male Cinderellas (see Schafer, 2003) his quest for maturity is explicitly tied to a set of physically aggressive challenges and its attainment is achieved through physical prowess and emotional stoicism. The final fight sequence in the film uses a highly mobile camera and intense rapid editing with the aim of maintaining a constant sense of momentum. The camera is constantly in the thick of the action. Close-up point-of-view shots work to create proximal intensity and flash frame white-outs are used to generate the jar and clash of the fight. The exaggerated use of sound effects, of fists hitting bodies and bones breaking, adds to the overall rendering of the visceral impact of the fight. Used in this boy teen film context, where action and physical force are the main spectacle, post-continuity techniques are used to generate kinaesthetic empathy of a kind that responds to the aggression, force and momentum of the fight.

In girl teen film the use of music video aesthetics – the specific combination of music and image – shifts the mode in which post-continuity techniques are employed. Music video sequences use the same post-continuity presentational strategies as those used in the impact spectacles of action cinema. However these techniques are employed in girl teen films, not to generate the same user excitement as a computer game but stylistically and affectively to render the feelings created by music and dance. The modes of spectacle table (Figure 6.2) provides a basic breakdown of how the impact mode of spectacle works in girl teen films. As a means of illustration the table compares (in a rudimentary way) the spectacles of action cinema to those of girl teen film. The comparison is made to demonstrate the generic and gendered construction of spectacle.

The table breaks the modes of spectacle down into three key areas: 1) the pro-filmic spectacle: what is presented for the camera as spectacle; 2) presentational strategies: the stylistic devises used to present spectacle; and 3) intended response: the desired effect that the combination of the first two categories encourages – by this I do not mean to suggest what these spectacles will do, but what they aim to do.

The table is supplied here as a means to break spectacle down into its component parts. In doing so we can see the similarities and differences between

	1. Pro-filmic spectacle		2. Presentational strategies		3. Intended response	
	Action cinema	**Girl Teen Film**	**Action cinema**	**Girl Teen Film**	**Action cinema**	**Girl Teen Film**
Impact spectacles	Explosions	Shopping	Rapid editing	Rapid editing	Shock	Exhilaration
	Car chases	Trying on clothes	Movement towards camera	Movement towards camera	Surprise	Excitement
	Fighting	Singing	Cut on movement	Quick fire series of shots showing same action from varied angles	Excitement	Amusement
	Running	Dancing	Quick fire series of shots showing same action from varied angles		Exhilaration	Astonishment
	Shooting	Laughing			Agitation	Admiration
	Parkour	Strutting			Astonishment	Desire
	Destruction	Applying make-up		Highly mobile camera	Desire	Tactile pleasure
	Elemental forces	Cleaning	Highly mobile camera	Reliance on CUs	Tension	Kinaesthetic empathy
	Fetish objects (e.g. guns)	'Girls' sports'	Reliance on CUs	Shallow lateral space	Tactile pleasure	Kinaesthetic sympathy
	The body	Parties	Shallow lateral space	Saturated colours	Kinaesthetic empathy	Kinaesthetic contagion
	Loud noises	The body	Saturated colours	Strong backlighting	Kinaesthetic sympathy	
	Forceful music	Audience	Strong backlighting	Intermedia aesthetics: music & visuals	Kinaesthetic contagion	
	Public sphere	Stage	Intense sound			
		Pop/hip-hop/r'n'b	Intense special effects	Hasty cuts from falling to rising action (little use of establishing shots)		
		Private/privatised -public space	Hasty cuts from falling to rising action (little use of establishing shots)			
			Rapid use of crosscutting			
			Bipolar extremes of lens length			

Figure 6.2 Modes of spectacle.

these generic and gendered spectacles. This stark comparison highlights the 'stuff' that Hollywood generates as part of the intimate public of girlhood. In the rest of this chapter I will use this breakdown of spectacle to explore the specificities of the types of pleasure that music video aesthetics create.

Intended response: Pleasure

The pleasures derived from the impact spectacles created by music video aesthetics in girl teen films are affectively linked to the unique pleasures of music and dance. Music video sequences render the experience of music and dance as much as display it. Michel Chion (1994) provides a way of thinking about sound that can be extended to the musical–visual relationship of music video aesthetics. Chion characterizes the verisimilitude of the film soundscape as a rendering of sensation, rather than as a reproduction of sound. In place of committing to straightforward representations of sound, the film soundscape aims to embody 'real'-world, multisensory experiences (ibid.: 107, 109). As Chion (ibid.: 113) explains: 'The thing is that sound … must tell the story of a whole rush of composite sensations, and not just the auditory reality of the event.' Music video aesthetics create a specific rush of sensations that is mutually constructed by music and visuals. Together music and image create an audiovisual spectacle that renders the feelings and sensations of music and dance. As I described in the previous chapter, music has the capability to create affective and emotional shifts. It can invite the body to take up specific modes of engagement (DeNora, 2000). Music and image together can similarly work on our bodies but their combination is potentially more intense. In girl teen film they promote an embodied engagement with the pleasures of energy, tension and release, control, freedom and mobility connected to music and dance. Like traditional musical numbers, music video sequences create experiences of expansion alongside the contradictory quality of confinement. Experiences of movement and change are fixed within a set of parameters, but they potentially feel good all the same.

In girl teen dance films the audio-viewer is invited to share in the joys of what bodies can do with music and dance. With a focus on rendering how the ideal body feels as it moves with music, music video sequences encourage kinaesthetic contagion. The pleasures of this type of kinaesthetic contagion are encouraged, not only with the body on display but also with how the dancing body is rendered by the fusion of music and image. These spectacles do not necessarily focus on the specific moves that the body makes but on generating the impact of how it feels to move to music. This is significantly different to the musical numbers explored in the previous chapter (except the number from *Stick It*, which also uses music video aesthetics). The musical moment in *Mean Girls* or the Record Hop in *Hairspray* (2007), for example, presents routines that can be imitated by audio-viewers, and consequently frequently are in video tutorials and fan videos (see for example 'Mean Girls Jingle Bell Rock', 2010 or 'Ladies Choice', 2008). Music video sequences in girl teen films are often less concerned with the pleasures of imitation and instead are constructed with a focus on the pleasures of muscular mimicry and kinaesthetic contagion. Though of course, many dance films aim to do both, in the girl teen film context, music video aesthetics are not just about presenting dance moves but concentrate on creating the feelings of dance and the pleasures of expansion, movement, control and power, as well as admiration of the performance.

Make It Happen

As a means of illustration *Make It Happen* offers a standard example of girl teen dance film and the music video sequence. Structured around set pieces of dance or burlesque, *Make It Happen* provides a narrative framework as motivation for each dance routine: having failed her audition to get into dance school, Lauryn

(Mary Elizabeth Winstead) takes a job at burlesque club 'Ruby's'. The dance routines are integrated as club numbers or rehearsals, with each consciously employing a music video aesthetic, as director Darren Grant states: 'Each little dance routine was going to be like its own little music video' ('The art of original filmmaking: Make It Happen,' accessed, 2013). Lauryn's first performance at 'Ruby's' provides a typical example. The pro-filmic elements of this spectacle include the space of the nightclub, the stage in particular and the body of the Cinderella character-icon. The mise en scène of the sequence includes a highly stylized proscenium arch, strong back lighting and saturated colours (Figure 6.1). This is a texturally loaded, glamorous space. The scene is perceived through a colourful veil with the use of materials that play with light, and lighting schemes that involve pronounced uses of light and shadow.

Initially Lauryn struggles to perform successfully. The diegetic music is a smooth jazz number, too slow for the character's form of dance. During this initial part of the scene, mid-to-long shots dominate to let the character's failure unfold. When the club DJ realizes Lauryn's predicament, he switches the diegetic track to the hip-hop/r'n'b-based 'Shawty Get Loose' (2008) by Lil Mama. The contrast between the two songs is central to the narrative of the scene. The use of music underscores the juxtaposition between maturity and youth. The jazz track has a swing beat that maintains a slow tempo, its lyrical flow emphasizes a mature sophistication. 'Shawty Get Loose' uses louder dynamics, the tempo is faster, the use of syncopation adds to the sense of speed, and the rap in the song stresses beat rather than lyrics. When the music changes, the sequence shifts to create music video aesthetics and at this point Lauryn manages to present an effective routine. Music video aesthetics create the spectacle and pleasures of a successful performance.

In this sequence music video aesthetics render an ideal body in control and generate the impact of a successful dance routine. The number is constructed with a focus on generating what it feels like to dance rather than displaying the specific choreography of the routine. Music and visuals work to generate kinaesthetic contagion, not with specific moves, but with the back and forth, tension and release, shift and swing of dance in general. The experience of pleasure in relation to music video aesthetics thus has less to do with the dance itself than with the intermedia relationship that creates an encounter with music and dance.

From the moment that 'Shawty Get Loose' kicks in, the sequence is cut around the beat of the music. The intense sense of speed and immediacy emphasized by the tempo and syncopation of the track is met by the use of rapid cutting and close-ups. At points the scene is cut around a series of seemingly disconnected close-ups – not revealing the flow from one move to another but accentuating the general pulse of music and dance. In places, the sequence abandons continuity to stress the rhythms of the music and make a further spectacle of specific dance tableaus. Similar to displays of spectacular physical feats in action cinema, consecutive shots show the same move twice: first, at twenty-four frames per second and then in slow motion and from differing angles. The sequence also aims to generate feelings of movement and alternation, echoing the configurations of tension and release central to music and dance. Dirty long shots (in which heads and shoulders obscure part of the shot) from the diegetic audiences' perspective act as counter shots to those close-ups on stage in conjunction with the counterpoint between melody and beat in the song.

This dance number aims to feel like promise but it essentially creates another form of modulation. The initial part of the scene sets up a contrast between maturity and youth, innocence and experience. The scene feels like 'becoming', but it is another expression of the combination of 'appropriate' contradictory qualities. Lauryn is incapable of dancing to the 'overly' sophisticated jazz music that opens the scene, which requires movement that is too overtly sexual for a Cinderella character-icon, especially in a film that is certified as a PG in the UK. Befitting of the certification and the Cinderella character, Lauryn's hip-hop dance is relatively tame. The use of the hip-hop track and music video aesthetics aim to give the routine a hint of sexuality, but not too much, and consequently create an 'appropriate' balance between innocence and experience. As I explained in the previous chapter, music and dance embody an affective tone and hip hop is imbued with musical and dance obscenity, not only (or necessarily) in lyrical content but also in the raced and gendered aesthetics of music and movement. Lauryn's sexuality is expressed, not explicitly as we may expect in the film's burlesque context, but implicitly through the use of music.

13 Going on 30

Fundamentally music video aesthetics can be applied to any sort of action to create spectacular impact. Music video aesthetics can make even the most 'ordinary' activities feel like music and dance without including dancing bodies at all. Music video sequences that do not involve dance routines can still create kinaesthetic pleasures. In the context of girl teen films these techniques are often used to create a spectacle around 'unremarkable' practices of femininity.

13 Going on 30 provides an illustrative example of a music video sequence that utilizes music video aesthetics to make a spectacle of the 'everyday'. The film follows Jenna (Jennifer Garner), who makes a wish on her thirteenth birthday and wakes to find herself trapped in her thirty-year-old body, seventeen years in the future. Consequently the film highlights the Hollywood version of girlhood in extreme. Like other body-swap film scenarios, stereotypes are played out to their zenith because it is the supposed contradictions between the mind and body (old mind in young body, man in woman's body and so forth) from which comedy is derived. Performed by an adult woman therefore, the Hollywood idea of what a thirteen-year-old girl is supposed to be is made stark. *13 Going on 30* is not exactly a girl teen film, the protagonist's narrative quest is fixed more heavily to the success of heterosexual romance, rather than the moments of triumphant recognition that organize girl teen film. The film is more accurately described as a romantic comedy that utilizes all girl teen film conventions. Nonetheless, the film provides a useful illustration of girl teen film's moments of 'fun' because it derives its comedy from the discrepancies between the ostensible sophistication of the adult Jenna and the innocence of her thirteen-year-old self, and the kinds of things the thirteen-year-old takes pleasure in. Because the film shows the adult Jenna having fun doing things that are at odds with her adulthood, those events and actions classed as 'girl fun' are very clearly articulated. Two moments of 'girl fun' in *13 Going On 30* are the makeover and catwalk, both of which are structured around music video aesthetics.

The sequence begins when Jenna – thirteen in the body of a thirty-year-old – gets ready for a party. This music video sequence is constructed to render the affects of music and dance, but it does not show dancing bodies. The loud dynamics of Whitney Houston's 'I Wanna Dance With Somebody' (1987) signal that the spectacle has begun. The pro-filmic aspects of the spectacle in this sequence include the domestic space of the flat, the body of the protagonist and 'everyday' commodity fetishes: clothes, accessories and make-up. The use of music video aesthetics in this example lends impact to otherwise relatively 'ordinary' activities and objects. The scene is a makeover and catwalk moment that, without music video aesthetics, would simply show a character getting dressed and putting make-up on – lacking any of the necessary enchantment essential to Cinderella moments. In this example music video aesthetics are the magic conjured by the commercial sphere – taking the place of the fairy godmother's magic. With the use of music video aesthetics the commercial products that adorn the Cinderella character-icon and her moment of visibility become enchanted and her makeover leaves a physical impression on the body of the audio-viewer.

One way that it does this is by generating a sense of constant forward and upward movement. The movement of the music itself is uplifting, but because the music does not work alone the movement that the music is 'doing' is intensified by its relationship with the image on screen. Despite the lack of dancing bodies in this sequence, the combination of image and music invites the audio-viewer to enjoy the kind of kinaesthetic contagion that is experienced in response to the rhythm, energy and movement of the scene as a whole. Kinaesthetic contagion is in reaction to the pulse of the entire sequence, rather than just the character's individual movements.

The scene begins by inviting the audio-viewer to adopt a familiar embodied watching position: a responsiveness to music and images that is similar to that offered by conventional music video. The music begins in combination with a graphic match between the front door of Jenna's apartment and the frame of the open bathroom door. The character emerges from billowing steam, reminiscent of the dry ice often used in music videos, making reference to a music video cliché. In combination the music introduction has a staggered entry of instruments – a build-up that gradually thickens the texture of the song. This visual and musical build-up acts as a transition point from classical continuity into the supra-diegetic space of the music video sequence, that aims to lead the audio-viewer into a mode of engagement that attends to the composite sensations of music and dance.

The sequence places a real emphasis on rhythm, with the aim of impacting upon the body of the audio-viewer. The synthesized handclap that opens 'I Wanna Dance With Somebody' is layered with the cross-rhythm of a synth drum and piano that uses a repetitive, syncopated rhythm based on one note. This lack of melody at the beginning of the sequence places full weight on beat and rhythm. Composer Howard Goodall (2006) explains that rhythm is the element of music that reacts most immediately with our bodies – it is the component of music that most directly impels us to move. In this sequence beats explicitly hit on the cut or in reference to movement in shot and the audio-viewer is invited to enjoy the kinaesthetic contagion of the musical and visual beat that the aesthetics create.

A little further into the sequence synth horns join in with an emphatic glissando (a slide up in pitch), which is echoed in Houston's vocals, ('Woo!'). The accompanying image works as an onomatopoeic imitation of the exhilaration and upward movement of the song. The aural and visual movement on screen

Figure 6.3 *13 Going on 30* (2004), onomatopoeic visuals.

implies movement beyond what we see – in combination music and image suggest an exhilarated 'jump'. All of the synthesized instruments and visuals have a high and bright colour tone – even the bass is bright. The elements work together to generate an upbeat, creating energy infused, ascendant movement. The flow of musical and visual movement invites the audio-viewer to experience the immediate pleasures of this energized, upward motion.

Finally, the construction of the sequence mirrors the configurations of tension and release fundamental to music and dance by emphasizing call and response and creating an ascending/descending/ascending pattern. Houston's vocals and synthesizer use call and response throughout the verse, and the visuals correspond to the motion of the synthesizer to answer the vocals. This call and response maintains a sense of momentum, echoing the back and forth of dance.

Visually and aurally the sequence also uses an ascending/descending/ascending pattern. As the song moves into its first verse and the visuals shift to a new location the dynamics become quieter and the pitch lower. In combination the camera tracks smoothly and the protagonist's body movements become relatively more fluid. At the end of the sequence the chorus kicks in with a horn slide. In combination the front door of the apartment opens and the camera tracks back and jibs up the protagonist's body as she struts down the corridor towards the camera. The quieter dynamics in the verse and visuals previous to this moment provide the necessary contrast that highlights the spectacle of the chorus and strut down the corridor. The build-up between verse and chorus/

makeover and catwalk, invite the audio-viewer to experience the patterns of tension and release key to music and dance.

Jenna's makeover and catwalk moment is double coded. Her excessively colourful costume and make-up is used for comic effect and consequently there is a discrepancy between the traditional makeover and this version of one. Jenna makes herself over in ways that make fun with the idea of the sort of makeover a thirteen-year-old from the 1980s might perform. Nonetheless the affective impact of music video aesthetics maintains the enchantment of the catwalk moment.

Adding spectacle to spectacles

Where the magic of other Cinderella moments is rendered by clothes, accessories, make-up and hair; the aesthetics of visibility or glamorous spaces and places; performances of sports, singing or dancing; music video aesthetics can make a spectacle and lend impact to any and all of these things. The basic shapes of girl teen films are given affective force through appeals to aesthetic pleasure. Music video aesthetics create encounters with impact and give further significance to these elements that contribute to the intimate public of girlhood, creating girl versions of fun.

The makeover and catwalk moment in *Wild Child*, for example, makes appeals to its audience using all of the tactility, glamour and techniques of address common to girl teen films. The group of friends move in time together to the music (not exactly a dance): they strut and sway to the music like a pop group ready to perform, standing in formation at the top of a flight of stairs (Figure 6.4). The staged staircase makes use of shimmering and layered surfaces and the play of light and shadow of glamorous spaces. The girls have undergone a self-devised glitzy makeover and the varied and abundant textures and colours add to the pleasurable tactility of the space that surrounds them. Similarly the quasi-magical material of hair (Warner, 1995: 372) is copiously present in different styles, colours and textures. As they strut down the stairs the scene uses a number of body tilts and the girls perform the effortless look back. Like the catwalk in *13 Going on 30* this moment is not actually witnessed by any diegetic characters, but the techniques of visibility render the experience as pleasurable all the same.

The scene cuts in with a dance song, 'Let me think about it,' by Ida Corr Vs Fedde Le Grand (2007). The sequence is cut to the beat of the track and movements in shot maintain and accentuate its fast tempo, syncopated rhythm

Figure 6.4 *Wild Child* (2008), pop-star line up.

and staccato beats. Music and image work together to emphasize a series of close-ups of commodity fetishes associated with femininity: lipstick, mascara, hair gel and hair spray. These close-ups work in combination with the music by cutting in with the divisible offbeat – in the spaces of the song in which the beat does not fall where it should – consequently these images lend spectacle to the song and the music lends the images impact.

In *Another Cinderella Story* (Santostefano, 2008) music and image work together to make cleaning fun. The Cinderella character, Mary (Selena Gomez), is told to clean the house by her Wicked Stepmother. The film is a musical and consequently musical address introduces this as a 'cleaning number'. The opening bars of a non-diegetic pop song begin the shift into the musical's supra-diegetic space and the characters' movements become increasingly rhythmical. The space is eventually infected by the rhythms and freedoms of musical address and everyday household items become part of the routine, lending the scene a sense of spontaneity. The scene also uses music video aesthetics, making a further spectacle of the cleaning in the number. The scene is cut around the beat of the music and movements are coordinated with rhythm and melody. Some shots do not abide by classical continuity but are cut to emphasize the rhythm of the song. Consequently the cleaning gains further excitement and impact.

In *Blue Crush* music video aesthetics make a spectacle of the ideal sports body. Rendering the feelings of music and dance, the impact of music video aesthetics is physical. Its pleasures are kinaesthetic but in the context of girl teen film these aesthetics do not make appeals to the 'real' fleshiness of our muscle and sinew in the way that kinaesthetic contagion with the perceived body does (explored in Chapter 4). The kinaesthetic contagion that music video aesthetics invite remains at the level of the ideal body. In *Blue Crush*, for example, music video aesthetics render the ideal surfing body. The 'Cruel Summer' sequence begins with a crash of waves in synchrony with the opening chords of the song: these techniques act as a curtain raise that leads the audio-viewer into the supra-diegetic space of the number. The scene is held together by the intermedia relationship of music and image. Structured by musical logic the scene is consistent, not through classical continuity, but through the music that weaves each shot together and makes post-continuity techniques such as speed ramping (a technique that shifts frame speed within a single shot) and sharp telescopic zooms, feel appropriate. These post-continuity techniques, combined with the beats and melody of the music, create an invitation to enjoy the high energy of the ideal, fun surf. The sequence makes appeals to the pleasures of sports flow as well as the movement of the dance on the waves that the characters perform, and the kinaesthetic contagion of the uplift and back and forth of the movement of music and image together. The scene lacks the weight of the perceived sports body but music video aesthetics give the sequence the impact of music and dance instead.

In *Mean Girls*, when Cady holds a house party, music video aesthetics lend spectacle to a scene that would otherwise seem 'domestic'. The song 'Fire' by Joe Budden and Busta Rhymes structures the sequence. The front door of Cady's house opens on the hook of the song and a Steadicam shot tracks in, through the party with the use of speed ramping. Edits hit on the beat and, as Cady walks through the party her movements work with the rhythm of the song while dancing bodies litter the frame. Mirroring the circularity of popular music, Cady and the camera come back to the front door and it opens again on the hook of the song. Without this intermedia relationship between music and visuals the scene would lack the necessary impact required to create the affective energy and attitude of the party.

It is worth noting that this music video sequence uses a Joe Budden/Busta Rhymes hip-hop track. The use of hip hop lends the scene a sense of danger, transgression and sexuality that it would otherwise lack. Through music, black, masculine aesthetics are brought into the domestic, feminized, white, middle-class space of the suburbs. Part of the scene's pleasure is derived from the transgressive affective states that are contained within the safe space of the white suburban home. It is worth noting here that all the music video sequences explored in this chapter, except the cleaning number in *Another Cinderella Story*, use hip-hop-influenced music. The use of hip hop is yet another way that girl teen films embody feelings of excitement, contained within a set of predetermined possibilities.

Conclusion

Girl teen films use post-continuity techniques that are usually associated with blockbusters and action cinema as a means of creating impact. These music video aesthetics invite the audio-viewer to experience the specific kinaesthetic pleasures of music and dance. Without necessarily presenting human bodies dancing these sequences themselves dance: rendering the sensations and pleasures of movement, tension and release fundamental to music and dance. Music video aesthetics are an intense example of the magic conjured by the commercial sphere, through which the dress, the strut, the move, the dance, the look, the lipstick and so forth, become meaningful, significant and compelling beyond their basic shapes. 'Girl fun' is limited, not only around the specific moments and 'stuff' that creates the intimate public of girlhood but also around the kinds of pleasures and affects that it aims to generate. The kinds of pleasure that girl teen films offer are grounded in modulations that constantly play out feelings of innocence and experience, expansion and confinement. Music video aesthetics are another aesthetic dimension that explains how these modulations potentially feel good.

7

Conclusions and Future Research

The House Bunny provides us with a very clear example of a film that represents post-feminist culture and neo-liberal ideals. When Natalie is made over, she goes from second-wave feminist to post-feminist via the magic of commercial culture. The film draws on feminism to disregard it and, as Joel Gwynne (2013) suggests, creates complex patterns whereby feminist and anti-feminist ideas sit side by side. Millennial girl teen film is distinct in its reflection of post-feminist and neo-liberal characteristics and values, embodied in the images of Natalie's before and after (Figures 7.1 and 7.2). These ideologies do not explain the pleasures that the film generates, though they do account for why this version of girlhood is designed as pleasurable.

This book has explored the aesthetic pleasures of girl teen film in order to understand what kinds of pleasures, experiences and versions of fun these films make available. The book demonstrates that the kinds of events and encounters created as 'appropriately' fun for girls are generally part of a normative model that stresses femininity as a bodily characteristic and visibility as the girl figures' only access to power and pleasure. The pleasures the films are designed to create, I suggest, lend affective force to scenarios, activities and actions that are restricted by gender norms. The films and their 'moments' are also generally organized by implicit exclusions and stereotypes connected to race, class, sexuality and (dis)ability. What we see here is that ideological implications are fundamental to understanding film but ideologies alone do not account for pleasure. By focusing on what pleasure is and how it is created, I have set out to understand what these films do, not in spite of or because of ideology but as well as. I have argued that ideologies do not explain pleasures but pleasures can explain why we are potentially drawn towards certain objects and the kinds of experiences these objects present.

Moments of 'girl fun' are made up of surfaces that appeal to tactile and kinaesthetic pleasures. These surfaces are: accessories, clothes, hair and skin; glamorous spaces and places; techniques of visibility; the phenomenal body;

Figures 7.1 and 7.2 *The House Bunny* (2008), second-wave feminist to post-feminist makeover.

music; and intermedia aesthetics. These surfaces work together in various combinations but they were explored separately in the book as a means to draw out their specific pleasures.

These surfaces also create pleasurable embodiments of feeling. The Cinderella character-icon is a version of girlhood constructed primarily by the contradictory qualities of innocence and experience, expansion and confinement. The character and the surfaces that make her embody these qualities, creating in their combination feelings of promise and possibility. In its design the traditional Cinderella costume, for example, holds these antinomies in a seemingly perfect balance to create this sense of promise. Celebrity glamour embodies feelings of potential because it gives enough for us to project our desires into but holds back enough to never dissolution. Similarly, the ways that the body is created as surface in these films, in sports, singing and dancing, creates feelings of freedom: of moving through the world unhindered, of expansion, stretching the body out and filling up space. In their moments of 'fun', girl teen films embody feelings of movement and change.

These feelings suggest more than they offer. The girl figure in these films is presented as though she expresses boundless transformation. As cited in Chapter 1, fairy tale is defined by metamorphosis but despite their fairy-tale influences, girl teen films are defined by modulation. Where metamorphosis gives the impression that anything could happen, that the possibilities of girlhood are limitless, modulation in comparison, presents forms of free-floating control (Deleuze, 1992: 4). Modulation is an incessantly shifting grid that creates states of steady metastability: 'like a self-deforming cast that will continuously change from one moment to the other, or like a sieve whose mesh will transmute from point to point' (ibid.). Girl teen films create forms of modulation: allowing for feelings of variety, difference, movement and change, while maintaining an underlying fixity; they frustrate the notion of transformation they are structured by.

As I have made clear throughout I do not suppose that the pleasures presented by girl teen films are necessarily taken up. Like fairy tales, these films require enchantment: complicity from the audience that goes along with the illusion put forward. Girl teen films invite us to take up the attitude of enchantment: a comportment that we are invited to adopt. The films ask us to go along with the promise of commercial magic. They aim to elicit an attitude that accepts that these things offer a new and better life in the worlds of girl teen film: that the right clothes or hair, for example, can create change. That being looked at means something, that it is important, or the illusion that shadow obscures the less salubrious elements of a space or place. In the sports performance the body as surface invites us to indulge the compositions of perfection that these moments create: to go along, momentarily, with the illusion of the ideal body. The musical number and music video sequences thrive on and invite us to go along with, the miracle of freedom that music and musical address seems to create. As I have suggested throughout, where these sentiments may seem too mawkish or 'already said', double coding makes enchantment easier. The audio-viewer of girl teen films does not have to necessarily subscribe to the worldview that these films produce but they do have to adopt an attitude of enchantment to enjoy the pleasures that they offer. For enchantment to work the audio-viewer does not have to *believe* these promises, nor do they have to want to wear Cinderella's gown or look like her (though they could), but they do need to go along, temporarily, with the promise that commercial magic presents.

Future research

Having re-positioned the Cinderella story and character-icon as essentially about pleasure, this book has presented a practical model for exploring pleasure in film. Focusing on tactility and kinaesthetics, 'Cinderella's Pleasures' offer a way to take account of the physical pleasures that costume on screen invites the audio-viewer to enjoy. This approach provides an example that could be employed in future research in relation to film surfaces. The aesthetic pleasures of hair, for example, offer an intriguing topic. Like clothes, hair has distinct social significance but our reactions to it are foremost visceral (see Postrel, 2003: 98; Warner, 1995: 372). Girl teen films often present hair in ways that make the most of its variations. In *Mean Girls* it is no coincidence that the Plastics have different hair colours: it does not just signify their differences it also makes of them, together, a scene of textural, colourful abundance. As Roach (2007: 117) suggests, hair has magical power greater than clothes or accessories, because it is both. Hair is an uncanny material that grows but can be cut, it survives decay, and it is a surface but also an intimate part of a person (see Roach 2007; Thrift, 2008; Warner, 1995). Hair also embodies contradictory qualities: it is animalistic but grooming it is social, it is fragile but also strong (Warner, 1995: 373). Hair can also have other glamorous qualities: when the Cinderella character-icon presents a seeming effortless aptitude to control her hair (for example, as it seems to respond gracefully to its own, isolated wind machine as she struts down corridors), her hair adds to her glamour. It should be no surprise then that when Regina in *Mean Girls* by increments loses her power, her hair is gradually pulled back into tighter hairstyles. Regina's hair signifies her power, sexuality and eventual containment but it also creates a physical impression of the character's glamour and her diminution. As we can see the aesthetic pleasures of hair have a lot to offer in regard to future research, not to mention the permutations of hair colour, the power of blonde hair, and the relationships between hair, race, class and sexuality in the girl teen film context. Likewise an exploration of the presentation of skin as a glamorous surface could yield an interesting study.

'Celebrity Glamour' deconstructs the component parts of celebrity in the worlds of girl teen film, defines the characteristics and pleasures of glamour itself and uses these to explore the typologies of glamorous space and place, and the slow-motion scene of visibility. In doing so this chapter provides a way of understanding how glamour is constructed and the kinds of pleasure it is used to produce. A potentially interesting comparison would be to examine if and how celebrity glamour is created in the worlds of boy teen film? How and why are the typologies of glamorous space and place different? What is the boy equivalent of the slow-motion scene of visibility? The framework also presents a way of examining the component parts of celebrity in other forms of popular culture aimed at girls. Combining elements of celebrity studies and film studies instigates questions that straddle the two disciplines. Do other media aimed at girls rely on structures of celebrity in the same way?

In 'Sporting Pleasures', I provide an overview of the strategies employed in the films to present the active, sporting girl body and the range of kinaesthetic pleasures that these strategies invite the audio-viewer to enjoy. It also offers an examination of how girl teen films create experiences of muscular bonding between girls. As I suggested, this muscular bonding is not at odds with the animosities apparent between female characters: it exists in addition, as something else to enjoy. Regarding girl teen films from these perspectives puts forward possible avenues of research that ask whether similar strategies are employed to present the active boy body in boy teen films? What are the implications of the ways that the boy body is utilized as a surface? Is muscular bonding employed as an experience in boy teen films? Where else (if at all) do we get an experience of muscular bonding in girls or women's culture? What do these experiences contribute to these other media?

Girl teen films involve lots of physical comedy. Reason and Reynolds' (2010) kinaesthetic pleasures, explored here in relation to the surfaces of the films, provide a framework for exploring and understanding the pleasures of other forms of activity in film. One particularly relevant area of further exploration would be the kinaesthetic pleasures of comedy and its development by different actors and filmic bodies. How is physical comedy designed to work on the body of the audio-viewer and what impact does this have on the kinds of pleasure on offer? In *The House Bunny*, for example, Anna Farris' performance of Shelley engages with what Lori Landay (2002) calls a 'ludic kinaesthetic': a playful embodiment of femininities, expressed and experienced in the body of the audio-viewer. In a scene in which Shelley goes on her first date outside of the Playboy mansion, she attempts to impress her love interest by mimicking Marilyn Monroe in *The Seven Year Itch* (Wilder, 1955). Tottering on high heels, Shelley steps on top of a manhole and steam pushes her dress up, but it also burns her legs and consequently she hollers, swears and grimaces.

Figures 7.3 and 7.4 *The House Bunny* (2008), kinaesthetic comedy.

The disparity between her intention and its failure creates humour, but her movements also invite us to experience the comedy physically. We can potentially enjoy a visceral awareness of the physical play that Shelley/Anna enacts. Her bodily comportment, facial expressions and gestures are over exaggerated. The switch between her excessive physical performance of femininity and her sudden awkward movements and unwieldy body, offers an embodied experience of the physical comedy on display. Girl teen films provide a potential site for exploring the pleasures of physical comedy and physical comedy presents another place from which to approach girl teen film.

Examining how music and dance are used in the films studied, the chapter on 'Musical Address' detailed the sanitized aesthetic mode of millennial girl teen films that, in part, explains their cheerfully affective attitude. I suggested that any sense of sexuality that the films create is often achieved through musical and dance obscenity, while the films still retain a highly polished finish. The chapter also pointed to the ways that music works on the body of the audio-viewer and acts as a prosthetic that, through kinaesthetic empathy, allows us to enjoy physical expansion beyond everyday limits. The research in this chapter points towards a number of questions that could be developed from here: is music and dance obscenity always related to race, and how else is it employed in girls' culture? Is musical obscenity exploited in boy teen films and what does this tell us about gender and race dynamics in teen film? How is music used in boy teen films to work on the body of the audio-viewer? Is it utilized to offer different kinds of pleasure? How do boy teen films use musical numbers, and to what narrative and pleasurable purposes? The framework provided in the musical address chapter could be employed to explore boy teen films from this standpoint.

'Music Video Aesthetics' offers a practical account of the intermedia relationship between music and image employed in the films studied. The chapter provides a breakdown of spectacle that illustrates the generic and gender-specific construction of spectacle and utilization of post-continuity techniques. This chapter established the different ways that post-continuity stylistics are brought into play: comparing the gaming aesthetic of a boy teen film fight sequence to that of the dance aesthetic in girl teen films. These findings again raise some questions. In what other ways are post-continuity techniques used in boy teen films? What else do they aim to make a spectacle of? To what else do they lend affective force? Are music video aesthetics used in other 'feminine' forms of popular culture and to what purpose? This chapter also establishes the idea of the intimate public of girlhood and raises a number of questions from this perspective: how do other modes of girl teen film contribute to the intimate public of girlhood? What do the modes share in common and in what ways do they diverge in their expressions of what is ostensibly common to girls? The romantic mode shares with its fun cousin the pleasures of visibility. In the first *Twilight* (Hardwicke, 2008) film, for example, the denouement centres on a dress, a prom and a dance. It is the romance however, with which affective force is placed. What other crossovers are there, and how does mode impact upon the inflections of pleasure and affect?

This book has identified a number of commonalities across girl teen films in the ways that cinematography is employed. Exploring music video aesthetics, for example, identified specific post-continuity techniques designed to generate impact. A further potential avenue for future research could develop this focus on cinematography. It is interesting to note that a number of cinematographers that work on the films explored here are predominantly employed to shoot other forms of exploitation film. Generic positioning and an industrial blueprint for how exploitation films of this kind are shot influence the look and feel of girl teen films. Exploitation films are made on a substandard budget, exploit fads, and are made with clear promotional tie-ins in mind. Daryn Okada, for example, who is director of photography for both *Mean Girls* and *Stick It* is also DoP for the horror-comedy *Lake Placid* (Miner, 1999) as well as stoner comedy *Harold and Kumar Escape from Guantanamo Bay* (Hurwitz and Schlossberg, 2008), among other exploitation films. What are the connections in the cinematography of these related exploitation films and girl teen film, what they aim to 'do', and the kinds of pleasures they invite?

As the book is structured by moments of 'fun' and their surfaces, it offers a potential model for other studies of pleasure and fun in 'feminine' film genres in the fun mode. In what ways does a makeover film such as *The Devil Wears Prada* (Frankel, 2006), for example, offer similar experiences? Is the Cinderella character-icon any different to her teen film counterpart, or do these older characters embody the same kinds of antinomies, simply situated within an adult landscape? What is representative of 'woman fun' in this kind of mainstream, Hollywood context and do these films utilize similar strategies to generate pleasure? Essentially, what kinds of pleasure do they invite us to enjoy? Likewise it would be interesting to consider whether a film such as *The Devil Wears Prada* relies on the same mode of enchantment and creates the same forms of modulation as girl teen films? Some films sit on the borderlands of teen film, asking of these films the same questions would tell us more about how Hollywood constructs fun and creates pleasure.

For a number of years Amy Heckerling has been working on turning *Clueless* into a stage 'jukebox' musical set in the original *Clueless* time period of the mid-1990s (Jones, 2009; Vineyard, 2012). As a 1990s predecessor to the films studied here it is significant that *Clueless* is recognizable as a film that 'feels' like a musical. Opening on Broadway in 2007 'Legally Blonde: the musical' is still on tour. 'Bring it on: the musical' (2011–) has also enjoyed a Broadway run, and *Mean Girls* creator Tina Fey is currently writing a stage musical version of the film (Vineyard, 2013). The mode of enchantment described in this book and the utilization of musical address techniques explains why girl teen films often 'feel' like a musical, even when they do not generically fit into the musical category. The number of girl teen films that have been adapted for the musical stage opens up another set of relevant questions: in what ways do the stage versions emulate or prolong the pleasures that the films offer? What is the relationship between the film pleasures and those of stage performance? What other connections are there between girl teen films and musicals? Do they engage with a similar audience?

These stage musicals also point towards other ways in which audiences engage with girl teen films as part of extra-textual practices. Girl teen films in the fun mode do not seem to lend themselves especially to extensive fan practices in the same ways that films such as *Twilight* do. However, films like *Bring It On* and *Mean Girls* have garnered a good deal of fan video tributes. Fans of *Mean Girls* have been especially prolific, creating, for example, online video tutorials that describe how to make a 'Burn Book' ('Make A Burn Book', 2013), how to copy Gretchen Weiners make-up ('Mean Girls – Gretchen Weiners Makeup + Hair [So Fetch!]', 2013), and mock-up trailers for 'Mean Girls 3' ('Mean Girls Trailer 2017', 2013). *Mean Girls, Bring It On, Legally Blonde,* (and *Clueless*) have also been presented in cinemas in recent years as part of 'quote a long' screenings. These events indicate language as another key pleasure of these films and demonstrate some of the ways that pleasures are prolonged and enjoyed collectively. What pleasures, evident in the films, do extra-textual practices aim to draw out or build on? What do they tell us about pleasures beyond film surfaces?

The sports film *Whip It* (Barrymore, 2009) complicates the boundaries I have set up around girl teen film in the fun mode and consequently raises some interesting questions. It is a girl teen film that works in the fun mode, and produced by Drew Barrymore's Flower Films and distributed by Fox, it is a Hollywood production. The film includes a Cinderella character-icon, moments of visibility and sports performance. All the same the film does not sit neatly with those explored throughout this book. Although it is a comic, 'feel good' film, it does not enact the same cheerfully affective attitude or tone. The film creates a post-punk stylistic and highlights a different kind of glamour; its surfaces are a little grimier and less polished. In practical terms the boundaries that I have set up were intended to act as markers that limit the study and highlight the kinds of pleasures Hollywood offers girls. *Whip It* points out that genres are fluid, but rather than argue around what those boundaries are I suggest that it would be more useful to ask whether the kinds of experience this film (and any like it) makes available are the same? Does a film like *Whip It* ask us to go along with the same kinds of enchantment? Does the film maintain the same version of girlhood in a different guise, or does it create transformations?

Looking at girl teen films from this perspective alludes to other questions and areas of possible research for which this book offers a potential starting point. Girl teen films in the 'indie' mode often invite us to enjoy different kinds of pleasure, but 'indie' is a relatively arbitrary label. Is it possible to ask of these films the same kinds of questions? If 'fun' is not the central concern of girl teen films in the 'indie' mode, what is? Do these films present a consistent version of girlhood? What kinds of experience do they offer? What kinds of pleasure? How do the surfaces that make up the 'indie' mode compare and to what do they lend affective force? I do not expect that there are any easy answers to these questions. Moving outside of Hollywood models means that direct parallels will not necessarily work in this context. Nonetheless, in raising questions about genre and gender-specific pleasures in ways that do not compound aesthetic and pleasure hierarchies the book offers a point of reference for exploring how girlhood is created elsewhere.

In 'Sporting Pleasures' I made passing reference to the questions around looking relations that girl teen films raise. In a 2012 thesis, Katherine Hughes explores the dynamics of looking relations between teens in film and the queer possibilities that teen friendships present. Hughes' work details the representational strategies that position teen friendships in a liminal and queer space. Focusing on dyadic teen friendships in film, Hughes demonstrates how the boundaries between homosociality and homosexuality are maintained and transgressed 'under the heteronormative surface' (2012: 237). This work, which provides a model for studies of friendships in film, could also be built on to explore the aesthetic dimensions of teen film friendships and relationships. What could the notion of muscular bonding, for example, add to Hughes' analysis of the ways that girl teen characters often mirror their friends/frenemies in attempts to gain admiration? How and what do tactile and kinaesthetic pleasures add to the queer possibilities that teen films present?

In a similar vein it would be interesting to come at girl teen films from an alternative character perspective. In 'Breaking the Disney Spell', Jack Zipes (1999: 349) criticizes Disney fairy-tale heroines, suggesting that 'despite their beauty and charm, these figures are pale and pathetic compared to the more active and demonic [female] characters'. These 'demonic' characters, he proposes, represent erotic and subversive forces that are more appealing to audiences (ibid.). The characters that Zipes describes that sit in opposition to the Disney 'princess', his witches and wicked stepsisters, are reincarnated in girl teen films as 'bitches' (Wood, 2003: 314). The 'bitch' can be an actual wicked stepsister character or the most popular girl in high school, but her powers always stem from her appearance: a masquerade of excessive femininity that, in narrative terms, positions the character as 'inauthentic', manufactured, hyper-feminine, villainous and power-hungry: a position that is ultimately punished (see Gwynne, 2013; Marston, 2012; Wood, 2003). Significantly millennial girl teen films have sometimes combined Cinderella and the 'bitch', or try to redeem the 'bitch' character. In *Mean Girls*, Cady gets to be both, although it is obviously to her Cinderella role that she has to return at the end. An interesting point of departure here would be to discover in what ways is the 'bitch' character potentially more aesthetically appealing than the Cinderella character-icon? In what ways is she interesting, not just for what she means but also in terms of what she creates? What kinds of aesthetic pleasure does this girl offer and what types of experience?

This book offers a practical model for a new methodological approach and a new attitude to girl teen films. This conclusion has raised a lot of questions because the book has pursued a line of enquiry that has tried to see pleasure in a new light. Understanding how girl teen films are designed with specific pleasures in mind introduces a way of looking at film that explains some of the reasons why we may be drawn towards certain objects, and how they are designed to 'tug' at us, but does not insist that what we like is tied to what we are like.

Filmography

10 Things I Hate About You (1999), Gil Junger, USA, Buena Vista
13 Going on 30 (2004), Gary Winick, USA, Sony Pictures
16 Wishes (2010), Peter DeLuise, USA, Disney Channel
A Cinderella Story (2004), Mark Rosman, USA, Warner Brothers
A Star is Born (1954), George Cukor, USA, Warner Brothers
A Walk To Remember (2002), Adam Shankman, USA, Warner Brothers
All Over Me (1997), Alex Sichel, USA, Fine Line
Angus, Thongs and Perfect Snogging (2008), Gurinda Chadha, UK, Paramount
Another Cinderella Story (2008), Damon Santostefano, USA, Warner Brothers
Aquamarine (2006), Elizabeth Allen, USA/AU, Twentieth-Century Fox
Beach Blanket Bingo (1965), William Asher, USA, American International Pictures
Beach Party (1963), William Asher, USA, American International Pictures
Bend it Like Beckham (2002), Gurinda Chandha, UK, Helkon SK
Bikini Beach (1964), William Asher, USA, American International Pictures
Black Swan (2010), Darren Aronofsky, USA, Twentieth-Century Fox
Blackboard Jungle (1955), Richard Brooks, USA, Warner Brothers
Blue Crush (2002), John Stockwell, USA, Universal
Bratz: the movie (2007), Sean McNamara, USA, Lionsgate/Momentum
The Breakfast Club (1985), John Hughes, USA, Universal Pictures
Bring it On (2000), Peyton Reed, USA, Universal
Bring it On Again (2004), Damon Santostefano, USA, Universal
Bring it On: all or nothing (2006), Steve Rash, USA Universal
Bring it On: fight to the finish (2009), Billie Woodruff, USA, Universal
Bring it On: in it to win it (2007), Steve Rash, USA, Universal
Bullet Boy (2004), Saul Dibb, UK, Verve Pictures
Burlesque (2010), Steve Antin, USA, Screen Gems/Sony Pictures
Cadet Kelly (2002), Larry Shaw, USA, Disney Channel
Camp Rock (2008), Matthew Diamond, USA, Disney Channel
Centre Stage (2000), Nicholas Hytner, USA, Columbia Pictures
Centre Stage: Turn It Up (2008), Steven Jacobson, USA, Sony Pictures Home Entertainment
Cinderella (1950), Clyde Geronimi, Wilfred Jackson, Hamilton Luske, USA, Walt Disney Pictures
The Clique (2008), Michael Lembeck, USA, Warner Brothers
Clueless (1995), Amy Heckerling, USA, Paramount

Confessions of a Teenage Drama Queen (2004), Sara Sugarman, USA, Walt Disney Pictures
Cruel Intentions (1999), Roger Kumble, USA, Columbia Pictures
Deuce Bigalow: Male Gigolo (1999), Mike Mitchell, USA, Buena Vista Pictures
Dirty Dancing (1987), Emile Ardolino, USA, Vestron Pictures
Drive Me Crazy (1999), John Shultz, USA, Twentieth-Century Fox
Drop Dead Gorgeous (1999), Michael Patrick Jann, USA, New Line Cinema
Easter Parade (1948), Charles Walters, USA, MGM
Easy A (2010), Will Gluck, USA, Sony Pictures
Ella Enchanted (2004), Tommy O'Haver, USA, Miramax
Fame (2009), Kevin Tanchareon, USA, MGM
Flashdance (1983), Adrian Lyne, USA, Paramount
Footloose (1984), Herbert Ross, USA, Paramount
Foxes (1980), Adrian Lyne, USA, United Artists
Foxfire (1996), Annette Haywood-Carter, USA, The Samuel Goldwyn Company
Freaky Friday (1979), Gary Nelson, USA, Walt Disney Pictures
Freaky Friday (2003), Mark Waters, USA, Walt Disney Pictures
Gidget (1959), Paul Wendkos, USA, Columbia Pictures
Gidget Gets Married (1972), E. W. Shwackhamer, USA, ABC
Gidget Goes Hawaiian (1961), Paul Wendkos, USA, Columbia Pictures
Gidget Goes to Rome (1963), Paul Wendkos, USA, Columbia Pictures
Gidget Grows Up (1969), James Sheldon, USA, ABC
Gidget's Summer Reunion (1985), Bruce Bilson, USA, Columbia Television
Ginger Snaps (2000), John Fawcett, CAN, Motion International
Girls Just Want to Have Fun (1985), Alan Metter, USA, New World Pictures
Girls Town (1996), Jim McKay, USA, October Films
Ghost in the Invisible Bikini (1966), Don Weis, USA, American International Pictures
Hairspray (1988), John Waters, USA, New Line Cinema
Hairspray (2007), Adam Shankman, USA, New Line Cinema
Hannah Montana: the movie (2009), Peter Chelsom, USA, Walt Disney Pictures
Harold and Kumar Escape from Guantanamo Bay (2008), Jon Hurwitz & Hayden Schlossberg), USA, New Line Cinema
Heathers (1988), Michael Lehmann, USA, New World Pictures
Her Best Move (2007), Norm Hunter, USA, Disney Channel
Herbie: Fully Loaded (2005), Angela Robinson, USA, Walt Disney Pictures
High School Musical (2006), Kenny Ortega, USA, Disney Channel
High School Musical 2 (2007), Kenny Ortega, USA, Disney Channel
High School Musical 3: senior year (2008), Kenny Ortega, USA, Walt Disney Pictures
The House Bunny (2008), Fred Wolf, USA, Columbia Pictures
How She Move (2007), Ian Iqbal Rashid, USA/CAN, Paramount Vantage
How to Stuff a Wild Bikini (1965), William Asher, USA, American International Pictures

Ice Castles (2010), Donald Wrye, USA, Sony Pictures
Ice Princess (2005), Tim Fywell, USA, Buena Vista
The Incredibly True Adventures of Two Girls in Love (1995), USA, Fine Line
Jawbreaker (1999), Darren Stein, USA, Columbia TriStar
John Tucker Must Die (2006), Betty Thomas, USA, Twentieth-Century Fox
Josie and the Pussycats (2001), Harry Elfont, USA, Universal Pictures
Kill Bill, Vol. 1 (2003), Quentin Tarantino, USA, Miramax
Kill Bill, Vol. 2 (2004), Quentin Tarantino, USA, Miramax
'Ladies Choice' (2008), http://www.youtube.com/watch?v=My6oI2tYro0, accessed 30 November 2016
Lake Placid (1999), Steve Miner, USA, Twentieth-Century Fox
Legally Blonde (2001), Robert Luketic, USA, MGM
Life-Size (2000), Mark Rosman, USA, ABC
Little Darlings (1980), Roland Maxwell, USA, Paramount
Little Nicky (2000), Steven Brill, USA, New Line Cinema
The Lizzie McGuire Movie (2003), Jim Fall, USA, Buena Vista
'Make A Burn Book' (2013), https://www.youtube.com/watch?v=1Xlx9op84CE, accessed 30 November 2016
Make It Happen (2008), Darren Grant, USA, The Mayhem Project
Material Girls (2006), Martha Coolidge, USA, MGM
Mean Girls (2004), Mark Waters, USA, Paramount
'Mean Girls – Gretchen Weiners Makeup + Hair (So Fetch!)' (2013), https://www.youtube.com/watch?v=CZ2w5kLawww, accessed 30 November 2016
'Mean Girls Jingle Bell Rock' (2010), http://www.youtube.com/watch?v=m8pyRFXxVTs, accessed 30 November 2016
'Mean Girls Trailer 2017' (2013), https://www.youtube.com/watch?v=-3FFxeD3o_k, accessed 30 November 2016
Meet Me in St. Louis (1944), Vincent Minnelli, USA, MGM
Muscle Beach Party (1964), William Asher, USA, American International Pictures
My Life As a Dog (1985), Lasse Hallstrom, SWE, Svensk Filmindistri
Never Back Down (2008), Jeff Wadlow, USA, Summit Entertainment
Never Been Kissed (1999), Roja Gosnell, USA, Fox
Not Another Teen Movie (2001), Joel Gallen, USA, Columbia Pictures
On the Town (1949), Stanley Donen & Gene Kelly, USA, MGM
Pajama Party (1964), Don Weis, USA, American International Pictures
The Piano (1993), Jane Campion, AUS, Miramax
Picture This (2008), Stephen Herek, USA, MGM
Pretty in Pink (1986), Howard Deutch, USA, Paramount
Pretty Persuasion (2005), Marcos Siega, USA, Samuel Goldwyn Films
The Prince and Me (2004), Martha Coolidge, USA, Paramount
The Princess Diaries (2001), Garry Marshall, USA, Walt Disney Pictures

Princess Diaries 2 (2004), Garry Marshall, USA, Walt Disney Pictures
Princess Protection Programme (2009), Allison Liddi, USA, Disney Channel
Raise Your Voice (2004), Sean McNamara, USA, New Line Cinema
Rebel Without A Cause (1955), Nicholas Ray, USA, Warner Brothers
Save the Last Dance (2001), Thomas Carter, USA, MTV Films/Paramount Pictures
Shakespeare's Romeo + Juliet (1996), Baz Luhmann, USA, Twentieth-Century Fox
She's All That (1999), Robert Iscove, USA, Miramax Films
She's the Man (2006), Andy Fickman, USA, Dreamworks
Singin' in the Rain (1952), Stanley Donen & Gene Kelly, USA, MGM
Sixteen Candles (1984), John Hughes, USA, Universal
Slap Her She's French (2002), Melanie Mayron, USA, ContentFilm
Sleepover (2004), Joe Nussbaum, USA, MGM
Some Kind of Wonderful (1987), Howard Deutch, USA, UIP
The Sound of Music (1965), Robert Wise, USA, Twentieth-Century Fox
Step Up 2: the streets (2008), Jon Chu, USA, Summit Entertainment
StreetDance (2010), Max Giwa, UK, BBC Films
Superbad (2007), Greg Mottola, Columbia Pictures
St Trinians (2007), Oliver Parker & Barnaby Thompson, UK, Entertainment Film Distributors
St Trinians 2: the legend of Fritton's gold (2009), Oliver Parker & Barnaby Thompson, UK, Entertainment Film Distributors
Starstruck (2010), Michael Grossman, USA, Walt Disney Pictures
Stick It (2006), Jessica Bendinger, USA, Spyglass Entertainment/Touchstone Pictures
Sugar and Spice (2001), Francine McDougall, USA, New Line Cinema
Sydney White (2007), Joe Nussbaum, USA, Morgan Creek/Universal
Thirteen (2003), Catherine Hardwicke, USA, Fox Searchlight
Times Square (1980), Allan Moyle, USA, Associated Films
Twilight (2008), Catherine Hardwicke, USA, Summit Entertainment
Water Lilies (2007), Celine Sciamma, FR, Haut et Court
What a Girl Wants (2003), Dennie Gordon, USA, Warner Brothers
Where the Boys Are (1960), Henry Levin, USA, MGM
Wild Child (2008), Nick Moore, UK, Universal Pictures
Wild Wild Winter (1966), Lennie Weinrib, USA, Universal Pictures

Television

American Idol (2002–), USA, Fox Network
Dancelife (2007–), USA, MTV Networks
Gidget (1965–6), USA, ABC

Gilmore Girls (2000–7), USA, WB Television Network
Hannah Montana (2006–11), USA, Disney Channel
Made (2002–), USA, MTV Networks
So You Think You Can Dance (2005–), USA, Fox Network
Supernatural (2005–), USA, Warner Brothers Television
Veronica Mars (2004–7), USA, UPN
X Factor (2004–), UK, ITV

Music

Cruel Summer (remix) (2002), Blestination/Bananarama, Warner
Fire (2003), Joe Budden, Def Jam
Good Morning Baltimore (2007), Nikki Blonsky, New Line
I Wanna Dance With Somebody (1987), Whitney Houston, Arista
Jingle Bell Rock (1957), Joe Beal and Jim Boothe, Decca Records
Ladies' Choice (2007), Zac Efron, New Line
Let Me Think About It (2007), Ida Corr Vs Fedde Le Grand, Lifted House, Ministry of sound, Flamingo Records
Madison Time (1959), Ray Bryant, Columbia Records
Nu Nu (Yeah Yeah) (2005), FannyPack, Tommy Boy Records
Pass That Dutch (2003), Missy Elliott, Goldmind, Atlantic
Shawty Get Loose (2008), Lil Mama, Jive Records

Bibliography

Aapola, S., Gonick, M. and Harris, A., 2005. *Young Femininity: Girlhood, Power, and Social Change*, Basingstoke: Palgrave Macmillan.

Abbott, S., 2009. Prom-Coms: Reliving the Dreams and Nightmares of High-School Romance. In S. Abbott and D. Jermyn, eds. *Falling in Love Again: Romantic Comedy in Contemporary Cinema*. London: I.B.Tauris, pp. 52–64.

Abbott, S. and Jermyn, D., 2009. *Falling in Love Again: Romantic Comedy in Contemporary Cinema*, London: I. B.Tauris & Co. Ltd.

Adkins, L., 2004. Introduction: Feminism, Bourdieu and After. In L. Adkins and B. Skeggs, eds. *Feminism After Bourdieu*. Oxford: Blackwell Publishing/The Sociological Review, pp. 3–18.

Adkins, L. and Skeggs, B., 2004. *Feminism after Bourdieu*, Oxford: Blackwell Publishing/The Sociological Review.

Adorno, T. W. and Horkheimer, M., 1997. *Dialectic of Enlightenment*, London: Verso.

Ahmed, S., 2004. *The Cultural Politics of Emotion*, New York: Routledge.

Ahmed, S., 2010. *The Promise of Happiness*, Durham, N.C.: Duke University Press.

Ahmed, S., J. Kilby, C. Lury, M. McNeill and B. Skeggs, 2000. *Transformations: Thinking Through Feminism*, London: Routledge.

Allen, K., 2011. Girls Imagining Careers in the Limelight: Social Class, Gender and Fantasies of 'success.' In S. Holmes and D. Negra, eds. *In the Limelight and Under the Microscope: Forms and Functions of Female Celebrity*. London: Continuum, pp. 149–73.

Allen, K. and Mendick, H., 2013. Young people's Uses of Celebrity: Class, Gender and 'Improper' Celebrity. *Discourse: Studies in the Cultural Politics of Education*, 34(1), pp.77–93.

Altman, R., 1981. *Genre, The Musical: A Reader*, London: Routledge & Kegan Paul.

Altman, R., 1989. *The American Film Musical*, London: British Film Institute.

Altman, R., 2002. The American Film Musical as Dual-Focus Narrative. In S. Cohan, ed. *Hollywood Musicals, the Film Reader*. London: Routledge, pp. 41–52.

Anderson, A., 1998. Kinesthesia in Martial Arts Films: Action in Motion. *Jump Cut*, 42(83), pp. 1–11.

Anderson, J. D., 1993. Sound and Image Together: Cross-Modal Confirmation. *Wide Angle*, 15(1), pp. 30–43.

Anderson, L., 2003. Case study 1: Sliding Doors and Topless Women Talk about Their Lives. In I. Inglis, ed. *Popular Music and Film*. London: Wallflower, pp. 102–16.

Anderson, L. M., 1997. *Mammies No More: The Changing Image of Black Women on Stage and Screen*, Lanham, MD: Rowman & Littlefield.

Andrew, D., 2010. *What Cinema Is!: Bazin's Quest and Its Charge*, Chichester, West Sussex: Wiley-Blackwell.

Ang, I., 1985. *Watching 'Dallas': Soap Opera and the Melodramatic Imagination*, London: Routledge.

Anon, The Art of Original Filmmaking: Make It Happen. *The Writing Studio*. Available at: http://www.writingstudio.co.za/page2366.html [Accessed 15 September 2013c].

Attwood, F., 2011. Through the Looking Glass?: Sexual Agency and Subjectification Online. In R. Gill and C. Scharff, eds. *New Femininities: Postfeminism, Neoliberalism, and Subjectivity*. Houndmills, Basingstoke, Hampshire: Palgrave Macmillan.

Barker, J. M., 2009. *The Tactile Eye: Touch and the Cinematic Experience*, Berkeley: University of California Press.

Barthes, R., 1990. *The Pleasure of the Text*, Oxford: Basil Blackwell.

Barthes, R., 1993. *Mythologies*, A. Lavers, ed., London: Vintage Classics.

Bauman, Z., 2005. *Liquid life*, Cambridge: Polity Press.

Beauvoir, S. de, 1953. *The Second Sex*, London: Vintage.

Beller, J., 2006a. Paying Attention. *Cabinet*, Winter(24). Available at: http://www.cabinetmagazine.org/issues/24/beller.php [Accessed 26 January 2012].

Beller, J., 2006b. *The Cinematic Mode of Production: Attention Economy and the Society of the Spectacle*, Hanover, NH: Dartmouth College Press.

Bennett, J., 2012. *Practical Aesthetics: Events, Affects and art After 9/11*, London: I. B. Tauris.

Benson, S., 2003. *Cycles of Influence: Fiction, Folktale, Theory*, Detroit: Wayne State University Press.

Benson-Allott, C., 2009. Camp Integration: The Use and Misuse of Nostalgia in John Waters' Hairspray. *Quarterly Review of Film and Video*, 26, pp. 143–54.

Berlant, L. G., 2008. *The Female Complaint: The Unfinished Business of Sentimentality in American Culture*, Durham, N.C.: Duke University Press.

Berry, S., 2000. *Screen Style: Fashion and Femininity in 1930s Hollywood*, Minneapolis, MN: University of Minnesota Press.

Betrock, A., 1986. *The I was a Teenage Juvenile Delinquent Rock 'n' Roll Horror Beach Party Movie Book: A Complete Guide to the Teen Exploitation Film, 1954-1969*, London: Plexus.

Bettelheim, B., 1976. *The Uses of Enchantment: The Meaning and Importance of Fairy Tales*, New York: Knopf: Random House.

Bordwell, D., 2006. *The Way Hollywood Tells It: Story and Style in Modern Movies*, Berkeley: University of California Press.

Bordwell, D., 2008. A Glance at Blows. Available at: http://www.davidbordwell.net/blog/?p=3208 [Accessed 16 June 2012].

Bordwell, D. and Thompson, K., 2004. *Film Art an Introduction* 7th ed., Boston: McGraw-Hill.

Bourdieu, P., 1989. *Distinction: A Social Critique of the Judgement of Taste*, London: Routledge.

Bowie, M., 2009. The Fate of Pleasure: An Update. *German Life and Letters*, 62(3), pp. 252–4.

Boyle, K. and Berridge, S., 2012. I Love You, Man. *Feminist Media Studies*, pp. 1–16.

Bozelka, K. J., 2010. The Musical Mode: Community Formation and Alternative Rock in Empire Records. In S. Cohan, ed. *The Sound of Musicals*. London: BFI, pp. 164–75.

Brewer, D., 2003. The Interpretation of Fairy Tales. In H. R. E. Davidson and A. Chaudhri, eds. *A Companion to the Fairy Tale*. Cambridge: D.S. Brewer, pp. 15–37.

Brinkema, E., 2014. *The Forms of the Affects*. Durham, NC: Duke University Press.

Brooker, P., 1992. *Modernism/Postmodernism*, London: Longman.

Bruno, G., 2011. Surface, Fabric, Weave: The Fashioned World of Wong Kai-Wai. In A. Munich, ed. *Fashion in Film*. Bloomington, Ind.: Indiana University Press, pp. 83–105.

Bruzzi, S., 1997. *Undressing Cinema: Clothing and Identity in the Movies*, London: Routledge.

Bruzzi, S. and Church Gibson, P., 2004. Fashion is the Fifth Character: Fashion, Costume and Character in Sex and the City. In K. Akass and J. McCabe, eds. *Reading Sex and the City*. London: I. B. Tauris.

Buckland, W., 1998. A Close Encounter with Raiders of the Lost Ark: Notes on Narrative Aspects of the New Hollywood Blockbuster. In S. Neale and M. Smith, eds. *Contemporary Hollywood Cinema*. London: Routledge, pp. 166–77.

Buckland, W., 2009a. *Film Theory and Contemporary Hollywood Movies*. New York: Routledge.

Buhler, J., Flinn, C. and Neumeyer, D., 2000. *Music and Cinema*, Hanover, NH: University Press of New England.

Buikema, R. and Smelik, A., 1995. *Women's Studies and Culture*, London: Zed.

Buikema, R. and Tuin, I. van der, 2009. *Doing Gender in Media, Art and Culture*, London: Routledge.

Bukatman, S., 2003. *Matters of Gravity: Special Effects and Supermen in the Twentieth Century*, Durham, N.C.: Duke University Press.

Butler, J., 1990. *Gender Trouble*, New York: Routledge.

Butler, J., 1993. *Bodies that Matter: On the Discursive Limits of 'sex'*, New York: Routledge.

Butler, J., 1998. Athletic Genders: Hyperbolic Instance and/or the Overcoming of Sexual Binarism. *Stanford Humanities Review*, 6 (2). Available at: https://web.stanford.edu/group/SHR/6-2/html/butler.html [Accessed 20 February 2013].

Caine, A. J., 2004. *Interpreting Rock Movies: The Pop Film and its Critics in Britain*, Manchester: Manchester University Press.

Callois, R., 1970. The Classification of Games. In E. Dunning, ed. *Sociology of Sport*. London: Frank Cass, pp. 17–39.

Carty, V., 2005. Textual Portrayals of Female Athletes: Liberation or Nuanced Forms of Patriarchy? *Frontiers - A Journal of Women's Studies*, 26(2), pp. 132–46.

Cashmore, E., 2000. *Sports Culture: An A-Z Guide*, London: Routledge.

Chamarette, J., 2012. *Phenomenology and the Future of Film: Rethinking Subjectivity Beyond French Cinema*, Basingstoke: Palgrave Macmillan.

Chion, M., 1994. *Audio-vision: Sound on Screen*, New York: Columbia University Press.

Chion, M., 2009. *Film, A Sound Art* English ed., New York: Columbia University Press.

Cohan, S., 2000. Case Study: Interpreting 'Singin' in the Rain. In C. Gledhill and L. Williams, eds. *Reinventing Film Studies*. London: Arnold, pp. 53–75.

Cohan, S., 2002. *Hollywood Musicals, The Film Reader*, London: Routledge.

Cohan, S., 2010. *The Sound of Musicals*, London: BFI.

Conlin, J., 2013. *The Pleasure Garden: From Vauxhall to Coney Island*, Philadelphia: University of Pennsylvania Press.

Connor, S., 1992. Aesthetics, Pleasure and Value. In S. Regan, ed. *The Politics of Pleasure: Aesthetics and Cultural Theory*. Buckingham: Open University Press.

Conrich, I., 2000. Merry Melodies: The Marx Bothers' Musical Moments. In B. Marshall and R. J. Stilwell, eds. *Musicals: Hollywood and Beyond*. Exeter: Intellect, pp. 47–54.

Conrich, I. and Tincknell, E. eds., 2006. *Film's Musical Moments*, Edinburgh: Edinburgh University Press.

Considine, D. M., 1985. *The Cinema of Adolescence*, Jefferson (NC): McFarland.

Couldry, N., 2001. The Hidden Injuries of Media Power. *Journal of Consumer Culture*, 1(2), pp. 155–77.

Couldry, N., 2004. Teaching Us to Fake It: The Ritualized Norms of Television's 'Reality' Games. In S. Murray and L. Ouellette, eds. *Reality TV: Remaking Television Culture*. New York: New York University Press, pp. 57–74.

Couldry, N., and McCarthy, A., 2004. *MediaSpace: Place, Scale and Culture in a Media Age*. London and New York: Routledge.

Cox, D., 2012. Speed Ramping. *Other Zine*. Available at: http://www.othercinema.com/otherzine/otherzine5/speedramp.html [Accessed 18 July 2012].

Cresswell, T., 2004. *Place: A Short Introduction*, Oxford: Blackwell Publishing.

Cronin, A. M., 2000. Consumerism and 'Compulsory Individuality': Women, Will and Potential. In S. Ahmed et al., eds. *Transformations: Thinking Through Feminism*. London: Routledge, pp. 273–87.

Cubitt, S., 2004. *The Cinema Effect*, Cambridge, Mass.: MIT Press.

Cummins, R. G., 2006. Sports Fiction: Critical and Empirical Perspectives. In A. A. Raney and J. Bryant, eds. *Handbook of Sports and Media*. New York: Routledge.

Cunningham, D., 2003. Warning: This Movie is Gross. *Senses of Cinema*, (October). Available at: http://sensesofcinema.com/2003/great-directors/waters/ [Accessed 14 March 2012].

Currid-Halkett, E. and Scott, A. J., 2013. The Geography of Celebrity and Glamour: Reflections on Economy, Culture, and Desire in the City. *City, Culture and Society*, 4(1), pp. 1–10.

Davidson, A. I. (Arnold I.), 2001. *The Emergence of Sexuality: Historical Epistemology and the Formation of Concepts*, Cambridge, Mass.: Harvard University Press.

Davidson, H. R. E. and Chaudhri, A., 2003. *A Companion to the Fairy Tale*, Cambridge: D.S. Brewer.

DeFrantz, T., 2004. *Dancing Revelations: Alvin Ailey's Embodiment of African American Culture*, New York: Oxford University Press.

Deleuze, G., 1992. Postscript on the Societies of Control. *October*, 59(Winter), pp. 3–7.

DeNora, T., 2000. *Music in Everyday Life*, Cambridge: Cambridge University Press.

Dickinson, K., 2001. Pop, Speed and the 'MTV Aesthetic' in Recent Teen Films. *Scope*, (June).

Dickinson, K., 2008. Music Video and Synaesthetic Possibility. In R. Beebe and J. Middleton, eds. *Medium Cool: Music Videos From Soundies to Cellphones*. Durham, N.C.: Duke University Press, pp. 13–29.

Doane, M. A., 1987. *The Desire to Desire: The Women's Film of the 1940s*. Basingstoke: Macmillan.

Doane, M. A., 1992. *Femmes Fatales: Feminism, Film Studies and Psychoanalysis*. London: Routledge.

Doherty, T. P., 2002. *Teenagers and Teenpics: The Juvenilization of American Movies in the 1950s* 2nd ed., Philadelphia: Temple University Press.

Dole, C. M., 2007. The Return of Pink: Legally Blonde, Third Wave Feminism, and Having It All. In S. Ferriss and M. Young, eds. *Chick Flicks: Contemporary Woman at the Movies*. New York: Routledge, pp. 58–78.

Donaldson, L., 2012. Effort and Empathy: Engaging with Film Performance. In D. Reynolds and P. Watson, eds. *Kinesthetic Empathy in Creative and Cultural Practices*. Bristol: Intellect, pp. 157–74.

Douglas, S., 1994. *Where the Girls Are: Growing up Female with the Mass Media*. New York: Times Books.

Driscoll, C., 2002. *Girls: Feminine Adolescence in Popular Culture and Cultural Theory*. New York: Columbia University Press.

Driscoll, C., 2011a. Modernism, Cinema, Adolescence: Another History for Teen Film. *Screening the Past*, (32). Available at: http://www.screeningthepast.com/2011/11/modernism-cinema-adolescence-another-history-for-teen-film/ [Accessed 21 January 2012].

Driscoll, C., 2011b. *Teen Film: A Critical Introduction*, Oxford: Berg.

Dyer, R., 1979. *Stars*, London: British Film Institute.

Dyer, R., 1993. The Colour of Virtue: Lillian Gish, Whiteness and Femininity. In P. Cook and P. Dodd, eds. *Women and Film: A Sight and Sound Reader*. Philadelphia: Temple University Press.

Dyer, R., 2002a. Action! In R. Dyer, ed. *Only Entertainment*. London: BFI, pp. 64–9.

Dyer, R., 2002b. Entertainment and Utopia. In *Only Entertainment*. London: Routledge, pp. 19–35.

Dyer, R., 2002c. *Only Entertainment* 2nd ed., London: Routledge.

Dyer, R., 2002d. The Sound of Music. In *Only Entertainment*. London: Routledge, pp. 46–59.

Dyer, R., 2004. *Heavenly Bodies: Film Stars and Society*, London: Routledge.

Dyer, R., 2007. *Pastiche*, New York: Routledge.

Dyer, R., 2012. *In the Space of a Song: The Uses of Song in Film*, London: Routledge.

Dyhouse, C., 2011. *Glamour: Women, History, Feminism*. London: Zed.

Eagleton, T., 1992. The Ideology of the Aesthetic. In S. Regan, ed. *The Politics of Pleasure: Aesthetics and Cultural Theory*. Buckingham: Open University Press, pp. 17–33.

Eco, U., 1992. Postmodernism, Irony, the Enjoyable. In P. Brooker, ed. *Modernism/Postmodernism*. London and New York: Peter Brooker, pp. 225–8.

Entwistle, J., 2000. *The Fashioned Body: Fashion, Dress, and Modern Social Theory*, Cambridge: Polity Press.

Erginel, M., 2011. Plato on the Psychology of Pleasure and Pain. *Phoenix*, 65(3/4), pp. 288–314.

Evans, C. and Gamman, L., 1995. The Gaze Revisited, or Reviewing Queer Viewing. In *A Queer Romance: Lesbians, Gay Men and Popular Culture*. London: Routledge, pp. 12–56.

Evers, C., 2009. 'The Point': Surfing, Geography and a Sensual Life of Men and Masculinity on the Gold Coast, Australia. *Social & Cultural Geography*, 10(8), pp. 893–908.

Faludi, S., 1991. *Backlash: The Undeclared War Against Women*. New York: Vintage.

Farrimond, K., 2013. The Slut That Wasn't: Virginity, (Post)Feminism and Representation in Easy A. In J. Gwynne and N. Muller, eds. *Postfeminism and Contemporary Hollywood Cinema [Kindle Edition]*. Basingstoke: Palgrave Macmillan, pp. 44–59.

Ferris, S., 2008. Fashioning Femininity in the Make Over Flick. In S. Ferris and M. Young, eds. *Chick Flicks: Contemporary Woman at the Movies*. New York and London: Routledge, pp. 41–57.

Ferriss, S. and Young, M., 2007. *Chick Flicks: Contemporary Women at the Movies*. New York and London: Routledge.

Feuer, J., 1977. The Self-Reflective Musical and the Myth of Entertainment. *Quarterly Review of Film Studies*, 2(3), pp. 313–26.

Feuer, J., 1993. *The Hollywood Musical* 2nd ed., Bloomington: Indiana University Press.

Fischer, L., 2000. Designing Women: Art Deco, The Musical and the Female Body. In J. Buhler, C. Flinn and D. Neumeyer, eds. *Music and Cinema*. Hanover, NH: Weslyan University Press, pp. 295–315.

Foster, S., 1997. Dancing Bodies. In J. Desmond, ed. *Meaning in Motion: New Cultural Studies of Dance*. Durham, N.C.: Duke University Press, pp. 235–57.

Fox, K., 2001. Space/Place. In P. Simpson and R. E. Pearson, eds. *Critical Dictionary of Film and Television Theory*. London: Routledge, p. 53.

Friedberg, A., 1994. *Window Shopping: Cinema and The Postmodern [Kindle Edition]*, Berkeley: University of California Press.

Frith, S., 1988. *Music for Pleasure: Essays in the Sociology of Pop*, Cambridge: Polity in association with Blackwell.

Frith, S., Goodwin, A. and Grossberg, L., 1993. *Sound and Vision: The Music Video Reader*, London: Routledge,.

Gaines, J., 1990. Costume and Narrative: How Dress tells the Woman's Story. In C. Herzog and J. Gaines, eds. *Fabrications*. London: Routledge, pp. 180–211.

Gaines, J., 2000. On Wearing the Film: Madam Satan (1930). In S. Bruzzi and P. Church Gibson, eds. *Fashion Cultures: Theories, Explorations and Analysis*. London: Routledge, pp. 159–77.

Galt, R., 2011. *Pretty: Film and the Decorative Image*. New York: Columbia University Press.

Gill, R., 2007a. *Gender and the Media*, Cambridge: Polity.

Gill, R., 2011 [2007]. Postfeminist Media Culture: Elements of a Sensibility. In M. Kearney, ed. *The Gender and Media Reader*. New York: Routledge, pp. 136–48.

Gilligan, S., 2011. Performing Postfeminist Identities: Gender, Costume, and Transformation in Teen Cinema. In M. Waters, ed. *Women On Screen*. Basingstoke; New York: Palgrave Macmillan, pp. 166–81.

Gledhill, C. and Williams, L., 2000. *Reinventing Film Studies*, London: Arnold.

Godard, J. L., Narboni, J. and Milne, T. 1972. *Godard on Godard : Critical Writings*, New York: Viking Press.

Gonick, M., 2006. Between 'Girl Power' and 'Reviving Ophelia': Constituting the Neoliberal Girl Subject. *NWSA Journal*, 18(2), pp. 1–23.

Goodall, H., 2006. How Music Works - Rhythm. Available at: http://www.youtube.com/watch?v=ZZJPnAer7EM [Accessed 27 March 2013].

Goodwin, A., 1992. *Dancing in the Distraction Factory: Music Television and Popular Culture*, Minneapolis, MN: University of Minnesota Press.

Goodwin, A., 1993. Fatal Distractions: MTV Meets Postmodern Theory. In S. Frith, A. Goodwin and L. Grossberg, eds. *Sound and Vision: The Music Video Reader*. London: Routledge, pp. 45–66.

Gorbman, C., 1987. *Unheard Melodies: Narrative Film Music*, London: BFI.

Gorbman, C., 1993. Chion's Audio-Vision. *Wide Angle*, 15(1), pp. 66–77.

Grossberg, L., 1993. The Media Economy of Rock Culture: Cinema, Post-modernity and Authenticity. In S. Frith, A. Goodwin and L. Grossberg, eds. *Sound and Vision: The Music Video Reader*. London: Routledge, pp. 185–209.

Gunning, T., 1990. The Cinema of Attractions: Early Film, Its Spectator and the Avant-Garde. In T. Elsaesser and A. Barker, eds. *Early Cinema: Space, Frame, Narrative*. London: BFI Pub, pp. 56–62.

Gunning, T., 1996. Now You See It, Now You Don't: The Temporality of the Cinema of Attractions. In R. Abel, ed. *Silent Film*. London: Athlone, pp. 71–84.

Gunning, T., 2000. *The Films of Fritz Lang*, London: British Film Institute.

Gwynne, J., 2013. The Girls of Zeta: Sororities, Ideal Femininity and the Makeover Paradigm in The House Bunny. In J. Gwynne and N. Muller, eds. *Postfeminism and Contemporary Hollywood Cinema [Kindle Edition]*. Basingstoke: Palgrave Macmillan.

Haase, D., 2004a. *Fairy Tales and Feminism: New Approaches*, Detroit: Wayne State University Press.

Haase, D., 2004b. Feminist Fairy-Tale Scholarship. In D. Haase, ed. *Fairy Tales and Feminism: New Approaches*. Detroit : Wayne State University Press, pp. 1–36.

Harris, A., 2004. *All About The Girl: Culture, Power, and Identity*. New York: Routledge.

Henderson, S., 2006. Youth, Excess and the Musical Moment. In I. Conrich and E. Tincknell, eds. *Film's Musical Moments*. Edinburgh: Edinburgh University Press, pp. 146–57.

Hentges, S., 2006. *Pictures of Girlhood: Modern Female Adolescence on Film*, Jefferson, NC: McFarland.

Herzog, A., 2010. *Dreams of Difference, Songs of the Same: The Musical Moment in Film*, Minneapolis, MN: University of Minnesota Press.

Heywood, L. and Dworkin, S. L., 2003. *Built to Win: The Female Athlete as Cultural Icon*, Minneapolis, MN: University of Minnesota Press.

Higonnet, A., 1998. *Pictures of Innocence: The History and Crisis of Ideal Childhood*, New York: Thames and Hudson.

Hollinger, K., 1998. *In the Company of Women: Contemporary Female Friendship Films*, Minneapolis, MN: University of Minnesota Press.

Holmes, S. and Negra, D., 2011. *In the Limelight and Under the Microscope: Forms and Functions of Female Celebrity*, London: Continuum.

Holmes, S. and Redmond, S., 2006. *Framing Celebrity: New Directions in Celebrity Culture*, London: Routledge.

Hopkins, S., 2002. *Girl Heroes: The New Force in Popular Culture*, Annandale: Pluto Press.

Howe, L., 2003. Athletics, Embodiment, and the Appropriation of the Self. *The Journal of Speculative Philosophy*, 17(2), pp. 92–107.

Hughes, K., Queer Possibilities in Teen Friendships in Film, 2000–9. PhD Thesis: University of Glasgow.

Inglis, I., 2003. *Popular Music and Film*, London: Wallflower.

Jackson, S. A. and Csikszentmihalyi, M., 1999. *Flow in Sports*, Champaign, IL: Human Kinetics.

James, R., 2013. Visual v Musical Obscenity. *It's Her Factory*. Available at: http://its-her-factory.blogspot.co.uk/2013/04/visual-v-musical-obscenity.html [Accessed 6 May 2013].

Jameson, F., 1985. Postmodernism and Consumer Society. In H. Foster, ed. *Postmodern Culture*. London: Pluto Classics, pp. 111–23.

Jencks, C., 1986. *What is Post-Modernism?*, London: Academy Editions.

Jenkins, H., 1992b. *What Made Pistachio Nuts?: Early Comedy and the Vaudeville Aesthetic*, New York: Columbia University Press.

Jones, G., 2008. In Praise of an 'Invisible Genre'? An Ambivalent Look at the Fictional Sports Feature Film. *Sport in Society: Cultures, Commerce, Media, Politics*, 11(2–3), pp. 117–29.

Jones, K., 2009. Clueless, the Musical, Will Get NYC Reading; Landau Directs. *Playbill.com*. Available at: http://www.playbill.com/news/article/131523-Clueless-the-Musical-Will-Get-NYC-Reading-Landau-Directs [Accessed 4 June 2013].

Kant, I., 2008. *Critique of Judgement*, Oxford: Oxford University Press.

Katz, L., 2009. Pleasure. *Stanford Encyclopedia Of Philosophy*. Available at: http://plato.stanford.edu/archives/fall2009/entries/pleasure/ [Accessed 3 February 2012].

Kaveney, R., 2006. *Teen Dreams: Reading Teen Film and Television from 'Heathers' to 'Veronica Mars'*, London: I.B.Tauris.

Kearney, M. C., 2002. Girlfriends and Girl Power. In F. K. Gateward and M. Pomerance, eds. *Sugar, Spice and Everything Nice: Cinemas of Girlhood*. Michigan: Wayne State University Press, pp. 124–44.

Kearney, M. C., 2006. *Girls Make Media*, New York: Routledge.

Kearney, M. C., 2012. *The Gender and Media Reader*, New York: Routledge.

Kearney, M. C., 2015. Sparkle: Luminosity and Post-Girl Power Media. *Continuum: Journal of Media and Cultural Studies*, 29(2), pp. 263–373.

Kennedy, E. and Hills, L., 2009. *Sport, Media, and Society*, Oxford: Berg.

Kerr, A., Kucklich, J. and Brereton, P., 2006. New Media – New Pleasures? *International Journal of Cultural Studies*, 9(1), pp. 63–82.

King, G., 2000. *Spectacular Narratives: Hollywood in the Age of the Blockbuster*, London: I. B. Tauris.

King, G., 2005. *The Spectacle of the Real: From Hollywood to 'Reality' TV and Beyond*, Bristol: Intellect.

Kitchin, R. and Hubbard, P., 2010. *Key Thinkers on Space and Place [Kindle Edition]* 2nd ed., London: SAGE.

Kracauer, S., 1995. *The Mass Ornament: Weimar Essays*. Cambridge, MA: Harvard University Press.

Krutnik, F., 1998. Love Lies: Romantic Fabrication in Contemporary Romantic Comedy. In P. W. Evans and C. Deleyto, eds. *Terms of Endearment: Hollywood Romantic Comedy of the 1980s and 1990s*. Edinburgh: Edinburgh University Press, pp. 15–36.

Landay, L., 2002, The Flapper Film: Comedy, Dance, and Jazz Age Kinaesthetics. In J. Bean and D. Negra, eds. *A Feminist Reader in Silent Film*. Chapel Hill: Duke University Press, pp. 221–48.

Lang, N., 2013. 40 'Mean Girls' Quotes That Make Everyday Life Worth Living. *Thought Catalog*. Available at: http://thoughtcatalog.com/2013/40-mean-girls-quotes-that-make-everyday-life-worth-living/ [Accessed 12 January 2014].

Langer, S. K., 1953. *Feeling and Form: A Theory of Art Developed from 'Philosophy in a New Key'*, London: Routledge and K. Paul.

Langer, S. K., 1957. *Problems of Art*, New York: Scribner.

Lee, C., 2010. *Screening Generation X: The Politics and Popular Memory of Youth in Contemporary Cinema*, Farnham: Ashgate.

Lev, P., 2000. *American Films of the 70s: Conflicting Visions* 1st ed., Austin, TX: University of Texas Press.

Levy, A., 2006. *Female Chauvinist Pigs: Woman and the Rise of Raunch Culture*, London: Pocket Books.

Lewis, J., 1992. *The Road to Romance and Ruin: Teen Films and Youth Culture*, New York: Routledge.

Lewis, L. A., 1990. Consumer Girl Culture: How Music Video Appeals to Girls. In M. E. Brown, ed. *Television and Women's Culture*. London: SAGE Publications, pp. 89–101.

Liebermann, M., 1972. 'Some Day My Prince Will Come': Female Acculturation through the Fairy Tale. *College English*, 3(34), pp. 383–95.

Lindner, K., 2009. Fighting for Subjectivity: Articulations of Physicality in Girlfight. *Journal of International Women's Studies*, 10(3), pp. 4–17.

Lindner, K., 2011a. Bodies in Action. *Feminist Media Studies*, 11(3), pp. 321–45.

Lindner, K., 2011b. Spectacular (Dis-) Embodiments: The Female Dancer on Film. *Scope*, (20), June, pp. 1–18.

Littler, J., 2003. Making Fame Ordinary: Intimacy, Reflexivity, and 'Keeping it Real'. *Mediactive*, 2, pp. 8–25.

Livingstone, S., 1994. The Rise and Fall of Audience Research: An Old Story with a New Ending. In M. Levy and M. Gurevitch, eds. *Defining Media Studies: Reflections on the Future of the Field*. New York: Oxford University Press, pp. 247–54.

Lurie, A., 1970. Fairy Tale Liberation. *New York Review of Books*, pp. 42–4.

Lury, K., 2010. *The Child in Film: Tears, Fears and Fairy Tales*, London: I. B. Tauris.

Maguire, J. A., 2011. Welcome to the Pleasure Dome?: Emotions, Leisure and Society. *Sport in Society: Cutltures, Commerce, Media, Politics*, 14(7–8), pp. 913–26.

Malabou, C., 2009. Plasticity and Elasticity in Freud's 'Beyond the Pleasure Principle'. *Parallax*, 15(2), pp. 41–52.

Manning, E., 2007. *Politics of Touch: Sense, Movement, Sovereignty*, Minneapolis, MN: University of Minnesota Press.

Marks, L. U., 2000. *The Skin of the Film: Intercultural Cinema, Embodiment, and the Senses*, Durham, N.C.: Duke University Press.

Marshall, P. D., 1997. *Celebrity and Power: Fame in Contemporary Culture*, Minneapolis, MN: University of Minnesota Press.

Marshall, P. D., 2010. The Promotion and Presentation of the Self: Celebrity as Marker of Presentational Media. *Celebrity Studies*, 1(1), pp. 35–48.

Marshall, P. D. and Redmond, S., 2015. *A Companion to Celebrity*, Chichester, UK: John Wiley & Sons, Inc.

Marston, K., 2012. Cinderella vs. Barbie: The Battle for Postfeminist Performance in Teen Transformation Narratives. *Scope*, (24), October, pp. 1–18.

Martin, A., 1989. The Teen Movie: Why Bother? *Cinema Papers*, 75, pp. 10–15.

Martin, A., 1994. *Phantasms*, Ringwood, VIC: McPhee Gribble.

Martin, A., 2003. Musical Mutations: Before, Beyond and Against Hollywood. In J. Rosenbaum and A. Martin, eds. *Movie Mutations: The Changing Face of World Cinephilia*. London: BFI Publishing, pp. 67–104.

Massumi, B., 1987. Notes on the Translation and Acknowledgements. In G. Deleuze and F. Guattari, eds. *A Thousand Plateaus*. Minneapolis, MN: University of Minnesota Press, pp. xvi–xix.

Massumi, B., 2002. *Parables for the Virtual: Movement, Affect, Sensation*, Durham, NC: Duke University Press.

McClary, S., 2002. *Feminine Endings: Music, Gender, and Sexuality* 2nd ed., Minneapolis, MN: University of Minnesota Press.

McDonald, T. J., 2010. *Hollywood Catwalk: Exploring Costume and Transformation in American Film*, London: I. B. Tauris & Co Ltd.

McNeill, W. H., 1995. *Keeping Together in Time: Dance and Drill in Human History*, Cambridge, Mass.: Harvard University Press.

McRobbie, A., 1991. *Feminism and Youth Culture: From 'Jackie' to 'Just Seventeen'*, Basingstoke: Macmillan Education.

McRobbie, A., 2004. Post-feminism and Popular Culture. *Feminist Media Studies*, 4(3), pp. 255–64.

McRobbie, A., 2005. Notes on What Not to Wear and Post-feminist Symbolic Violence. In B. Skeggs and L. Adkins, eds. *Feminism After Bourdieu*. Oxford: Blackwell, pp. 99–109.

McRobbie, A., 2009. *The Aftermath of Feminism: Gender, Culture and Social Change*, Los Angeles: SAGE Publications.

Merleau-Ponty, M., 2002. *Phenomenology of Perception*, London: Routledge.

Metter, A., 1985. *Girls Just Want to Have Fun*, USA: New World Pictures.

Metz, C., 1986. The Imaginary Signifier (exerpts). In P. Rosen, ed. *Narrative, Apparatus, Ideology*. New York: Columbia University Press, pp. 244–78.

MGA, Bratz webpage. http://www.bratz.com/en-us/section/about/ [Accessed 14 February 2014].

Mitchell, C., and Rentschler, C., 2016. *Girlhood and the Politics of Place*, Oxford: Berghahn Books.

Modleski, T., 1982. *Loving with a Vengeance: Mass-Produced Fanstasies for Women*, New York: Methuen.

Modleski, T., 1991. *Feminism Without Women: Culture and Criticism in a 'Postfeminist' Age*, New York: Routledge.

Modleski, T., 2000. The Terror of Pleasure: The Contemporary Horror Film and Postmodern theory. In K. Gelder, ed. *The Horror Reader*. London: Routledge, pp. 285–93.

Monteyne, K., 2013. *Hip-Hop on Film: Performance Culture, Urban Space, and Genre Transformation in the 1980s*, Jackson: University Press of Mississippi.

Morris, G., 1998. Beyond the Beach: AIP's Beach Party Movies. *Bright Lights Film Journal*, May(21). Available at: http://brightlightsfilm.com/surfs-beyond-beach-aips-beach-party-movies/#.WIjmFWNb67Y [Accessed 29 August 2014].

Moseley, R., 2002. Glamorous Witchcraft: Gender and Magic in Teen Film and Television. *Screen*, 43(4), pp. 403–22.

Moseley, R., 2005a. Dress, Class and Audrey Hepburn: The Significance of the Cinderella Story. In R. Moseley, ed. *Fashioning Film Stars: Dress, Culture, Identity*. London: BFI, pp. 109–20.

Moseley, R., 2005b. *Fashioning Film Stars: Dress, Culture, Identity*, R. Moseley, ed., London: BFI.

Mulvey, L., 1986. Visual Pleasure and Narrative Cinema. In P. Rosen, ed. *Narrative, Apparatus, Ideology*. New York: Columbia University Press, pp. 198–209.

Mulvey, L., 2004. Looking at the Past from the Present: Rethinking Feminist Film Theory of the 1970s. *Signs: Journal of Women in Culture and Society*, 30(1), pp. 1286–92.

Mulvey, L., 2006. *Death 24 × A Second: Stillness and The Moving Image*, London: Reaktion.

Mundy, J., 1999. *Popular Music on Screen: From Hollywood Musical to Music Video*, Manchester: Manchester University Press.

Mundy, J., 2006. Television, the Pop Industry and the Hollywood Musical. In I. Conrich and E. Tincknell, eds. *Film's Musical Moments*. Edinburgh: Edinburgh University Press, pp. 42–55.

Munich, A., 2011. *Fashion in Film*, Bloomington, Ind.: Indiana University Press.

Nash, I., 2006. *American Sweethearts: Teenage Girls in Twentieth-Century Popular Culture*. Bloomington: Indiana University Press.

Neale, S., 2002. *Genre and Contemporary Hollywood*, London: BFI.

Neale, S., Neale, S. and Smith, M., 1998. *Contemporary Hollywood Cinema*, London: Routledge.

Negra, D., 2009. *What a Girl Wants: Fantasizing the Reclamation of Self in Postfeminism*, London: Routledge.

Nichols, B., 1991. *Representing Reality: Issues and Concepts in Documentary*, Bloomington: Indiana University Press.

Nichols, B., 2000. Film Theory and the Revolt Against Master Narratives. In C. Gledhill and L. Williams, eds. *Reinventing Film Studies*. London: Arnold, pp. 34–52.

O'Connor, B. and Klaus, E., 2000. Pleasure and Meaningful Discourse: An Overview of Research Issues. *International Journal of Cultural Studies*, 3(3), pp. 369–87.

Ormrod, J., 2002. Issues of Gender in Muscle Beach Party (1964). *Scope*, December.

Osumare, H., 2007. *The Africanist Aesthetic in Global Hip-Hop: Power Moves*, Basingstoke: Palgrave Macmillan.

Palmer, G., 2004. The New You: Class and Transformation in Lifestyle Television. In S. Holmes and D. Jermyn, eds. *Understanding Reality Television*. New York: Routledge, pp. 173–90.

Perrault, C., [1697] (2002). Cinderella; or The Little Glass Slipper. In M. Tatar, ed. *The Annotated Classic Fairy Tales*. New York: Norton. pp. 28–40.

Petrie, D. and Warner, M., 1993. *Cinema and the Realms of Enchantment*, London: BFI.

Philip, N., 2003. Creativity and Tradition in The Fairy Tale. In H. R. E. Davidson and A. Chaudhri, eds. *A Companion to the Fairy Tale*. Cambridge: D.S. Brewer, pp. 39–55.

Plantinga, C., 2009. *Moving Viewers: American Film and The Spectator's Experience*, Berkeley & Los Angeles: University of California Press.

Podilchak, W., 1991. Distinctions of Fun, Enjoyment and Leisure. *Leisure Studies*, 10(2), pp. 133–48.

Postrel, V. I., 2003. *The Substance of Style: How the Rise of Aesthetic Value is Remaking Commerce, Culture, and Consciousness*, New York, N.Y.: HarperCollins.

Postrel, V., 2013. *The Power of Glamour: Longing and the Art of Visual Persuasion*, New York: Simon & Schuster.

Preston, C. L., 2004. Disrupting the Boundaries of Genre and Gender: Postmodernism and the Fairy Tale. In D. Haase, ed. *Fairy Tales and Feminism: New Approaches*. Detroit: Wayne State University Press, pp. 197–212.

Projansky, S., 2007. Mass Magazine Cover Girls: Some Reflections on Postfeminist Girls and Postfeminism's Daughters. In D. Negra and Y. Tasker, eds. *Interrogating Postfeminism: Gender and the Politics of Popular Culture*. Durham, NC: Duke University Press, pp. 40–72.

Projansky, S., 2014. *Spectacular Girls: Media Fascination and Celebrity Culture*. New York and London: New York University Press.

Propp, V., 2000. Fairy Tale Transformations. In D. Duff, ed. *Modern Genre Theory*. Harlow: Longman, pp. 50–67.

Propp, V. Y. and Scott, L., 1968. *Morphology of the Folktale*, Austin, TX: University of Texas Press.

Purse, L., 2009. Gestures and Postures of Mastery: CGI and Contemporary Action Cinema's Expressive Tendencies. In S. Balcerzak and J. Sperb, eds. *Cinephilia in the*

Age of Digitial Reproduction: Film Pleasure and Digital Culture. London: Wallflower Press, pp. 214–34.

Purse, L., 2011. *Contemporary Action Cinema*, Edinburgh: Edinburgh University Press.

Radner, H., 1995. *Shopping Around: Feminine Culture and the Pursuit of Pleasure*, New York: Routledge.

Radner, H., 2010. *Neo-Feminist Cinema: Girly Films, Chick Flicks and Consumer Culture*, London: Routledge.

Railton, D. and Watson, P., 2011. *Music Video and the Politics of Representation*. Edinburgh: Edinburgh University Press.

Reason, M. and Reynolds, D., 2010. Kinesthesia, Empathy, and Related Pleasures: An Inquiry into Audience Experiences of Watching Dance. *Dance Research Journal*, 42(2), pp. 49–75.

Reason, M., and Reynolds, D., 2012. *Kinesthetic Empathy in Creative and Cultural Practices*, Bristol: Intellect.

Redmond, S., 2015. The Passion Plays of Celebrity Culture. *European Journal of Cultural Studies*, 19(3), pp. 1–16.

Reed, J. W., 1989. *American Scenarios: The Uses of Film Genre*. Middletown, CT: Weslyan University Press.

Regan, S., 1992. *The Politics of Pleasure: Aesthetics and Cultural Theory*, Buckingham: Open University Press.

Renold, E. and Ringrose, J., 2011. Schizoid Subjectivities? Re-theorizing Teen Girls' Sexual Cultures in an Era of 'Sexualization', *Journal of Sociology*, 47(4), pp. 389–409.

Reynolds, D., 2012. Kinesthetic Empathy and the Dance's Body: From Emotion to Affect. In D. Reynolds and M. Reason, eds. *Kinesthetic Empathy in Creative and Cultural Practices*. Bristol: Intellect, pp. 122–36.

Rigakos, G. S., 2008. *Nightclub: Bouncers, Risk, and the Spectacle of Consumption*, Montréal: McGill-Queen's University Press.

Ringrose, J., 2007. Successful Girls? Complicating Post-feminist, Neo-liberal Discourses of Educational Achievement and Gender Equality. *Gender and Education*, 19(4), pp. 471–89.

Roach, J. R., 2007. *It*, Ann Arbor: University of Michigan Press.

Rojek, C., 2001. *Celebrity*, London: Reaktion.

Rose, T., 1994. *Black Noise: Rap Music And Black Culture in Contemporary America*, Hanover, NH: University Press of New England.

Ross, M., 2011. Spectacular Dimensions: 3D Dance Films. *Senses of Cinema*, (61). Available at: http://sensesofcinema.com/2011/feature-articles/spectacular-dimensions-3d-dance-films/ [Accessed 13 January 2012].

Rushton, R., 2013. *The Reality of Film: Theories of Filmic Reality*, Manchester: Manchester University Press.

Rutsky, R. L., 1999. Surfing the Other: Ideology on the Beach. *Film Quarterly*, 52(4), pp. 12–23.

Rutsky, R. L. and Wyatt, J., 1990. Serious Pleasures: Cinematic Pleasure and the Notion of Fun. *Cinema Journal*, 30(1), pp. 3–19.

Schaefer, P., 2003. Unknown Cinderella: The Contribution of Marian Roalfe Cox to the Study of Fairy Tale. In A. Chaudhri and H. R. E. Davidson, eds. *A Companion to the Fairy Tale*. Cambridge: D. S. Brewer, pp. 137–48.

Scott, C., 1996. Magical Dress: Clothing and Transformation in Folk Tales. *Children's Literature Association Quarterly*, 21(4), pp. 151–7.

Shary, T., 2002. *Generation Multiplex: The Image of Youth in Contemporary American Cinema*, Austin, TX: University of Texas Press.

Shary, T., 2003. Teen Films: The Cinemaic Image of Youth. In B. K. Grant, ed. *Film Genre Reader III*. Texas: University of Texas Press, pp. 490–511.

Shary, T., 2005. *Teen Movies: American Youth on Screen*, London: Wallflower.

Shary, T., 2011. Buying Me Love: 1980s Class-Clash Teen Romances. *Journal of Popular Culture*, 44(3), pp. 563–82.

Shaviro, S., 1993. *The Cinematic Body*, Minneapolis, MN: University of Minnesota Press.

Shaviro, S., 2009. *Without Criteria: Kant, Whitehead, Deleuze, and Aesthetics*, Massachusetts: MIT Press.

Shaviro, S., 2010. *Post Cinematic Affect*, Winchester: Zero Books.

Shilling, C., 2012. *The Body and Social Theory* 3rd ed., London: SAGE.

Shinkle, E., 2013. Uneasy Bodies: Affect, Embodied Perception and Contemporary Fashion Photography [kindle]. In B. Papenburg and M. Zarzycka, eds. *Carnal Aesthetics: Transgressive Imagery and Feminist Politics*. London: I. B. Tauris.

Short, S., 2006. *Misfit Sisters: Screen Horror as Female Rites of Passage*, New York: Palgrave Macmillan.

Shouse, E., 2005. Feeling, Emotion, Affect. *M/C Journal*, 8(6). Available at: http://journal.media-culture.org.au/0512/03-shouse.php [Accessed 30 November 2012].

Skeggs, B., 2004a. Context and Background: Pierre Bourdieu's Analysis of Class, Gender and Sexuality. In L. Adkins and B. Skeggs, eds. *Feminism After Bourdieu*. Oxford: Blackwell Publishing/The Sociological Review, pp. 19–33.

Skeggs, B., 2004b. Exchange, Value and Affect: Bourdieu and 'The Self'. In L. Adkins and B. Skeggs, eds. *Feminism After Bourdieu*. Oxford: Blackwell Publishing/The Sociological Review, pp. 75–95.

Skeggs, B., 2005. The Making of Class and Gender Through Visualizing Moral Subject Formation. *Sociology*, 39(5), pp. 965–82.

Skeggs, B., 2010. The Value of Relationships: Affective Scenes and Emotional Performances. *Feminist Legal Studies*, 18, pp. 29–51.

Smelik, A., 1995. What Meets the Eye: Feminist Film Studies. In R. Buikema and A. Smelik, eds. *Women's Studies and Culture*. London: Zed, pp. 66–81.

Smelik, A., 2009. Lara Croft, Kill Bill, and The Battle for Theory in Feminist Film Studies. In R. Buikema and I. Van Der Tuin, eds. *Doing Gender in Media, Art and Culture*. Oxon: Routledge, pp. 178–92.

Smelik, A., 2011. The Performance of Authenticity. *Address*, 1(1), pp. 76–82.

Sobchack, V., 2004. *Carnal Thoughts: Embodiment and Moving Image Culture*. Berkeley: University of California Press.

Sobchack, V., 2006. Cutting to the Quick: Techne, Physis, and Poiesis and the Attractions of Slow Motion. In W. Strauven, ed. *The Cinema of Attractions Reloaded*. Amsterdam: Amsterdam University Press, pp. 337–54.

Sobchack, V., 2012. Fleshing Out the Image: Phenomenology, Pedagogy, and Derek Jarman's 'Blue'. *Cinema: Journal of Philosophy and the Moving Image*, (3), pp. 19–38.

Spielmann, Y., 2001. Intermedia in Electronic Images. *Leonardo*, 34(1), pp. 55–61.

Stacey, J., 1988. Desperately Seeking Difference. In L. Gamman and M. Marshment, eds. *The Female Gaze: Woman as Viewers of Popular Culture*. London: The Women's Press Limited, pp. 112–29.

Stacey, J., 1994. *Star Gazing: Hollywood Cinema and Female Spectatorship*. Oxon: Routledge.

Stam, R., 2000. *Film Theory: An Introduction*, Malden, Mass: Blackwell.

Stewart, K., 2007. *Ordinary Affects*, Durham, N.C.: Duke University Press.

Street, S., 2001. *Costume and Cinema: Dress Codes in Popular Film*, London: Wallflower.

Swindle, M., 2011. Feeling Girl, Girling Feeling: An Examination of 'Girl' as Affect. *Rhizomes*, (22). Available at: http://www.rhizomes.net/issue22/swindle.html [Accessed 21 August 2016].

Tasker, Y. and Negra, D., 2005. Postfeminism and Contemporary Media Studies. *Cinema Journal*, 44(2), pp. 107–10.

Tasker, Y. and Negra, D., 2007. *Interrogating Postfeminism: Gender and the Politics of Popular Culture*, Durham, N.C.: Duke University Press.

Tatar, M., 1999. *The Classic Fairy Tales: Texts, Criticism*, New York: Norton.

Tatar, M. M., 1987. *The Hard Facts of the Grimm's Fairy Tales*, Princeton (N.J.): Princeton U.P.

Tatar, M. M., 2002. *The Annotated Classic Fairy Tales*, New York: Norton.

Teller, J., 2005. Kristen McMenamy: Marc Jacobs. *Purple Fashion*, Fall/Winte(4), pp. 396–415.

Thomas, D., 2000. *Beyond Genre: Melodrama, Comedy and Romance in Hollywood Films*. Moffat: Cameron & Hollis.

Thompson, K., 1977. The Concept of Cinematic Excess. *Cine-tracts*, 1(2), pp. 54–63.

Thrift, N. J., 2007. *Non-Representational Theory: Space, Politics, Affect*, London: Routledge.

Thrift, N., 2008. The Material Practices of Glamour. *Journal of Cultural Economy*, 1(1), pp. 9–23.

Tiffin, J., 2009. *Marvelous Geometry: Narrative and Metafiction in Modern Fairy Tale*, Detroit: Wayne State University Press.

Tolkien, J. R. R., 1966. On Fairy Stories. In *The Tolkien Reader*. New York: Ballantine Books, pp. 2–84.

Trilling, L., 1972. *Sincerity and Authenticity*, Cambridge, Mass.: Harvard University Press.

Trilling, L., 1980. *Beyond Culture*. Oxford: Oxford University Press, pp. 50–76.

Truffaut, F., 1982. *The Films in My Life*, Harmondsworth: Penguin.

Turim, M., 1984. Designing Women: The Emergence of the New Sweetheart Line. *Wide Angle*, 6(2), pp. 4–11.

Turner, G., 2004. *Understanding Celebrity*, London: SAGE.

Turner, G., 2010. *Ordinary People and the Media: The Demotic Turn*, Los Angeles: SAGE.

Turner, V., 1967. *Forest of Symbols: Aspects of Ndembu Ritual*, Ithaca: Cornell University Press.

Veblen, T., 1925. *The Theory of the Leisure Class: An Economic Study of Institutions*. London: Unwin.

Vineyard, J., 2012. Vamps Director Amy Heckerling on Her Clueless Reunion and Paul Rudd's AOL account. *Vulture*. Available at: http://www.vulture.com/2012/10/vamps-amy-heckerling-interview.html [Accessed 4 June 2013].

Vineyard, J., 2013. Everything You Need to Know About 'Mean Girls' Musical (So Far). *Vulture*. Available at: http://www.vulture.com/2013/03/whats-going-on-with-the-mean-girls-musical.html [Accessed 4 June 2013].

Waitt, G., 2008. 'Killing waves': Surfing, Space and Gender. *Social & Cultural Geography*, 9(1), pp. 75–94.

Warner, M., 1993. The Uses of Enchantment. In D. Petrie, ed. *Cinema and the Realms of Enchantment*. London: BFI, pp. 13–35.

Warner, M., 1995. *From The Beast To The Blonde: On Fairy Tales and Their Tellers*. London: Vintage.

Waxman, L., 2011. *Through the Looking-Glass with Heart Shaped Sunglasses: Searching for Alice and Lolita in Contemporary Representations of Girls*, C. Grant and L. Waxman, eds., Bristol: Intellect.

Waxman, L. and Grant, C., 2011. *Girls! Girls! Girls! in Contemporary Art*, Bristol: Intellect.

Weber, B., 2009. *Makeover TV: Selfhood, Citizenship, and Celebrity*, Durham, NC: Duke University Press.

Weber, B., 2011. Imperialist Projections: Manners, Makeovers, and Models of Nationality. In M. Waters, ed. *Women On Screen*. Basingstoke; New York: Palgrave Macmillan, pp. 136–52.

Whannel, G., 2008. Winning and Losing Respect: Narratives of Identity in Sport Films. *Sport in Society: Cultures, Commerce, Media, Politicsltures, Commerce, Media, Politics*, 11(2–3), pp. 195–208.

Whitson, D., 2002. The Embodiment of Gender: Discipline, Domination, and Empowerment. In S. Scraton and A. Flintoff, eds. *Gender and Sport: A Reader*. London: Routledge, pp. 227–40.

Williams, K. C., 2003. *Why I (still) Want My MTV: Music Video and Aesthetic Communication*, Cresskill, N.J.: Hampton Press.

Williams, L., 1990. *Hard Core: Power, Pleasure and 'Frenzy of the Visible'*, London: Pandora.

Williams, L., 1991. Film Bodies: Gender, Genre, and Excess. *Film Quarterly*, 44(4), pp. 2–13.

Williamson, M., 2010. Female Celebrities and the Media: The Gendered Denigration of the 'Ordinary' Celebrity. *Celebrity Studies*, 1(1), pp. 118–20.

Wilson, E., 1985. *Adorned in Dreams*, London: Virago.

Winch, A., 2011. 'Your New Smart-Mouthed Girlfriends': Postfeminist Conduct Books. *Journal of Gender Studies*, 20(4), pp. 359–70.

Winch, A., 2012a. The Girlfriend Gaze. *Soundings*, 52, pp. 21–32.

Winch, A., 2012b. 'We Can Have It All' The Girlfriend Flick. *Feminist Media Studies*, 12(1), pp. 69–82.

Winch, A. and Webster, A., 2012. Here Comes the Brand: Wedding Media and the Management of Transformation. *ContinuumL Journal of Media and Cultural Studies*, 26(1), pp. 51–9.

Wiseman, R., 2002. *Queen Bees & Wannabes: Helping Your Daughter Survive Cliques, Gossip, Boyfriends, and Other Realities of Adolescence*, New York: Crown Publishers.

Wood, R., 2003. *Hollywood from Vietnam to Reagan.. And Beyond: A Revised and Expanded Edition of the Classic Text* 2nd ed., New York: Columbia University Press.

Yolen, J., 1977. America's Cinderella. *Children's Literature in Education*, 8, pp. 21–9.

Young, I. M., 2005. *On Female Body Experience: 'Throwing Like a Girl' and Other Essays*. Oxford: Oxford University Press.

Young, L., 1996. *Fear of the Dark: 'Race', Gender, and Sexuality in the Cinema*, London: Routledge.

Zarzycka, M. and Papenburg, B., 2013. *Carnal Aesthetics: Transgressive Imagery and Feminist Politics [Kindle]*, London: I.B. Tauris.

Zipes, J., 1979. *Breaking the Magic Spell: Radical Theories of Folk and Fairy Tales*, London: Heinemann Educational Publishers.

Zipes, J., 1983. *Fairy Tales and the Art of Subversion: the Classical Genre for Children and the Process of Civilization*, London: Heinemann.

Zipes, J., 1999. Breaking the Disney Spell. In M. Tatar, ed. *The Classic Fairytales: Texts, Criticism*. New York: Norton, pp. 332–52.

Zipes, J. D., 1988. *The Brothers Grimm: From Enchanted Forests to The Modern World*, New York: Routledge.

Index

13 Going on 30 22, 115, 123–7

aesthetics 14–15, 19–20, 42, 49–50, 51, 99–100, 103, 118
　of teen film 3
affect 1, 4–5, 6, 9, 10, 14–16, 18–19, 20, 27, 28, 30, 36, 38, 40–1, 43, 45, 46, 48, 49, 54, 62, 72, 78, 92, 94, 97–100, 103, 105, 107, 111, 114, 115, 117, 118–19, 120, 123, 130, 137
Ahmed, Sara 18–19

Barker, Jennifer 14, 105
becoming 35, 77, 80–3, 123
Berlant, Lauren 22, 116–17
Bourdieu, Pierre 10
Bratz 48, 54–5
Brinkema, Eugenie 14

catwalk 6, 7, 35, 43–4, 45, 50, 52, 62–70, 73, 89, 117, 124, 126–7
celebrity 21, 30–1, 45–6, 47–70, 71, 89, 95, 100, 116, 132, 134–5
Chion, Michel 15, 120
Cinderella 2, 7, 20–1, 23–46, 48, 49, 50, 51, 57, 60, 61, 64, 66, 68, 71, 89, 90, 103, 119, 124, 127, 132, 133–4, 140
　character-icon 21, 28, 29, 31, 32, 35, 39, 40, 49, 51, 55, 56, 60, 67, 68, 71, 74, 75, 76, 78, 80, 87, 100, 116, 122, 123, 124, 132, 134, 138, 139, 140
Cinderella Story, A 21, 24, 27–8, 38–40, 43, 44, 45, 61
cinematography 62, 68, 137
Clueless 3, 8, 9, 138, 139
coming-of-age 2, 35, 51, 74, 80
Confessions of a Teenage Drama Queen 21, 61–2
costume 21, 32–45, 55, 69, 75, 85, 96, 104, 126, 134

Deleuze, Gilles 34, 133
double coding 7, 8–9, 10, 11, 26–8, 40–5, 103, 133
Driscoll, Catherine 3, 4, 5, 7, 11
Dyer, Richard 9, 16, 53, 54, 95–6, 97, 102, 103, 106–7

Easy A 7, 21, 65–6
Eco, Umberto 8, 9, 27
embodiments of feeling 16, 31, 132
enchantment 25–8, 32, 33, 39, 40–2, 44–5, 49, 52, 45, 49, 52, 68, 85, 90, 100, 101, 102, 106, 112, 113, 117, 124, 127, 133, 138, 139

fairy-tale realism 26, 27, 85
Freaky Friday 26, 59, 144
fun 1, 2, 4, 6–7, 12, 15, 18, 19, 20, 22, 47, 52, 87, 92, 94, 95, 99–100, 104, 108–9, 114, 115, 117, 119, 124, 127, 131–2, 138
　mode 6, 9, 8, 9, 10–11, 24, 30, 75, 85, 139

Gidget 7, 80
girl teen film, definition 2–9
glamour 1, 21, 24, 26, 28, 32, 33, 36, 39, 42, 45, 46, 48, 50, 55–6, 78, 73, 74, 75, 76, 78, 89, 100, 116, 127, 132, 134, 139
　definitions of 52–5
　and space and place 55–65
　and visibility 65–70

hair 28, 32, 33, 35, 36, 45, 68, 69, 127, 131, 133, 134
Hairspray (1988) 22, 95, 97–8, 100
Hairspray (2007) 22, 92, 93, 97, 99, 101, 102–3, 109, 110, 111, 121
Heathers 8, 9, 47

Index

Hilary Duff 39, 48, 60
homosociality 140
House Bunny, The 21, 40–1, 43–5, 47, 131, 132, 135–6
Hughes, John 3, 8

Ice Princess 72, 78–9
intermedia aesthetics 22, 115, 122, 129, 132, 137
intimate public of girlhood 22, 116–18, 120, 127, 130, 137

kinaesthetic empathy 31, 33, 44, 78–9, 84, 87, 89, 110, 111, 119, 136
Kracauer, Siegfried 86

Langer, Susanne 15–16, 110
liminality 5, 58, 140
Lizzie McGuire Movie, The 60
Lohan, Lindsay 1, 26, 48, 59, 61
looking relations 81, 82, 140

McNeill, William 87
Make It Happen 22, 60, 121–3
makeover 6, 7, 28–9, 35, 39, 42–4, 45, 47, 50, 58, 63, 64, 65, 66, 67, 68, 77, 88, 89, 124, 126, 127, 132, 138
Martin, Adrian 3, 4, 5
Mean Girls 1–2, 5, 6, 20, 22, 30, 35–6, 47, 52, 65, 66, 89–90, 93, 95, 96–7, 103–4, 106, 107–8, 109, 121, 129, 134, 137–8, 140
modulation 34–5, 39, 42, 43, 45, 59, 62, 65, 68, 70, 100, 116, 123, 130, 133, 138
Mulvey, Laura 12–13
muscular bonding 87–9, 91, 106, 135, 140

neo-liberalism 11, 12, 13, 29, 30, 34, 46, 49, 88, 89, 95, 131
Never Back Down 118–19

pastiche 8–9, 35, 40, 103–4, 106
place 48, 49, 55–6, 58, 59, 60–2, 67, 70, 131, 133, 134

Plantinga, Carl 12, 14
pleasure
    definitions of 16–20
    hierarchies of 10–1, 13, 19, 140
post-feminism 11–12, 13, 29, 40, 42, 46, 49, 88–9, 131–2
Princess Diaries, The 58
public intimacy 52, 53, 54, 64, 65, 70

representation. *See* Mulvey, Laura
Roach, Joseph 4, 33, 52, 53, 54, 62, 134
Rushton, Richard 12–13

St Trinians 66–7
Shaviro, Steven 12, 14, 22, 34–5, 53, 118
Shinkle, Eugenie 36, 38
Sleepover 6–7
slow motion 62–7, 78, 79, 84, 86, 123, 134
Sobchack 14, 15, 86, 105
space 21, 32, 48, 49, 54–60, 70, 109–11, 122, 124, 127, 129, 131, 132, 133, 134
sparkle 67–8
spectacle 22, 33, 38, 45, 46, 49, 50, 55, 56–7, 58, 60, 62, 67, 68, 77, 78, 79, 81, 86, 93, 94, 108, 113, 114, 115–16, 117, 118–30, 137
Starstruck 57, 60
Stick It 21, 83–4, 85, 86–7, 108–9, 111–12, 121, 137
Superbad 6–7
Swindle, Monica 4

teen film, definitions of 2–6

visibility 6–7, 20, 21, 29–30, 42, 43, 45, 47, 48–57, 59, 60, 62–70, 71, 75, 80, 95, 116, 124, 127, 131, 134, 137, 139

What a Girl Wants 67–70
Whip It 139

Young, Marion 71–3, 75, 110

Lightning Source UK Ltd.
Milton Keynes UK
UKHW020648030620
364291UK00009B/133